Property Loss Adjusting

Volume II

Property Loss Adjusting

Volume II

Edited by

James J. Markham, J.D., CPCU, AIC, AIAF
Vice President
Insurance Institute of America

Second Edition • 1995

Insurance Institute of America
720 Providence Road, Malvern, Pennsylvania 19355-0716

Second Edition • July 1995

Library of Congress Catalog Number 95-77155
International Standard Book Number 0-89462-091-6

 Printed in the United States of America on recycled paper.

Contents

7 **Preparation of Estimates**   *1*

The Scope and
Estimating Process   1

Estimating Procedures   9

Summary   28

Appendix   31

8 **Residential Construction Losses and Estimates**   *33*

Painting   33

Wallpapering   52

Drywall   58

Exterior Siding   62

Roofing   68

Summary   78

9 **Residential Construction Losses and Estimates, Continued**   *81*

Frame Carpentry   81

Finish Carpentry   101

Mechanical Systems   116

Summary   129

10 **Merchandise Losses**   *133*

Insured Value of
Merchandise   134

Books and Records   139

Salvage   146

Reporting Form Policies   151

Loss Adjustment   158

Summary   163

11 **Time Element Losses**   *165*

What Happens to an
Organization After a Loss?   166

Insurance for Loss of
Business Income and Extra
Expense   176

Homeowners Loss of Use   202

Summary   207

12 **Specialty Losses**   **209**

Inland Marine Losses   209

Losses Under the
National Flood Insurance
Program   219

Condominium Losses   228

Builders' Risk Losses   234

Summary   239

13 **Specialty Losses,
Continued**   **241**

Crime Losses   241

Boiler and Machinery
Coverage   255

Computer Losses   261

Contamination Claims   273

Summary   278

Bibliography   **281**

Index   **283**

Chapter 7

Preparation of Estimates

Estimating building damages is a basic skill that property loss adjusters should master. This chapter introduces the theoretical and practical foundations for estimating building damages. Chapters 8 and 9 apply these principles to some common building components.

This chapter discusses the important preliminaries to good estimating: preparing a proper scope of damage at the scene of a loss and knowing the basic cost elements of all estimates. The chapter also discusses the essential estimating methods; ways to resolve differences in estimates; the coverage aspects of estimating; and two important estimating tools, computerized programs and basic mathematics.

The Scope and Estimating Process

Estimating damages is a two-step process. The first step is preparing the scope of damage at the loss scene. The second step is pricing the work determined by the scope into a repair estimate.

Scope of a Building Loss

The adjuster itemizes the damage elements, or scopes, to establish the extent of the insured's loss. The **scope** details the damage to each building component. Some property adjusters substitute other terms for "scope." Common synonyms are "take-off," "survey," "specifications," or "field notes." Regardless of the name, the scope is the first and most crucial step in preparing a repair estimate.

For smaller losses, the adjuster prepares the scope and writes the estimate at the scene of the loss. For larger losses, trying to finish the estimate at the scene is impractical. Although completing the scope and estimate in a timely manner is important, the adjuster must use references to find labor and material usage rates and current prices.

Elements of a Proper Scope

The scope must contain enough detail to calculate loss restoration costs. For each damaged building component, the scope must describe the following three things:

1. **Degree of damage**, usually stated as a method of repair
2. **Quality of the materials** and workmanship of damaged property
3. **Raw counts or measurements** needed to calculate quantities

For example, assume that an interior water loss has occurred. The entire ceiling in a small bedroom is bowed, and the walls are stained. The scope entries for the damage in that room are as follows:

> Bedroom 9 feet x 10 feet x 8 feet
>
> Replace ⅝ inch ceiling drywall, complete
>
> Seal and paint walls and ceiling, flat latex

The room's dimensions provide the raw measurements needed to calculate the surface areas that determine the amount of material needed. Replacing the drywall and sealing and painting the surfaces are the repair methods that indicate the damage degree. Finally, the thickness of the drywall and the type of paint describe the quality of the damaged component.

Contrast to Finished Estimate

The scope differs from the finished estimate in two ways. First, the scope does not necessarily list any prices, although prices can be used to describe quality. Second, the scope does not list the calculated quantities. It includes just the raw counts and measurements needed to calculate quantities for the estimate. Calculators are not needed to prepare a scope. The quantities should be calculated as the adjuster extends and prices the scope into a finished estimate.

Suggested Sequence for a Scope

Following a set sequence in inspecting the loss and preparing the scope is important. The sequence suggested here works well for larger fire losses, and it can be tailored to fit other types of losses. For smaller losses, some of the steps can be combined or eliminated. The steps in a first inspection and scope include the following:

Step I—Conduct the initial survey

Step II—Prepare diagrams and sketches

Step III—Scope the damage

Step IV—Consider coverage

Step V—Document with photographs

Step I—Conduct the Initial Survey

The adjuster should inspect the building to get an idea of construction type, damaged areas, condition before the fire, and any building hazards. The adjuster should enter the building below the lowest damaged floor to check the condition of the floors above. Once the point of origin of the loss has been established, the adjuster can decide whether to call in expert help to confirm the cause. Partly as a result of the **initial survey**, coverage issues that demand immediate attention might become apparent. Whenever possible, the adjuster should finish the scope during the initial inspection.

Step II—Prepare Diagrams and Sketches

After preparing a perimeter diagram, the adjuster can draw in the interior walls. Starting with the perimeter helps ensure that the interior dimensions will all fit. Next, the adjuster should measure and sketch exterior elevations, trusses, cabinets, doors, and windows. Thoroughness here makes the final detailed scope easier to prepare.

Step III—Scope the Damage

Conducting an organized scope of the damage ensures that nothing is missed. Whenever possible, the adjuster should complete the scope with the insured or with the insured's contractor. One of the purposes for preparing the scope is to agree on the damage extent. Insureds typically want to discuss every detail, so the insured and the adjuster should agree on anything that might become an issue. If the insured's contractor is present, he or she can be part of the agreement on the major unit costs and labor rates as well as on each repair item. Experts should resolve uncertainties or legitimate differences of opinion.

Step III of the inspection should include examining the following five categories in the following order. The adjuster should consider only one category at a time, necessitating five complete tours of the loss scene:

1. Structural components
2. Exterior, including insulation

3. Room by room (architectural items, finishes, fixtures, and components of building systems completely contained within the room)
    a. Floor
    b. Walls
    c. Trim, doors, and windows
    d. Ceiling
    e. Fixtures, appliances, built-ins, and cabinets
4. Building systems that cross room boundaries (plumbing, electrical, and heating and air conditioning)
5. General considerations (debris removal, access, and permits)

There are two reasons for beginning with the structural components. First, they are difficult to scope on a room-by-room basis. Second, structural component damage might require removing an undamaged component. Exterior items are next because they span room boundaries and cannot be seen from the inside. In the detailed scope of each damaged room, besides the finished ceiling, walls, and floors, the adjuster should also scope the fixtures, ducts, pipes, outlets, and wiring within the room. The next category, scoping the plumbing, electrical, and heating systems, is limited to the components that cross room boundaries. Once these systems have been scoped, the adjuster should evaluate debris removal, permits, access items, and equipment rental.

For smaller or different losses, common sense often dictates a different sequence. For instance, if the insured reports a wind loss with interior water damage, starting on the inside to get an idea of where the roof damage is would make sense.

Step IV—Consider Coverage

The adjuster should consider code requirements, damage from excluded causes, and damage to excluded property. The adjuster should also gather enough information to calculate the building's value before the loss to establish that the insured has complied with the coinsurance or replacement cost requirements.

Step V—Document With Photographs

The final step is to photograph the important items to the adjustment. There are two reasons for taking photographs. First, the important items might not be apparent until the whole loss has been seen. Second, another tour of the scene ensures that the scope is complete.

Whether the adjuster writes the estimate or submits it for contractors bids, a detailed scope of damage is essential to gain control of any building loss.

Pricing an Estimate

The second step in the estimating process is pricing out the scope into a final repair estimate. The adjuster estimates the loss restoration cost on the basis of the damage as itemized in the scope document. This section discusses construction costs and explains some specific estimating methods. Any construction operation involves the following types of costs:

1. Materials
2. Labor and employer's burden
3. Tools and equipment
4. Overhead and profit
5. Miscellaneous direct costs, such as permits and sales taxes

Materials

Establishing the cost of materials involves two steps. First, the adjuster must identify the materials, their quality, and the quantities needed to make the repair. Second, the adjuster must obtain current local prices for those materials.

Several sources can identify the items and quantities needed. *How to Estimate Building Losses and Construction Costs* by Paul Thomas and *Walker's Building Estimators Reference Book* by Frank R. Walker Company are two recognized sources (those and others are listed in the Appendix to this chapter). For each construction or repair operation, these references identify the materials needed and provide usage factors to convert the sale unit into the units used for estimating. For example, these books reveal that a gallon of latex wall paint covers 450 to 500 square feet of smooth walls.

Waste

The material usage information is sometimes described as a "waste factor." There are two kinds of waste. The first is **cutting and fitting waste**, which can occur, for example, when installing a ceramic tile floor. The references indicate that an additional 5 to 10 percent of material should be added to the estimated quantity, allowing for breakage and cutting of tiles to fit the room. Cutting and fitting waste is also a factor in the estimation of required quantities of drywall, roofing, wallpaper, wood siding, paneling, and plywood.

Another way to handle cutting and fitting waste is to consider waste causes while determining the quantity needed. For example, some references state that the waste in drywall should be allowed by including door and window openings in the surface area measurements unless these spaces are larger than one full 4 ft. x 8 ft. sheet of drywall. If this method is used, adding a percentage of material might not be appropriate.

The second type of waste is more difficult to understand because it does not appear in the scrap pile. It is called **milling waste.** Milling waste is the difference between the actual size and the **nominal size** of a piece of material and is often associated with lumber. The nominal size of, say, a piece of lumber is the measurements that are commonly used to describe it. These might differ from the actual measurements. A piece of 1 in. x 3 in. oak flooring actually measures $^{25}\!/_{32}$ in. thick by $2\frac{1}{4}$ in. wide. The milling waste occurred because some of the width of the 3 in. board was removed when the tongue and groove were formed. The piece is called a 1 x 3, but it is actually smaller, which means that it will cover a smaller area. In this case, $33\frac{1}{3}$ percent more material is needed to cover the nominal width of 3 in. with $2\frac{1}{4}$ in. material. As a result, a 33 percent milling waste factor should be added to the actual floor area when determining the quantity of material required.

Material Prices

The second step in estimating the cost of materials is to obtain local prices. Although reference sources exist, the best way to get current costs is to contact local suppliers. The adjuster should determine the contractor's price for the material delivered to the site. In many cases, this price is close to the price charged to the public without the delivery service. For small jobs, the contractor picks up the material at the lumberyard and pays the retail price.

Contractors who pay their bills on time might receive time payment discounts. On very large jobs, a contractor receives an additional quantity discount. If the job requires a carload lot of one material type, there should be some discount. The type of material often dictates the discount. Construction materials range from commodity items such as lumber and nails to specialty items such as lighting fixtures and cabinets. Because of their generic nature, commodity items carry a relatively small markup, resulting in minimal discounts. However, specialty items often carry higher markups and, as a result, higher discounts.

Labor

Estimating labor costs consists of two steps similar to determining material costs: (1) determine the quantity of labor and (2) determine the price of labor. The quantity of labor is the number of hours needed to perform the operation. The price is the cost of each hour.

Quantity of Labor

The amount of labor required can be obtained from several reference sources. The Appendix to this chapter describes the standard reference sources for estimating construction costs, including *The Means Repair and Remodeling Estimator, How to Estimate Building Losses and Construction Costs*, and *Walker's Building Estimators Reference Book*. These sources give the amount of labor associated with any construction operation. For example, these references indicate that hanging, taping, and finishing 100 square ft. of drywall require 2.5 hours.

Published production rates reflect the average labor required for a usual quantity of new construction. If the job is very large or very small, the production rates should be adjusted accordingly. On small jobs, the adjuster should add the additional time needed for setup, preparation, and cleanup. On large jobs, the highest productivity figure given in ranges is usually appropriate.

Some repair operations require two or more skills. For example, a job might require a plumber and an assistant. The labor times quoted might refer to the crew. In this case, the crew is two workers. The adjuster might accidentally overestimate a plumbing loss if the plumber's rate is allowed when half of the hours should have been figured at the helper's rate. The standard references indicate whether the operation requires more than one labor type and more than one worker.

Employer's Burden

The price of a labor hour can be obtained from references or computed according to local rates. The most important part of accurately computing labor costs is understanding and accounting for the difference between the worker's wage and the contractor's hourly price. This difference is a group of costs called **employer's burden**. The employer's burden costs are as follows:

1. Taxable fringe benefits such as vacation and sick leave
2. Nontaxable fringe benefits (health and life insurance plans and so forth)
3. State and federal unemployment tax
4. Employer's Social Security tax
5. Workers compensation costs
6. Liability insurance costs

To arrive at a price of labor, add these costs to the base wage.

If a subcontractor is performing the work, the labor price might also be marked up to include the subcontractor's overhead and profit. The total costs to the general contractor produce the labor price to the public. The percentage of burden varies by trade and locale. Both *National Construction Estimator* and *Means Repair and Remodeling Cost Data* provide factors for each of these cost components.

Tools and Equipment

The cost of most tools and equipment is either borne by the worker or included in the contractor's overhead. However, some jobs require specialty equipment such as scaffolding, a floor sander, or heavy equipment such as a crane or a bulldozer. The best way to estimate the cost of specialty equipment is to allow a daily or hourly rental charge quoted by a local supplier. The labor associated with erecting scaffolding or using equipment comes from the same references as any other labor factor.

Overhead and Profit

Overhead and profit are distinct elements of cost, though they are frequently referred to together.

Overhead

Overhead encompasses the fixed costs for any business. It does not involve costs associated with a specific job. Overhead exists whether or not the contractor is working on a project. Some examples of overhead items are the salaries of estimators, job supervisors, and office personnel; office rent; utilities; and business licenses. The contractor usually recovers these costs by charging a flat percentage on each estimate. For example, if the fixed operating costs of the business are $100,000 per year and the contractor expects to do $1 million worth of work, then the contractor recovers the annual overhead by adding a 10 percent overhead charge to every job.

Profit

Profit is the amount over the costs of a job that the contractor expects to earn for his or her services. General contractors perform several services. The primary ones are to coordinate, schedule, and supervise the activities of the various subcontractors. Contractors customarily add a percentage to the total estimate to cover their overhead and profit. (The adjuster would also add a percentage to the estimate to reflect the contractor's costs.) The usual amount varies by the locale, the size of the job, the contractor's desire to get the job, and the methods used to bill the other costs used in the estimate. A common allowance is "ten and ten," which is 10 percent overhead and 10 percent profit. In some areas, contractors routinely use the "ten on ten" method, which results in a total of 21 percent. In other areas, a flat 15 percent to cover both overhead and profit is common. Regardless of local practices, competitive pressures can dictate a different amount.

Application of Overhead and Profit

As a rule, the general contractor's markup is justified if restoring the loss requires three or more trades. However, little scheduling or coordinating is usually required on a loss involving three trades, such as roofing, drywall, and painting. The insured might be willing to deal directly with roofing and decorating subcontractors in many cases. The amount of markup on a small loss probably does little more than cover the general contractor's costs.

Charges for overhead and profit are not always listed only as separate items at the end of the estimate. Estimating methods taught by the insurance industry assume that labor and material unit costs are bare costs. In many areas, the usual labor rates and unit costs contain at least some elements of profit. The adjuster's ability to apply burden to obtain a fair price for labor and to derive unit costs from labor and materials is the only way to ensure that the customary prices are truly bare costs.

The percentage added to the estimate is for the general contractor's overhead and profit. Most larger losses involve work that is usually performed by subcontractors, such as electrical, plumbing, heating and air conditioning, and masonry work. On large losses, subcontractors might be used for other trades to maximize the economies of scale that can be achieved through specialized skills and equipment. The subcontractor's overhead and profit might be shown as a separate item on the bid, but they are more likely to be handled by marking up the labor rate by an additional percentage. On the general contractor's bid, the subcontracted work is often a single flat figure that includes the subcontractor's direct costs, overhead, and profit.

Miscellaneous Direct Costs

Building permits and engineering fees are examples of other direct costs. These costs should be directly related to the individual job rather than to the cost of operating the contracting business.

Estimating Procedures

The same process of scoping the loss scene damage and pricing the estimate always applies, but preparing the estimate itself can involve different procedures, depending on the nature and size of the loss. Although some estimates must be developed by using the labor and materials method, the unit cost method is more efficient in other situations. Estimates themselves might differ because of scope differences of the loss or price differences applied, and the adjuster must reconcile the differences. Insurance policy provisions also affect estimate preparation. Finally, the adjuster might be able to apply computerized tools as well as standard mathematical formulas to prepare estimates.

Estimating Methods

Adjusters use two primary methods to estimate the repair cost. They are not mutually exclusive; in fact, most estimates use both approaches depending on the item. Neither method is inherently more accurate than the other because both methods rely on the same data. They use the same labor and material usage factors and the same local labor and material prices.

The first method is the **labor and materials method** or the **time and materials method**. The cost estimation with this method is based on the number of labor hours and the amount of material for each repair item. For instance, for a painting job, the estimate shows the number of hours and the gallons of paint required to paint each room. The labor and materials method is best for estimating the restoration cost of unique or unusual items such as elements of a house's frame, cabinets, fixtures, doors, and windows.

The second method is the **unit cost method**. A **unit** is the most common way of counting or measuring the quantity of material needed. The estimate shows the number of these units and a single price that represents the cost of labor and material for one unit. For instance, for painting, the estimate shows the square footage of an area to be repainted and the cost to paint one square foot.

Application of Estimating Methods

The best way to describe the two methods is to estimate an item of repair both ways. Ceramic tile is a good example. Ceramic tile can be set in mortar or set directly on smooth plywood, drywall, or concrete by using an adhesive. The latter method is called "thin set." How much will replacing a thin set, ceramic tile floor in a room that is 8 ft. x 10 ft. cost? Assume that the local labor tile setter rate is $20 per hour and that the local material cost is as follows:

1 in. x 1 in. white ceramic tile, 1 square foot paper-backed sheets, $1.75

Tile adhesive, 1 gallon, $10.00

Grout, 25 pounds, $11.00

How much of each material is necessary?

The Labor and Materials Method

First, the repair is estimated using the labor and materials method from the data found in *Walker's Building Estimators Reference Book*.

Materials   The area of the 8 ft. x 10 ft. floor is 80 square feet. Add 10 percent cutting and fitting waste to arrive at a quantity of 88 square feet. Since the tile is sold in square-foot sheets, 88 sheets will be needed. The cost for 88 sheets at

$1.75 per sheet is $154. For the adhesive, the reference book says that a gallon covers 40 to 50 square feet. Two gallons are needed to cover the 80 square feet. The cost for 2 gallons at $10 per gallon is $20. For the grout, 1 pound is needed for 4 square feet of 1 in. x 1 in. tile. By dividing 4 into 80 square feet results in 20 pounds to grout 80 square feet. If 25 pounds costs $11, how much would 20 pounds cost? A simple formula that works when the quantity needed and the quantity of sale are stated in the same units of measure is as follows:

$$\frac{\text{Quantity needed}}{\text{Sale quantity}} \times \text{Sale price} = \text{Cost of quantity needed}$$

or in this case,

$$\frac{20}{25} \times \$11 = \$8.80$$

Labor   For the labor in this job, the reference sources indicate that 8 hours of tile setter's labor are necessary to install 100 square feet of thin set ceramic tile. How many hours are needed for 80 square feet if 8 hours are needed to set 100 square feet? A version of the above formula can be used:

$$\frac{\text{Quantity needed}}{\text{Standard quantity}} \times \text{Hours required for standard quantity}$$

or in this case,

$$\frac{80}{100} \times 8 = 6.4 \text{ hours}$$

The adjuster should allow for 6.4 hours at the tile setter's rate of $20. The labor cost to set 80 square feet is $128.

Final Estimate   The finished labor and materials estimate for this item is $310.80, as shown in Exhibit 7-1.

Exhibit 7-1
Labor and Materials Estimate

	Quantity	Materials	Labor	Total
Replace 1" x 1"				
Ceramic Tile	88 sq. ft. @ 1.75	154.00	6.4 @ 20. = 128.	$282.00
Adhesive	2 gal. @ 10.00	20.00		20.00
Grout	20#	8.80		8.80
Total				$310.80

The Unit Cost Method

If the adjuster must estimate the cost to repair or replace a ceramic tile floor a second time for another loss or in another room, he or she could repeat the labor and materials process or develop a **unit cost** to streamline the estimating process. From estimating the first job, the adjuster knows replacing 80 square feet would cost $301.80. Dividing $310.80 by 80 provides the cost per square foot, $3.89. This is a unit cost that represents the labor and materials to replace one square foot of 1 in. x 1 in. white ceramic tile. The next time this tile is used in a repair, the adjuster can use the unit cost method. If the next room is 6 ft. x 9 ft., the estimate would read:

Replace 54 square feet of 1 in. x 1 in. white ceramic tile @ $3.89 = $210.66.

Additional Items and Unit Cost   The procedure used to estimate the floor repair can be used to estimate the cost of repairing base tiles around the perimeter of the room. Once the adjuster uses the labor and materials method, he or she can apply a unit cost for a linear foot of wall to determine the cost for that item.

In estimating the cost to repair a bathroom floor, the adjuster must allow for access time—in this case, removing and resetting the toilet to replace the tile underneath it. The **access time** should be stated as a separate item using the labor and materials method. The references estimate that the work would take 1.0 hours and that the only material required is a wax ring.

The estimate would therefore include the following:

Remove and reset toilet, 1.0 hours @ $20 + $1 material = $21

The adjuster would not build that item into the unit cost for three reasons: (1) the access cost does not vary with the room size, (2) the cost might be used in rooms other than the bathroom, and (3) including access or preparation time in the unit cost can lead to counting the cost to gain access twice. The best approach is to keep unit costs as simple as possible. The adjuster should separately estimate and show extra labor and materials needed to gain access in a particular work area.

Choice of Estimating Methods

Which estimating method is better? Unit costs work well with common generic items such as paint, drywall, and floor coverings. Unit costs do not work as well with uncommon items because developing the unit cost takes as much time as using the labor and materials method. The time to develop a unit cost for common items is justified by the long-term time savings realized by applying that unit cost to similar items in that particular project or in subsequent projects, thus eliminating the time needed to recompute labor and materials. However, no time savings can be realized in computing a unit cost for uncommon items such as the installation of a furnace, because difference in items makes applying one item's unit cost to another item difficult. In this case, computing a unit cost simply adds to the time it takes to recompute labor and materials for each item.

For some components, the labor and materials method is clearly more satisfactory. One is framing. Although estimating a set of unit costs for different types of framing is possible, the unit costs do not help much because the labor factor depends on so many variables. Rafters can help to illustrate the point. There are different factors for 2 ft. x 6 ft. rafters and 2 ft. x 8 ft. rafters. Installing rafters on hip roofs takes more time than installing them on gable roofs, which in turn takes more time than installing them on flat roofs. Depending on the design of the roof and the assessment of the job, some rafters are supported by collar beams. If the same variables were applied to the other framing components, the huge collage of unit costs would be more confusing than revealing. If the adjuster tried to simplify the unit costs for framing by developing an average cost, this average cost would be too much in some cases and too little in others. When properly used, the unit cost method is not an average cost method. Each unit cost should be tailored to a specific component, rather than to a class of similar components.

Unique items should also be estimated using the labor and materials method. Lighting fixtures, which come in a variety of types and qualities, are a good example. However, the labor to install the fixtures is relatively constant. The most accurate way to estimate the cost to replace light fixtures is to price the fixture and add the labor to install it. The same holds true for cabinets, plumbing fixtures, and appliances.

The unit cost method should produce the same estimate as a pure labor and materials method. The only difference is that the adjuster does not spend the extra time calculating the number of gallons of paint or rolls of dry wall tape needed in each room. Unit cost estimating has fallen into disfavor with some companies because some adjusters do not take the time to verify the unit cost quoted by a contractor. If the contractor's labor rates and production figures are routinely accepted, the adjuster might also be making a mistake in using the labor and materials method.

Other Considerations in Estimating

Other considerations include demolition, debris removal, and the cost effect of very small or very large jobs.

Demolition and Tear Out

Demolition is the removal of damaged components from their original place in the building. Demolition yields debris, which must be removed from the site (as explained in the following section). This work is generally figured using a laborer's wage rate rather than a skilled worker's rate. The adjuster can estimate demolition on either a labor and materials or a unit cost basis. Unit removal costs can be added to the unit item replacement cost to arrive at a remove and replace unit cost. Theoretically, the unit cost method should be as accurate as any other approach. Nevertheless, it can lead to serious overestimating, especially on larger losses, for the following reasons:

1. Some components are "out-of-sight," requiring no tear out.
2. Demolition of one component often includes demolition of another. To estimate both with a remove and replace cost duplicates the cost of the demolition.
3. The remove and replace cost tends to become the accepted norm and is often used without careful analysis.
4. On larger losses, unit cost fails to recognize economies of scale. A few hours with heavy equipment can replace days of manual labor.
5. Many of the tear-out figures in the labor references are appropriate for careful remodeling demolition rather than for the gross sort of demolition involved in larger losses.

The labor and materials method is the best approach to use for demolition. If that method is used, the unit costs used in the rest of the estimate should not include removal.

Experience is necessary to estimate the number of work hours or days of demolition. The references contain enough information to get the adjuster started, but duplications are still possible. The tear-out time for the most significant item in a building assembly should be used. The labor factor usually includes secondary components. For instance, if 2.5 hours are allowed to tear out 100 square feet of partition wall, additional time to remove the drywall, wallpaper, switch plates, or heating vents should not be allowed.

One approach to checking the demolition portion of a contractor's estimate is dividing the amount by the local common labor rate. The result approximates the number of hours of demolition labor. If the hours seem excessive, negotiating time is usually easier than negotiating dollars.

Debris Removal

Debris removal cost is the labor and expense involved in removing debris from the site. The two types of debris are (1) the debris of the damaged property and (2) the waste produced by repairs. The demolition labor figures include the time needed to pile the debris on the premises. The debris removal cost represents the additional cost to remove it from the site and properly dispose of it.

The best approach to estimating the cost of debris removal is to estimate the number and size of boxes or trash bins needed to handle the debris and apply the fee quoted by a local waste disposal company. Disposal companies quote a single price to place the bin on the site and to pick it up when it is full. Trying to estimate debris removal costs by truckloads, hours of driving time, mileage allowances, and dump fees is an exercise in futility.

Small Losses

The labor tables in most references allow time for normal setup, preparation, and cleanup. For small jobs, this allowance might be inadequate. Drywall repair is a good example. Even if the damage is less than one square foot and the actual repair time is less than one hour, completing the repair is more time-consuming because the drywall compound has to dry between coats. Even the smallest repair might require an additional trip or two, unless other work can be done while the compound dries. On a large job, the worker would have other things to do while waiting for the compound to dry or could return to the job site later without the extra travel time affecting the cost too much.

One approach to estimating a small job is to allow for driving time in addition to the time required to do the work. The more popular approach is to allow a minimum charge. The minimum charge quoted by a contractor usually represents two to four hours of labor and a small amount of material. Minimum charges are convenient but should be used with caution. The adjuster should consider whether separate trades are necessary when a small job involves minimum charges for several trades. If there are several small items for a single trade, a better approach is to estimate the damage using the labor and materials or unit costs method. When the estimate is completed, the adjuster should check to see whether the total for that trade exceeds the usual minimum charge.

Large Losses

An adage states that the only difference between estimating a $10,000 loss and a $100,000 loss is one zero. Although those words might comfort a new adjuster, they are also misleading. Large jobs involve economics of scale. Subcontractors with specialized skills and equipment can produce significant savings. Material discounts for large quantities are possible. Finally, competition can play a greater role in larger losses.

The adjuster should analyze the unit costs and production rates used on smaller losses. If the loss involves painting the interior of an apartment building, the unit cost should be based on spray painting rather than brush or roller painting. Drywall specialists, who might be engaged for a large job, can work more efficiently than the carpenter who only occasionally does a room or two. In addition, drywalling a large space is usually easier because it involves less cutting, fewer odd shapes, and more standard seams. The adjuster should check unit costs by talking with specialty subcontractors about pricing for the quantity of work involved. Finally, an adjuster might want to approach demolition as a single labor and material item, avoiding the possibility of redundancy in remove and replace unit costs.

Negotiating Building Losses

Estimators looking at the same loss would develop two different repair figures for only two reasons. The first reason is scope differences, including measurement and quantity errors, as well as divergent opinions on the quality and the type of repair. The second reason is price.

Resolving Differences in the Scope

Estimating is not an exact science, and legitimate differences are common. Negotiating a repair figure begins with the first inspection. If the scope is agreed on early, the pricing issues are relatively easy to resolve through negotiation or competitive bidding. The easiest way to reach an agreement on a scope is for the adjuster to prepare it jointly with the insured or the insured's choice of contractor. An adjuster should find a way to resolve any differences in scope before an estimate is written. Following are some approaches to resolving scope-related issues:

1. If the adjuster is scoping with a contractor, each should keep separate notes and diagrams, which help to identify differences more quickly, unless the contractor wants to work from the adjuster's notes.

2. The adjuster should resolve any question of hidden damage by arranging for some quick demolition or by doing a more complete inspection.

3. Some scope questions require an expert, such as a structural engineer. A common question is the degree of fire damage to concrete, masonry, or steel. Although building inspectors usually have an opinion, they might not have the training and resources to make an accurate decision.

4. Other differences in scope can be resolved by calling in a subcontractor. Most insurance repair contractors are general contractors who rely heavily on their subcontractors for technical expertise. Scope issues involving

electrical, plumbing, and heating and air conditioning can be resolved by consulting a specialty subcontractor.

5. Test repairs can be made on a small area to determine whether a repair option would work.

6. Competitive bids can resolve scope problems in a few specific situations. If the insured has chosen a contractor who usually deals in remodeling or new construction, that contractor might want to tear out and replace everything. A more experienced contractor in damage restoration might be needed to identify more conservative yet equally effective alternatives.

Resolving Price Differences

Resolving price-related differences can begin only after the scope has been agreed on. Some contractors charge higher prices than others. If a contractor with a reputation for quality work charges a higher price, the adjuster might decide to pay that price. Although no single price is correct, some ranges are acceptable. Following are general guidelines for negotiating price:

1. Unit costs are difficult to negotiate. The adjuster should suggest the unit costs as the scope is prepared. Most contractors have a range of unit costs they will accept. If the adjuster suggests a price on the lower side of the range, the contractor will be more likely to accept it during the scope phase than after the estimate is written. The same holds true for labor rates. If the adjuster and contractor can agree on the price of labor in advance, they can then negotiate the labor production rates based on published sources.

2. If unit costs are not agreed to in advance, the labor and materials methods can be used to analyze and negotiate the unit cost. For larger losses, the standard labor production rates are usually on the high side, just as they are on the low side for small jobs.

3. For trades in which the involvement of a subcontractor is expected, the adjuster should ask the general contractor to confirm the price with the subcontractor. That gives the general contractor a chance to reduce the price without losing face. If the price still seems high to the adjuster, another subcontractor can be asked to bid on the repair. The difference might be an additional markup by the general contractor.

4. As a general rule, negotiating from a known quantity such as the adjuster's detailed estimate is more effective than negotiating without an agreed scope. Simply comparing estimates from contractors can cause errors if there is no established norm. The electrical portion of two general contractors' bids could have been prepared by the same subcontractor who accidentally hit the wrong key on the calculator. The two amounts will be

similar, but both will be wrong. Bid comparisons are effective as long as everyone works from the same scope and presents the bid in roughly the same format. In each bid, some items will be higher and some will be lower. The adjuster should address the bigger discrepancies. Trying to get a contractor to agree to the lowest price for every item is rarely successful.

Coverage Aspects of Estimating

Insurance policy provisions affect the preparation of estimates in several important respects.

Code Requirements

Without endorsement, most policies exclude the additional repair costs needed to bring a damaged building up to current codes. These codes might require demolishing and replacing undamaged components, replacing obsolete components with new ones, or even adding new items. Determining the additional cost resulting from the codes involves determining the difference between the cost of replacing the damaged portion with items or material of like kind and quality and the cost of replacing with items or materials to meet the current code. In some situations, the amount is obvious. In others, it is not so clear. Because the extra cost will come out of the insured's pocket, an expert opinion might be warranted.

Alternative Repairs

In general practice, most adjusters estimate the cost of repairs using like kind and quality. Creative adjusters sometimes identify repair methods that add value to the insured yet cost less than the usual replacement with like kind and quality. Carpet damaged by a burning log rolling out of the fireplace is a good example. For wall-to-wall carpet, many companies pay to replace carpet in the damaged room and any area that cannot be closed from view. The insured, however, might choose to replace the burned area in front of the fireplace with quarry tile rather than replacing several rooms of carpet. Installing drywall instead of plaster or using a butcher block to cover a small burned area on a counter top are other examples of alternative repairs. Although these approaches make sense, the usual policy language does not specifically address the issue of alternative repairs. The adjuster might suggest an alternative repair, but the insured must decide whether to accept that option. If necessary, the adjuster might rely on the policy provision of paying only the actual cash value until repairs are completed, which can prevent an overpayment.

Determining the Actual Cash Value of a Repair Estimate

Determining the **actual cash value (ACV)** of a repair estimate requires knowing the useful life of building components as well as the court decisions dealing with ACV in the jurisdiction. Most policies do not define ACV. Although the insurance industry has historically thought of ACV as replacement cost less depreciation, the courts tend to use the broad evidence rule to include market value factors. Depreciation is warranted only when repairs leave the insured in a better situation than he or she was in before the loss. The notion of betterment is not only a good way to explain ACV to insureds, but it is also a good way to test whether depreciation is warranted.

Determining ACV involves examining each item of repair and quantifying the extent of betterment. The age, condition, and expected use of the item all affect the amount of betterment. For example, if a house is two years old, if the condition of the paint in the garage was the same as the paint in the foyer, and if both were damaged and needed repainting, the adjuster would probably charge more betterment in the foyer because it would enhance the value of the house more than new paint in the garage. If the paint in a family room was badly worn before a loss and the loss required that the room be repainted, it would be subject to greater depreciation than the paint in a guest room, which would show little or no evidence of wear. The process of making an objective judgment on betterment follows no set rules, only general principles.

In determining ACV of a repair item, the adjuster must understand what causes building components to lose value. Following are some reasons:

1. Physical wear is the most obvious reason. Paint, wall and floor coverings, roofing, and mechanical appliances wear out over time. The *Repair and Remodeling Quarterly* by Marshall and Swift (see the Appendix to this chapter) contains a list of the expected life for some common building components. Another source of determining useful life is the manufacturer's warranty, although the useful life can be expected to be longer than the warranty period. These items are generally depreciated on a straight line basis; thus, if a component has a useful life of 10 years, it will depreciate in value 1/10th per year. Items that do not wear out are rarely subject to depreciation. There are exceptions. Evidence of rot or termite damage in framing would justify depreciation if the loss were caused by fire and damaged components were to be replaced with new ones.

2. Obsolescence also contributes to loss in value. As building materials and techniques change, features of older buildings lose value. A good example is piping for gas lights in an old building. Although the lines might be functionally sound, they add no value to the building. However, obsoles-

cence can be an elusive concept. The nine- and ten-foot ceilings that were becoming obsolete during the energy crisis of the 1970s are again considered a sign of superior construction as well as an aesthetic advantage.

3. Partial repairs usually do not improve the insured's financial position. As a result, they are rarely subject to depreciation. Replacing a few shingles causes no betterment, but replacing the entire roof usually does. Between the extremes of partial repair and total replacement, the adjuster must decide each case on its merits. Replacing only the damaged slope of a roof might not increase the value of a house. However, it would reduce the ultimate cost of replacing the rest of the roof at a later date.

4. In large losses involving older buildings, the ACV of the entire building might be the measure of loss. The market eventually devalues building components that do not wear out. The old notion that ACV of the entire building should reflect the same reduction in value as the depreciated repair estimate is simply incorrect. The effective building age depends on factors beyond the simple deterioration of the components.

Estimating the Value at Risk

Confirming that a building meets coinsurance or replacement cost requirements involves a different sort of cost estimating. Most insurers use either the Marshall & Swift or Boeckh publications to verify the insured value. The simplest methods use square-foot costs for several classes and qualities of construction for each type of occupancy. The more complex methods come close to the detail of the stick-by-stick estimate. These publications can also be used to set reserves, settle total losses, and verify value.

The key to using these references is to identify the *class*, *quality*, and *occupancy* of the building correctly. The books define these three terms. Adjusters must study and apply these definitions rather than rely on what they think a term or terms might mean. For example, an office in a good quality warehouse is different from a good quality medical office. Another example of differences in definition is the case of an adjuster trying to determine whether the cost to replace a fitness club building includes the cost of a pool. The answer to this question depends largely on whether the publisher defines a fitness club as including a pool. The adjuster must be sure to interpret this definition as the publisher intends.

Computer Estimating Systems

Computer-prepared estimates are an important loss adjusting tool. Most computer programs rely on a special scope sheet through which the adjuster collects data at the loss scene. Scope sheets are preprinted, with common construction operations arranged in a logical sequence of inspection. Instead of writing a description of the item, the adjuster marks the sheet to indicate the scope of damage for each component. That data is entered into the computer, which automatically computes area and quantities. The system draws pricing information from a construction cost database tailored to the location of the property. The computer can be a lap-top model used at the scene, a desk-top personal computer that remains in the office, or a remote mainframe that is accessed by modem. The data from the scope sheet can be entered by the adjuster or, more commonly, by a designated data entry person.

Advantages of Computer Estimating

The most obvious computer advantage is the easy to read and review printed estimate. Other advantages are the automatic extensions and totals, which are free of the errors in arithmetic that can creep into manual estimates. The computerized calculation of areas from dimensions can also eliminate arithmetic errors and save time. Some programs allow dimensions to be entered in feet and inches. The program then computes and uses the decimal equivalents. Using estimates can also save money; for example, computers can provide exact measurements, rather than rounding to the nearest half-foot.

Some of the systems have a database of local construction costs. Others rely on the adjuster's knowledge of local costs to provide the data. Even those with a built-in database allow the pricing to be tailored to the situation. Although some believe that control of the prices is an advantage, most eventually decide that flexibility to use the built-in data or to insert costs is the overriding need. Most systems mark or flag items for which the adjuster has overridden the built-in data.

Training

The structure of a computer system emphasizes following procedures, but computer systems cannot teach judgment. Computerized systems prompt inexperienced adjusters to consider things that they might have overlooked. Such discipline can create some good habits, leading to a more complete scope. However, the detail can lead to over-itemization and duplications if an adjuster is not completely familiar with the system and construction techniques. The cost data can provide some confidence, but the machine relies on the adjuster to make scope decisions. Making the right decision requires the adjuster to have the same training and experience as if he or she were preparing a manual estimate. If the adjuster chooses to replace some drywall that could have been cleaned and painted, the program will not correct the error.

To an experienced adjuster, computer systems can immediately provide increased efficiency. Realizing the full benefits of the system often requires the adjuster to do things differently, such as following a different sequence of inspection, using a different form for scoping the loss, or using a different method of approaching some repair items. For experienced adjusters, the training must emphasize the flexibility allowed by the system. Experienced adjusters will embrace the system only when they see that they, not the system, control the final estimate. A good flexible computer program can make an experienced, well-trained adjuster more efficient. In the hands of an untrained adjuster, it simply makes an untrained adjuster faster.

Cost Data

Most computer programs use unit cost data. Many create their unit costs from the labor and material costs method in much the same manner as the adjuster would do it manually. In some systems, the adjuster uses location modifiers and does not research costs in every possible place. At the very least, a good system offers some breakdown, if not complete disclosure, of the prices and usage rates that make up the unit costs. Without this information, checking or negotiating individual items is difficult. Many systems use quality codes to indicate the relative cost and quality of an item. However, more often than not, the adjuster must manually determine the cost of an unusual item and then look for the quality code that produces that same cost. A more direct approach is to override the built-in costs for unusual items.

Other Features

Another major advantage of a computerized system is the control that the adjuster gains by being able to obtain the scope and estimate almost immediately. If the insured's contractor finishes his or her estimate first, the adjuster would need to negotiate from the contractor's figures. With an estimate in hand, the adjuster negotiates from his or her figures. In competitive bid situations, the system helps control the form and format of the bids. Several programs print a scope that lists only the items and quantities, without pricing or extensions.

Another feature that helps negotiations is the automatic trade breakdown. Most programs print a trade estimate as well as a detailed room-by-room estimate. The **trade estimate** summarizes the detailed estimate by totaling the repairs for each trade. The trade estimate makes comparing the adjuster's estimate to a contractor's estimate that is itemized by trade easy.

A variety of features distinguish property estimating systems. The programs preferred by contractors usually have no built-in cost data, allowing the contractor to tailor the estimate to his or her usual charges. Some systems have only residential data, but others do a fair to thorough job of covering commercial building components as well. Several provide a method for calculating the value at risk. Some systems include cost data and reports for personal property. At least one system has a built-in routine for preparing bid comparisons between contractor estimates. An adjuster who can write a good manual estimate can, with some additional training, prepare the same estimate, in less time, using one of the computerized systems.

Arithmetic for Estimating

This section summarizes the formulas needed to calculate quantities in estimating property losses. This basic mathematics is of fundamental importance in preparing estimates.

Decimal Equivalents

Tape measures read feet and inches, but calculators use **decimal equivalents**. To develop speed in estimating, adjusters need to commit these decimal equivalents to memory. If the table presented below is used often enough, it will be learned quickly. If adjusters try to shorten the process by rounding up to the next foot or half-foot, however, estimates can be significantly higher when the loss involves many surface items like paint and drywall.

Inches	Decimal Equivalent (in feet)
1	.08
2	.17
3	.25
4	.33
5	.42
6	.50
7	.58
8	.67
9	.75
10	.83
11	.92
12	1.00

Surface Area

This section contains the basic formulas for calculating area. Subsequent chapters will describe specific techniques applicable to different building components.

Parallelogram, Rectangle, and Square

A **parallelogram** is a four-sided plane figure whose opposite sides are parallel to each other. A **rectangle** is a type of parallelogram whose sides meet at a ninety-degree angle. A **square** is a type of rectangle with four sides of equal length. As Exhibit 7-2 illustrates, the area of these figures is found by multiplying the base by the height. For instance, the area of a 4 ft. x 8 ft. sheet of plywood is 32 square feet.

Exhibit 7-2
Area of a Parallelogram

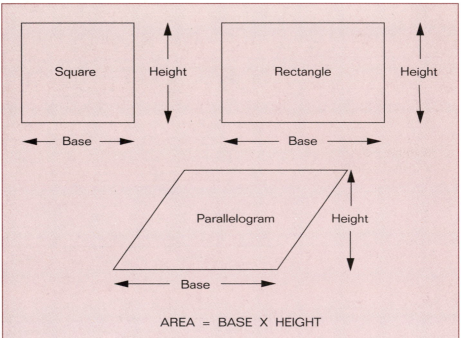

Trapezoid

A **trapezoid** is a four-sided plane figure with two parallel sides. The area of a trapezoid, shown in Exhibit 7-3, is one half of the sum of the parallel sides multiplied by the height.

Triangle

A **triangle** is a three-sided plane figure. As shown in Exhibit 7-4, the area of a triangle is one-half the base times the height.

Square Feet Versus Square Yards

The area of a surface is expressed in **square feet** for the purpose of determining how much material will be needed to restore that surface. There are, however,

Exhibit 7-3
Area of a Trapezoid

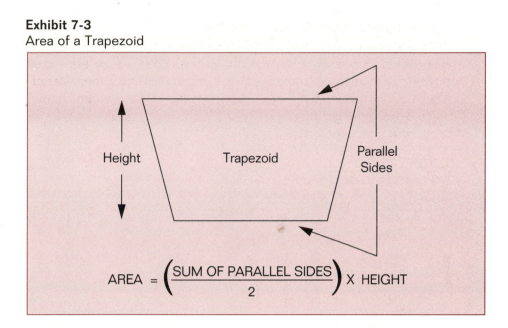

$$AREA = \left(\frac{SUM\ OF\ PARALLEL\ SIDES}{2} \right) \times HEIGHT$$

Exhibit 7-4
Area of a Triangle

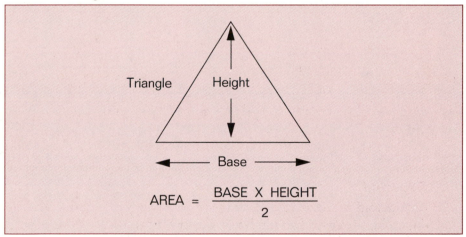

$$AREA = \frac{BASE \times HEIGHT}{2}$$

some exceptions. The amount of surface area to be covered by carpet, plaster, and stucco, for example, is typically expressed in square yards. In some areas of the country, contractors also quote an amount of paint needed by the number of square yards it must cover. The number of square yards is obtained by dividing the area in square feet by 9.

For example, the area of a floor 10 ft. x 12 ft. is 120 square feet. Dividing 120 by 9 expresses the same area as 13 ⅓ square yards.

Volume calculations for loss or repair estimates are much less common, but they are necessary. For example, to know the amount of poured concrete needed to restore a patio, the adjuster must determine the volume of the patio. Volume is calculated by multiplying the surface area of the patio (or other solid) by its depth or thickness. The units of measure should be consistent. For instance, in calculating the volume of a 10 ft. x 12 ft. patio that is 4 in. thick, the depth must be converted to feet. Four inches is $\frac{4}{12}$, or $\frac{1}{3}$, feet. The volume of the patio is calculated as follows:

Surface area 10 ft. x 12 ft. = 120 square feet
Volume 120 ft. x $\frac{1}{3}$ ft. = 40 cubic feet

Because concrete is quoted in cubic yards, the volume of this patio must be converted to cubic yards. Like a cubic foot, a cubic yard is a unit of measurement that expresses the volume of a solid. It is one-yard wide, one-yard high, and one-yard deep. Expressed in feet, a cubic yard is 3 ft. wide, 3 ft. high, and 3 ft. deep. The volume of an object that is one yard wide, one yard high, and one yard deep is one cubic yard (1 x 1 x 1) or 27 cubic feet (3 x 3 x 3). To convert 40 cubic feet into cubic yards, 40 must be divided by 27, which equals 1.48 cubic yards of concrete.

Rafter Length

There are three ways to determine the length of a rafter. If the roof is accessible and sound, the best way is to measure it. If not, the adjuster can look up rafter length in a rafter table or calculate rafter length. Exhibit 7-5 shows the end of a plain gable roof. The rafter length is the hypotenuse of the right triangle formed by the rise and the run. The run of a roof should not be confused with the span. For clarity, both terms are shown in Exhibit 7-5, even though the span is not used to calculate the rafter length. The rafter length is equal to the square root of the sum of the squares of the rise and the run. The example is simple because the roof has no overhang. If the eaves extended beyond the exterior wall, the length of the overhang would be added to get the full length of the rafter.

Board Feet

Many home centers sell lumber by the piece. A 2 x 4 that is 10 feet long might cost $2.10. A 2 x 4 that is 12 feet long might be priced at $2.52. Yet a lumber yard that deals with contractors might say that 2 x 4s, 8 to 14 feet long, cost $315.00 per thousand board feet.

These prices represent the same cost although they are stated in different units. Although the board foot terminology is becoming archaic in the retail

Exhibit 7-5
Rafter Length of a Gable Roof

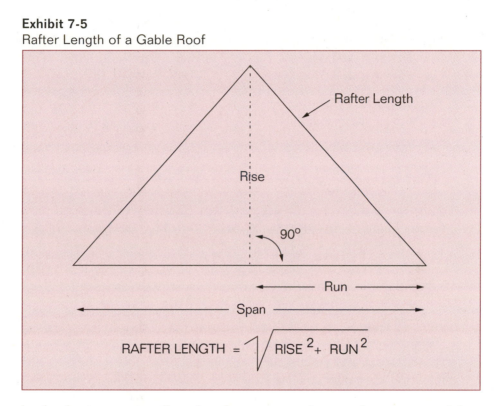

$$\text{RAFTER LENGTH} = \sqrt{\text{RISE}^2 + \text{RUN}^2}$$

lumber business, it is still used in the estimating business because many labor tables quote labor requirements in hours per thousand board feet. the traditional abbreviation for a board foot is "fbm," which stands for "foot board measure." Although the abbreviation "BF" is becoming more common, the abbreviation MBF also appears in some labor tables. The Roman numeral for 1,000, M, is used to abbreviate 1,000.

Nominal Versus Actual Dimensions

A 2 x 4 is not 2 inches by 4 inches, but the nominal size, meaning that is what this piece of lumber is called. It is actually ½ inch less on each dimension, or 1½ in. x 3½ in. The lumber was a full 2 in. x 4 in. before it was planed at the mill. After it was smoothed or dressed, the piece lost ¼ in. on each side, or ½ in. on each dimension. The same holds true for any type of milled lumber. The actual measurements of wood paneling, siding, and flooring are less than the nominal size. In some older buildings, framing members are full size. They are called **true dimension** or **full dimension lumber**.

When estimating building losses, adjusters should use the nominal dimensions rather than the actual measurement when calculating board feet. If a joist measures 1½ in. x 9 ¼ in., it is a 2 x 10 for the purpose of calculating board feet.

A board foot is a measure of the volume of a piece of lumber, so a piece of wood 12 in. square and 1 in. thick is one board foot. A 1 in. x 12 in. piece that is 10 ft. long is 10 board feet. A 2 in. x 12 in. piece of the same length is 20 board feet because it is twice as thick.

The Board Feet Formula

Board feet equal the number of pieces times the length of each piece times the nominal dimensions divided by 12:

$$\text{Board feet} = \frac{\text{Number of pieces} \times \text{Length of each piece} \times \text{Nominal dimensions}}{12}$$

If the scope calls for replacing 20 rafters, each 16 feet long, of 2 in. x 6 in. nominal lumber, the quantity can be converted to board feet as follows:

$$\frac{20 \times 16 \times 2 \times 6}{12} = 320 \text{ BF}$$

Lumber is usually sold in even lengths. As far as waste is concerned, if the length of the piece required is not an even number, the adjuster should round up to the next even length before converting to board feet. If the example above involved 15-foot rafters, the adjuster would round to 16 feet and arrive at the same quantity requirement, 320 board feet of 16-foot 2 x 6s. Other than rounding to even lengths, no other waste factor is used. Once the amount has been converted to board feet, looking up the labor required in a labor table is easy. If the table says that installing 2 x 6 rafters in a plain gable roof requires 30 hours per 1,000 board feet and the job requires only 320 board feet, the adjuster should divide 320 by 1,000 and multiply by 30 hours:

$$\frac{320}{1,000} \times 30 \text{ hours} = 9.6 \text{ hours}$$

Summary

All property loss adjusters need to know how to estimate building damages. The two steps in the estimation process are (1) preparing the scope of damage at the loss scene and (2) pricing the work determined by the scope into a repair estimate.

A scope is a detailed list of damage to each building component. The scope consists of a description of the degree of damage to each component, the quality of the materials of the damaged property, and the raw counts of the materials necessary for the repairs. Unlike a finished estimate, a scope does not list any prices or the calculated quantities. This chapter described a recommended method for inspecting a loss site and preparing a scope.

Pricing an estimate involves estimating the loss restoration cost by using the itemized damage in the scope. Construction operations typically include costs for materials, labor and employer's burden, tools and equipment, overhead and profit, and other miscellaneous direct costs (such as building permits and engineering fees). Adjusters can use reference materials such as those listed in the Appendix to this chapter to identify the materials and quantities needed and to estimate other construction costs.

The process of scoping the loss scene and pricing the estimate is similar for most losses, but the process of preparing the actual estimate can differ depending on the nature and size of the loss. The two primary methods for estimating repair costs are the labor and materials method (also called "the time and materials method") and the unit cost method.

The labor and materials method relies on data contained in *Walker's Building Estimators Reference Book*. That manual lists information such as the number of square feet that a gallon of paint will cover and how long a worker would need to paint a wall of a certain size. The unit cost method calculates the labor and materials necessary to repair one unit, such as one square foot of white ceramic tile. Once the adjuster has determined the unit cost for a job, he or she can multiply that cost by the number of units that the job include. Depending on the circumstances of the job, either the labor and materials method or the unit cost method might be the more appropriate estimating choice. Unit cost estimating is much quicker, but adjusters must understand its limitations to apply it correctly.

This chapter also discussed other considerations in estimating, such as demolition, debris removal, and the cost effect of very small and very large jobs. Demolition, the removal of damaged components from their original place in the building, can lead to overestimating, so the labor and materials method is usually the best approach for estimating the cost of demolition.

Demolition yields two types of debris: the debris of the damaged property and the waste produced by repairs. The best approach for estimating the cost of debris removal is to estimate the number and size of boxes or trash bins necessary to handle the debris and to apply a fee quoted by a local waste disposal company. Disposal companies charge a flat fee for placing a bin on site and removing it when it is full.

One popular approach for estimating small losses is to allow a minimum charge that represents two to four hours of labor and a small amount of material, but adjusters can also use the labor and materials or unit cost method. For large losses, adjusters might be able to take advantage of discounts for the purchase of large quantities.

Estimators studying the same loss might develop different repair figures either because of scoping differences or because of different opinions on the quality and type of repairs. The best way for an adjuster to resolve scoping differences is to prepare the scope jointly with the insured or the insured's contractor. After the scope has been agreed to, the adjuster can begin to resolve the difference in price by using the methods described in this chapter.

Adjusters should be aware that policy provisions can affect the preparation of estimates. For example, most policies exclude the additional repair costs needed to bring a damaged building up to current codes. In addition, an adjuster might be able to identify repair methods that add value but that cost less than the usual replacement with like kind and quality. Adjusters should also be aware that although the insurance industry has historically considered actual cash value, the basis of estimating repairs, to be equal to replacement cost less depreciation, the courts have used the broad evidence rule to include market value factors that can affect the amount of the cost to repair.

Adjusters can use computer estimating systems to prepare scopes. Those systems can produce easy-to-read printed estimates that are free of mathematical errors, but they cannot replace human judgment. The final section of this chapter summarized basic mathematical formulas that adjusters need to know to calculate quantities and estimate property losses. Chapter 8 will apply some of those formulas to hypothetical losses.

Appendix

Estimating References

How to Estimate Building Losses and Construction Costs, Paul I. Thomas, 4th ed., 1983, Prentice Hall, Inc., Englewood Cliffs, NJ, 471 pages.

The definitive work on estimating property losses. It contains information on damage and repair techniques as well as the necessary labor and material usage data needed to prepare an estimate.

Walker's Building Estimators Reference Book, ed. by Robert Siddens et al., 24th ed., 1992, Frank R. Walker Publishers, Chicago, IL.

Covers an extremely broad range of components providing labor and material usage data as well as more general information on residential and commercial construction methods.

Means Repair and Remodeling Cost Data, 1994 ed., Howard Chandler and David Tringale, 1993, R. S. Means Company, Kingston, MA 02364, 480 pages.

A unit cost reference covering residential and commercial components. It contains detailed labor factors. Location modifiers are presented by trade. Updated annually.

The Repair and Remodeling Quarterly, Marshall & Swift, Los Angeles, CA.

A detailed unit cost reference with complete labor factors that can be used in labor and material estimates. Covers residential and commercial components. Loose leaf format, updated quarterly.

National Construction Estimator, 1994, ed. by Martin D. Kiley and Will Moselle, 1993, Craftsman Book Company, Carlsbad, CA 92008, 592 pages.

A unit cost reference covering a broad range of residential, commercial, and industrial building components. Updated annually.

Wood-Frame House Construction, L. O. Anderson, U. S. Department of Agriculture, Agriculture Handbook No. 73, 1975, U. S. Government Printing Office, Washington, DC 20402, 223 pages.

This well-illustrated book covers all aspects of residential frame construction. Although it is written to show how to build a house rather than how to estimate losses, it is a good reference for terminology and construction methods.

This Old House Guide to Building and Remodeling Materials, 1986, Bob Villa with Norm Abram, Stewart Byrne, and Larry Stains, Warner Books, Inc., New York, NY 10103, 496 pages.

An easy-to-read, well-illustrated reference covering residential building materials. The emphasis is on the various types and quality of materials. It also contains some material usage information.

Property Damage Repair, National Property and Casualty Claims Research Service, Inc., 541 Catherine St., Chambersburg, PA 17201.

A bimonthly pamphlet, prepunched for ring-binder storage, provides excellent up-to-date information on construction materials, methods, damageability, and methods of repair. Each pamphlet is devoted to a particular subject.

Residential Building Cost Guide, Boeckh, an operating unit of American Appraisal Associates, Inc., Milwaukee, WI.

An annual publication that enables users to estimate the replacement cost of any residential structure. Boeckh also publishes similar services for commercial, agricultural, mobile-home, and high value residential structures. Several Boeckh services are available on computer software.

Chapter 8

Residential Construction Losses and Estimates

Property loss adjusters should have a working knowledge of methods of construction, methods of repair, and methods of estimating for residential structures. This chapter and Chapter 9 discuss the basics of these subjects. This chapter addresses painting, wallpapering, drywall, exterior siding, and roofing; Chapter 9 will address frame carpentry, finish carpentry, cabinets, and electrical and mechanical systems. These two chapters treat only residential losses, which account for most property losses. Commercial structures are too varied and too complex to be discussed adequately in this textbook, but many of the principles of adjusting losses to residential constructions apply to adjusting losses to commercial structures as well. These chapters describe the fundamentals, but adjusters can learn much more about construction material, methods, damageability, and costs, especially adjusters who prepare damage scopes and estimates.

Painting

In adjusting losses involving damage to painted surfaces, adjusters must determine how much area has been damaged and the cause of the damage (which will often determine the type of necessary remedy). After having determined those, an adjuster must prepare an estimate for the painting by considering the preparation for painting, the type of surface to be painted, the materials necessary for the painting, and labor. This section also discusses other considerations in adjusting painting losses: varnish, shellac, and stains, and exterior painting.

Determining the Method of Repair

Damage to painted surfaces can be repaired by cleaning, repainting, or sealing over and repainting. The degree of damage to interior finishes is closely related to their location relative to the cause of loss. Adjusters must be aware of this relationship when examining damages to interior painted surfaces. Water, heat, smoke, grease, soot, and fire can all affect paint. When examining the damage to interior paint surfaces, adjusters will find that the cause of the damage will, in many instances, determine the remedy.

Water Stains

Water stains to walls and ceilings are common. When water such as overspray from water hoses, use of fire extinguishers, or seepage of water from outside damages painted surfaces, the result is generally a stain or multiple spots. Depending on the type of painted surface, the area might be cleaned with a mild detergent. The adjuster should wipe the surface with a dampened cloth in an out-of-view area, a lower corner, or around a far window frame to determine whether the painted surface can be cleaned. With experience, adjusters will begin to recognize the relatively few times that such water stains or spots can be cleaned.

Water Stains on Ceilings

Water stains or spots on fiber material ceiling tiles have a brownish color. Most tiles discolored by water are not distorted or warped, but the stains cannot be removed. Covering the stained area with a sealer and painting the entire ceiling area can effectively hide the stains. A clear shellac or sealer additive in the paint prevents the stain from bleeding through the coat of paint. Unless such a sealer is used, the stain will continue to show no matter how many coats of paint are applied. As long as the tile is not itself bowed or warped, sealing and repainting the ceiling help to avoid extensive renovations.

Some areas are repeatedly affected by water seepage, such as from ice buildup along the eaves that forces water back into the interior or from rain driven under roof shingles by severe winds. In these cases, the tiles affected not only show several shades of brownish staining, but are also probably be bowed or warped. Replacement is the only appropriate solution for bowed or warped tiles.

Coverage Questions

When confronted with what appears to be a repeated exposure to seepage or other water problem, adjusters should question the owner about previous occurrences. Insurance coverage excludes losses caused by repeated exposures. Inadequate maintenance probably causes such problems, and related repairs require attention by and at the expense of the owner of the property.

Water Damage to Drywall

Unless continuously and repeatedly exposed to water or moisture, drywall ceilings and walls should not require tear-out and replacement. Drywall will dry and maintain its integrity unless it is exposed to so much water than the entire drywall panel is saturated, causing it to warp or pull through the nailed areas. If the shape of the drywall has been altered, replacement is the only appropriate way to repair the damage. If the only damage is stain to the painted surface, sealing and painting the drywall can be an effective method of repair. If an area of drywall must be replaced, the damaged area alone can be patch-repaired, smoothed, cleaned, and primer-sealed. The entire wall or ceiling area can then be painted to match the rest of the room.

Smoke Damage

In addition to damage by water, interior wall surfaces are subject to smoke damage. Smoke damage can occur from a fire, a furnace malfunction, or cooking grease fires. Smoke residue from sources other than grease fires or soot must be carefully examined and evaluated. Applying a light cleanser to an out-of-view area, such as over door trim, can determine whether the smoke residue can be removed. If the surface appears to clean readily, a cleaning allowance should be considered instead of repainting the surface. A professional cleaning service can provide an expert opinion when an interior cleaning an interior appears possible. Generally, smoke from wood stoves and heating surfaces is cleanable, but it might not be covered. Because wood stoves and fireplaces are inherently dirty, their continued use deposits smoke on interior surfaces.

Soot

Greasy or oily soot deposits are generally not completely cleanable. Soot clings to drywall nailheads and settles in cracks and crevices and between ceiling tiles and paneling on the walls. Flat painted surfaces can be washed when rubbed briskly with detergents, but semi-gloss and gloss-painted areas are more resilient and might require detergent cleaning. Because over-wetted soot tends to smear and streak, the cleaning of soot is best left to professional cleaners.

Paneling, including marlite surfaces and ceramic tiles, though, can be cleaned easily.

Fire and Heat

Direct fire always severely damages painted surfaces, either by burning it off or by blistering or scorching it. Damage from heat alone can also require repainting. Heat damage will be most severe at the ceiling, on the upper walls, and especially around door and window openings. If the paint is bubbled or blistered, it must be completely removed, and the entire area must be thoroughly cleaned and then repainted.

Factors in Painting Estimates

The important factors that adjusters need to consider in preparing estimates for painting are (1) preparation before painting, (2) the type of surface to be painted, (3) materials, and (4) labor.

Preparation Before Painting

Examples of the types of preparation work and the estimated amount of work in square feet that can be done in an hour of labor are presented in Exhibit 8-1. Estimates of painting costs should show a separate breakdown for unusual amounts of preparation time, covering of walls, moving of furnishings, or cleaning.

Exhibit 8-1
Preparing Time Estimates

Approximate Number of Square Feet per Hour To Prepare Surfaces for Painting	
Kinds of Work	**Sq. Ft. per Hour**
Washing smoked, calcimined walls, ceilings, and trim	100
Washing smoked painted smooth walls, ceilings, and trim	150
Washing smoked painted rough walls, ceilings, and trim	125
Washing floors	300
Removing floor varnish with liquid remover	50
Removing paint or varnish from trim with torch	25
Sanding trim	150

Adapted from Paul I. Thomas, *How to Estimate Building Losses and Construction Costs*, 1st ed. (Englewood Cliffs, NJ: Prentice Hall, 1960), p. 296.

Paint should never be applied to any smoke- or soot-covered surface. The surface to be painted must be clean, dry, and smooth for best results. Nailheads should be spackled, and all drywall joints must be compounded and sanded. If new drywall has been applied, a sealer coat will be needed, followed by at least one and possibly two additional coats of paint. Cracked or peeling paint must be removed.

Types of Surfaces

Interior surfaces to be painted are usually plaster, drywall, wood trim, or ceiling tiles. In general, surfaces not previously covered by paint absorb the first coat, and subsequent coats are needed to achieve a more finished and color-rich appearance. When estimating materials, adjusters must remember that completely new surfaces require more paint because of their tendency to absorb it. The additional cost created by the need for more materials is offset by the ease of applying those coats, thereby reducing the time and the cost of labor to apply the paint.

Masonry, or block walls, textured finishes, and metal ceilings are more difficult interior surfaces to paint. The rougher and more absorptive the surface is, the more labor and material will be required. Some masonry materials contain water-soluble salts, which, if not washed down by muriatic acid or a similar product and rinsed thoroughly, can form white or powdery deposits on the surface. Existing high-gloss surfaces of some masonry might have to be sanded lightly to ensure better adhesion.

Paint

Depending on the type of paint covering, the materials for any job might range in price from $10 to $18 a gallon. Sale prices of paint are not relevant in cost estimates since losses do not always coincide with sales. Interior paint is generally less expensive than exterior paint. Color and gloss are important factors. Although color is a matter of personal preference, gloss affects both appearance and wear. Adjusters can determine the average price range for paint in a locale and can usually use that price in their estimate. The most commonly used paints are latex, oil, and alkyd for interior and exterior finishes; rubber base and cement paints for masonry; and epoxy and urethane for those surfaces subjected to the toughest treatment and requiring the most protection from moisture, such as hardwood flooring.

One coat is generally enough to paint over a cleaned surface. If a sealer is used to cover a stain, one coat is also typically adequate. For heavily soot-damaged areas, two coats are usually needed despite the initial cleaning of the surface. This fact might justify reducing the cleaning allowance because the cleaning has not removed the need for two coats. If the soot is not as heavy, the cost of more extensive cleaning might be justified because either paint will not be needed at all or, more likely, only one coat will be needed because cleaning has effectively repaired the damage.

Primers are used for the first coat over new woodwork or new drywall. The new woodwork or drywall will absorb some of the primer, so each gallon of paint used on those surfaces will cover less square footage than normally.

Labor

Exhibit 8-2 presents the approximate number of square feet per hour for the application of paint or other materials to different surfaces. In the painting and decorating trades, labor represents approximately 70 percent of the total cost. Painting jobs, especially interior ones, can typically be handled by one person. In a given geographic area, wage rates are set by trade custom or by local economics. Wages per hour for a painter tend to be a few dollars less than for a roofer or general carpenter. In some areas of the country, union contracts might affect the number of workers hired for a job.

In most small residential losses, the time for preparation, set-up, cover-up, and other elements should be included in the estimate. Also included should be any unusual circumstances, such as extraordinary travel distance, very high or inaccessible areas, special types of surfaces, or material that would increase the time for the job.

Working on ladders reduces mobility, thereby reducing the area painted per hour. If a room has no furnishings, a quicker pace is possible. Moving and covering furnishings and removing draperies and wall decorations all require extra time. A spray gun is faster than a brush or roller, but the time involved in properly covering and protecting areas not to be painted could offset the time saved by using such a device. Of course, the experience of the painter also affects the rate of work.

Painting an area that is flat, smooth, and accessible requires less time than painting an area with windows, trim, cupboards, built-in shelving, and similar features. If the trim is a different color than the walls or needs to be covered with high-gloss paint as opposed to an alkyd or a latex paint, additional time will be required. Lack of space can present difficulties and slow down the rate of work. If an adjuster believes that a painting contractor's preliminary estimate figure is not justified, perhaps the adjuster has not fully considered the difficulties and limitations of the particular area involved.

Estimating Methods

This section explains three methods of measuring areas that need to be repainted. The first two, the gross area method and the net area method, are based on the time and materials method described in Chapter 7. The third method, the unit cost method, is appropriate for larger jobs.

Exhibit 8-2
Painting Time Estimates

Approximate Number of Square Feet per Hour To Apply Painting Material For Various Kinds of Work	
Kinds of Work	**Sq. Ft. per Hour**
Interior	
Painting smooth walls and trim (including openings)	150
Painting smooth walls only (excluding openings)	200
Painting windows, doors, and trim only	125
Painting rough plaster walls	125
Painting wood floors	200
Calcimine and casein painting	200
Staining trim and paneling	150
Shellacking floors	250
Liquid filler on floors	300
Varnishing trim and paneling	150
Varnishing floors	200
Waxing floors, paste and polish	200
Exterior	
Painting smooth walls (including openings)	125
Painting rough walls (including openings)	100
Painting smooth walls only (excluding openings)	175
Painting windows, doors, and trim only	100
Painting smooth concrete or masonry	125
Painting rough concrete or masonry	100
Staining wood shingle roofs	200
Painting solid board fences	200
Windows and Doors Separately	
Allow 1/3 hour per opening for each side.	

Adapted from Paul I. Thomas, *How to Estimate Building Losses and Construction Costs*, 1st ed. (Englewood Cliffs, NJ: Prentice Hall, 1960), p. 285.

Gross Area Method

Exhibit 8-3 shows a room for which the gross area method can be used. The floor of the room in the exhibit is 28' long x 15' wide, and the ceiling is 10' high. The door is 7' high x 3' feet wide. The room has three windows: two are 3' high x 5' wide, and the third is 3' high x 6' wide.

Exhibit 8-3
Example of Gross Area Method

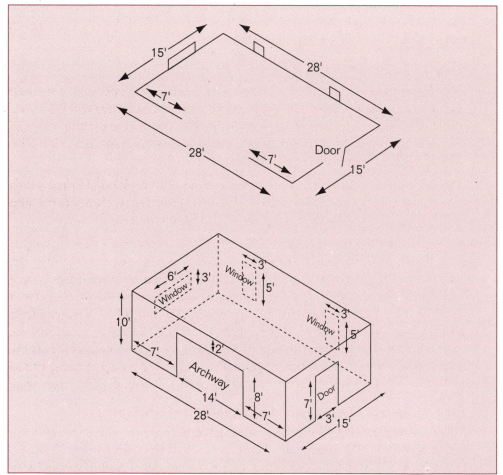

The gross area method does not deduct openings of less than 100 square feet from the total wall area of the room. (Square footage is calculated by multiplying height by width.) In effect, this method assumes that the door surface (21 square feet) and the three window areas (15 square feet, 15 square feet, and 18 square feet, for a total of 48 square feet) are to be painted. This method therefore provides an allowance for the extra time needed to paint the trim around the windows and door.

The steps in calculating the gross area of a room are as follows:

1. Calculate the surface area
2. Deduct openings of 100 square feet or more
3. Estimate the materials
4. Estimate the labor
5. Total the estimate

This section will describe each of those steps in detail. Once adjusters have learned the methods, however, they will not need to perform the painstaking calculations that this section describes.

Step 1: Calculate the Surface Area

For the purposes of painting, the surface area in any room is the sum of the wall area and the ceiling area. The wall area equals the perimeter of the room, which is simply the sum of the lengths of the four walls multiplied by the height of the room. In this case, the perimeter equals 86 lineal feet (28 + 28 + 15 +15), so the wall area is 860 square feet (86 x 10).

The ceiling area equals the length of the ceiling (28') multiplied by the width of the ceiling (15'), or 420 square feet. The total gross area is therefore the sum of 860 square feet and 420 square feet, or 1,280 square feet.

Adjusters must measure rooms precisely, and not simply pace them, guess, or even accept a homeowner's estimate. Even minor measurement errors can prove costly later. For example, an error of only two additional feet in the linear dimensions of this room would result in a wall area of 940 square feet and a ceiling area of 510 square feet, resulting in a gross area of 1,450 square feet, which equals approximately 12 percent more area. If this miscalculation were multiplied by several rooms and multiple claims files, the potential for distortion would be enormous. Adjusters must also remember to deduct non-painted surfaces (such as those which are paneled or papered) from the total gross area.

Step 2: Deduct Openings of 100 Square Feet or More

In this example, only the archway is deducted because the three windows are all smaller than 100 square feet. The gross area of the archway is 112 square feet (14' x 8'). The total gross area (1,280 square feet) minus the archway (112 square feet) equals 1,168 square feet, which is the gross area that must be painted. The area of the archway should include the moldings around the opening.

Step 3: Estimate the Materials

Labels on most paint cans estimate approximately 400 square feet of coverage per gallon. Given that estimate, 2.9 gallons of paint (rounded to 3 gallons) are necessary to paint the room in this example (1,168 square feet divided by

400 square feet per gallon). If two coats are required, six gallons of paint would be necessary (2 coats x 3 gallons per coat).

When several rooms will be painted the same color, a more accurate method for estimating the materials is to total the gross area of all the rooms to be painted, divide by the number of square feet per gallon, then multiply by the number of coats before rounding off to the nearest gallon.

Step 4: Estimate the Labor

Exhibit 8-2 presented the approximate number of square feet of painting material that can be applied per hour to different surfaces. According to that schedule, 150 square feet of paint can be applied per hour to cover smooth walls and trim (including openings) with one coat of paint. Based on this rate, the labor for the sample room can be estimated at 7.8 hours (1,168 square feet gross area divided by 150 square feet per hour).

Included in the average rate is the time required for normal preparation such as dusting, sanding trim, and patching minor surface cracks. Not included, however, are any openings larger than 100 square feet and unusual items such as radiators and built-in book shelves. Those items should be deducted from the gross area and considered as separate items. Also not included are preparatory tasks such as washing soot from walls and ceilings; removing furnishings such as draperies, light fixtures, and furniture; covering furnishings and wall-to-wall carpeting; and anything other than minor filling, sanding, and patching. Finally, ceilings and walls higher than nine feet might slow the rate of painting.

Step 5: Total the Estimate

The cost to apply one coat of paint to the room in the example is calculated as follows:

3 gallons of paint x $18.00 per gallon	= $ 54.00
7.8 hours of labor x $20.00 per hour	= 156.00
Remove/replace furnishings, cover floor, flooring, and fixtures as needed:	
1.2 hours x $20.00 per hour	= 24.00
Gross area method total	$234.00

For a small residential loss, the labor rate for the removal and replacement of furnishings will be the same as the painter's trade rate because the painter will be the only laborer on the job. For very large losses, those non-trade duties can be negotiated at a lower hourly rate.

Net Area Method

Most of the steps in the net area method are the same as the corresponding steps of the gross area method. The only difference between the two is that the net area method deducts from the total actual area the true size of all openings. The net area method uses the multiple system of measurement to calculate separately the size of all openings, and those areas are added to the adjusted area to estimate the materials.

In general, an estimate based on net area plus a separate calculation for each opening will be higher than an estimate based on the gross area method. If a room has more than four windows and two doors, the net area method would probably be more appropriate than the gross area method.

Step 1: Calculate the Surface Area

The first step is to calculate the *net* wall and ceiling areas in the room. The room in this example is 28' x 15' x 10'. The gross area of the walls is 860 square feet, but the room has five openings: an archway, a door, and three windows. The archway is 14' x 8', or 112 square feet. The door is 7' x 3', or 21 square feet. Two of the windows are 3' x 5', or 15 square feet apiece and 30 square feet combined. The third window is 3' x 6', or 18 square feet. Altogether, the openings represent 181 square feet of area. When that figure is subtracted from the 860 gross square feet of surface area, the result is 679 net square feet of area.

The last step in the calculation of the surface area in the net area method is to add the net wall square footage to the ceiling square footage, which, in this example, was 420 square feet. The total net area is the sum of 679 square feet and 420 square feet, or 1,099 square feet.

Step 2: Calculate the Openings

The **multiple system of measurement** adds a percentage or multiple of the actual size of a surface to the actual size to arrive at an effective size that reflects the time needed to paint such a surface. The adjustments to the actual openings can be considered a "difficulty factor." Exhibits 8-4 and 8-5 present difficulty factors that affect the amount of labor needed for different jobs.

According to the multiple system of measurement, no opening should be calculated at less than 40 square feet. Therefore, the openings in the sample room would be calculated as follows (the numbers in the parentheses are the adjustments made based on the directions presented in Exhibit 8-4):

- Archway   14' (+ 2') x 8' (+ 1') = 16' x 9' = 144 square feet
- 2 Windows   3' (+ 2') x 5' (+ 2') = 5' x 7'   = 80 (40 minimum x 2)
- 1 Window   3' (+ 2') x 6' (+2') = 5' x 8'   = 40
- Door   7' (+ 1') x 3' (+ 2') = 8' x 5'   = <u>40</u>

Effective area for calculating labor and time   304 square feet

Exhibit 8-4
Methods of Measuring and Listing Painting Quantities

The most accurate and perhaps the best method of estimating painting is to find the actual surface area to be painted from the plans and specifications or to take actual field measurements. As in everything else, painting costs are based on two major items, namely, labor and material. The cost of labor depends on the present-day labor scales, and the cost of material depends on the grade, or quality, and quantity of paint used. Estimating the quantities of material by finding the surface areas to be painted is relatively simple, but the labor quantities present a much more difficult problem.

For example, a plain wall surface might have the same surface area as a cornice, but it takes much longer to paint the cornice because of its height, which requires the erection of scaffolding. Care must be taken in pricing any piece of work, because conditions on each job are different. The following table, giving methods of measuring and listing painting quantities, is based on the actual performance of numerous jobs and represents a fairly accurate method of establishing quantities.

DESCRIPTION OF ITEM	UNIT OF MEASURE	DIFFICULTY FACTOR
Bevel or drop siding (NO deductions for areas less than 10' x 10')	Find actual area	Add 10% to surface
Shingle siding (NO deductions for areas less than 10' x 10')	Find actual area	$1\frac{1}{2}$ times area
Bricks, wood, stucco, cement, stone walls (NO deductions for areas less than 10' x 10')	Find actual area	
Eaves—plain, painted same color as side walls	Find actual area	$1\frac{1}{2}$ times area (no cornice)
Eaves—different color from side walls	Find actual area	2 times area (no cornice)
Eaves—with rafters running through	Find actual area	3 times area (overhanging; no cornice)

DESCRIPTION OF ITEM	UNIT OF MEASURE	DIFFICULTY FACTOR
Eaves—over bricks, stucco, or stone walls	Find actual area	3 times area
Exterior cornices:		
Plain	Find actual area	2 times area
Fancy scalloped	Find actual area	3 times area
Down spouts and gutters:		
Plain	Find actual area	2 times area
Fancy	Find actual area	3 times area
Blinds and shutters:		
Plain	Area of outer faces	2 times area
Slatted	Area of outer faces	4 times area
Columns and pilasters:		
Plain	Area sq. ft.	
Fluted	Area sq. ft.	$1\frac{1}{2}$ times area
Paneled	Area sq. ft.	2 times area
Moldings:		
If under 12" in girth	Figure 1 sq. ft. per linear ft.	
If over 12" in girth	Take actual area	
Exterior doors and frames:		
Figure no door less than 3' x 7', allow for frame, add 2' to width and 1' to height	Figure all doors at minimum of 40 sq. ft.	2 times area for both sides (no additional for one side)
Containing small lights of glass	Add 2 sq. ft. for each additional light	2 times area for both sides
Interior doors, jambs, and casings:		
Figure no door less than 3' x 7' , allow for frame, add 2' to width and 1' to height	Figure all doors at minimum of 40 sq. ft.	Do not deduct for glass in doors— 2 times area for both sides
Containing small lights of glass	Add 2 sq. ft. for each additional light	2 times area for both sides
Door frames only (NO DOOR)	Allow area of opening for both sides	

Continued on next page

DESCRIPTION OF ITEM	UNIT OF MEASURE	DIFFICULTY FACTOR
Exterior windows: Figure no window less than 3' x 6'; and 2' to both width and height of opening	Figure all windows at minimum of 40 sq. ft.	
Sash containing more than one light	Add 2 sq. ft. for each additional light	
Stairs: Add 2' to length of treads and risers to allow for stair strings. Figure 2' width of tread and riser	Multiply width (2') by length of tread. Then multiply by number of treads for total sq. ft.	
Wood ceilings	Find actual area	No deductions for openings less than 10' x 10'
Plastered walls and ceilings	Actual area of wall and ceiling, sq. ft.	Do not deduct for door and window openings
Floors	Find actual area	
Radiators	Find sq. ft. face area	Mulitply sq. ft. face area by 7
Cabinets, cupboards, bookcases	Find sq. ft. face area	Multiply sq. ft. face area by 3; WITH DOORS by 5
Wainscoting: Plain	Find actual area	
Paneled	Find actual area	2 times area

Step 3: Estimate the Materials

The difficulty factors added through the multiple system of measurement only affect labor, so the actual square footage is used for determining materials.

Net area of walls	679 square feet
Actual area of openings	181
Ceiling area	420
Total area	1,280 square feet

The method for estimating the materials involves dividing the total number of square feet by the number of square feet that one gallon of paint can cover, rounding that number to the next half gallon, and multiplying that figure by the cost of a gallon of paint. In this example, one gallon of paint covers 400 square feet and costs $18, so the materials estimate is calculated as follows:

$$\frac{1{,}280 \text{ square feet}}{400 \text{ square feet}} = 3.2 \text{ gallons, 3.5 when rounded to the next half-gallon}$$

Total materials = $63 (3.5 gallons x $18)

Step 4: Estimate the Labor

Exhibit 8-2 shows that the hourly rate to paint smooth walls only, excluding openings, is 200 square feet per hour. The hourly rate to paint trim only is 125 square feet per hour. Because the multiple system of measurement has already accounted for the difficulty of the trim, the rate for smooth walls can be used for the trim. Because the ceiling is higher than normal, the rate for smooth walls should be reduced to 150 square feet per hour. Based on these figures, the labor hours are estimated as follows:

Net area of walls	$\dfrac{679 \text{ square feet}}{200 \text{ square feet/hour}}$	= 3.4 hours
Rate for windows, door (trim)	$\dfrac{304 \text{ square feet}}{200 \text{ square feet/hour}}$	= 1.5 hours
Ceiling	$\dfrac{420 \text{ square feet}}{150 \text{ square feet/hour}}$	= 2.8 hours
Total labor	7.7 hours x $20/hour	= $154

Step 5: Total the Estimate

The estimate for the whole job is the sum of the cost of the materials ($63), the cost of the labor (7.7 hours at $20 per hour = $154), and the cost of removing and replacing the furnishings (1.2 hours at $20 per hour = $24). For this job, the estimate based on the net area method is $241.

Unit Cost Method

The unit cost method (which was described in Chapter 7) is most appropriate when several areas of damage or large areas of damage must be repaired. Once the cost per square foot to paint one room has been determined, that unit cost can be applied to similar rooms. Only one additional step is need to determine unit cost once the time and material figures have been calculated. That step is to divide the total cost by the total area:

Gross area method totals $234/1,168 square feet = $.20 per square foot

Net area method totals $241/1,280 square feet = $.188 ($.19) per square foot

Exhibit 8-5
Painting Difficulty Factors

The factors are based on the time necessary to paint irregular surfaces compared to painting a simple wall or ceiling area. For example, the factor of "4" allowed for painting a picket fence indicates that four times as much time is necessary to paint a fence than is necessary to paint a wall area of the same dimensions.

All of these factors are for one coat of paint.

The actual measurements of the item should be shown in the Description column of your estimate. The Square Foot Equivalent should be shown in the quantity column of the estimate. For example, to paint a 50' section of $3^1/2'$ high picket fence, 50 x 3.5 x 4 = 700 SF is necessary.

Item	Square Foot Equivalent
Cabinets with doors	L x H x 5
Bookcase, shelves, cupboards	L x H x 3
Lattice	L x H x 3
Drop or bevel siding less than 5"	L x W + 20%*
Drop or bevel siding 5" or wider	L x W + 10%*
Corrugated metal	L x W x 10%*
Eaves with open rafters	L x W x 3
Cornice (plain)	L x W x 2
Cornice (fancy)	L x W x 3
Gutters (outside only)	LF = SF
Steam radiators	L x H x 7
Picket fence (both sides)	L x H x 4
Chain link fence (both sides)	L x H x 3
Gratings/grille work	L x H x 4
Pipe less than 4" diameter	LF = SF
Pipe 4" to 8"	LF x 2
Pipe 8" to 12"	LF x 3
Pipe 12" to 16"	LF x 4
Balustrade	L x H x 4 = SF
Stairs	No. of risers x W (in feet) x 8
Structural steel	Actual area + 5%
Open trusses	L x H x 2
Masonry or stucco	L x H + 30%

*Deduct for large openings greater than 100 SF (10' x 10')

Adapted from *Estimating Guide*, 14th ed. (Falls Church, VA: Painting and Decorating Contractors of America), 1984, p. 15.

The unit cost method might not be accurate for smaller jobs (that is, those requiring fewer than three working days or twenty-four labor hours). Even though less time is needed to complete smaller jobs, contractors have fixed overhead costs, so a five- or six-hour job might not be calculated at less than an eight-hour job.

Varnish, Shellac, and Stains

Clear finishes like varnish and shellac not only enhance the natural colorings of wood, but also provide needed protection. Stain enhances the grain of wood by altering its color. Because the process of varnishing and refinishing solid wood surfaces is similar to painting, the labor and material computations are identical to those used for painting.

Varnish

Varnish is moisture-resistant and produces a tougher surface than most paints. Because of its durability, it provides excellent protection for hardwood flooring, wood furniture, and staircases, and it can also cover painted areas if the paint needs to be protected. Several coats are usually applied. The basic kinds of varnish are alkyd and phenolic, polyurethane, epoxy, and moisture-cured urethane. As more coats are applied, the surface becomes glossier. Before an additional coat is applied, the initial surface must be allowed to dry and finely sanded to remove imperfections.

Although multiple coats of any kind of varnish will improve the wood's durability, the alkyd and phenolic base is the least durable. Polyurethane, epoxy, and moisture-cured urethane give increasingly tougher protection. Pricing for varnishes ranges widely, so the adjuster should try to determine, if possible, the kind of material and the number of coats that were previously applied.

Scratches can be difficult to touch up. If damage is extensive, a complete resanding or stripping and application of new varnish is the most appropriate way to repair a surface. Because varnish is protective, water spills can be easily cleaned from it, as can smoke and soot. Heat, however, can cause the material to melt and run down cupboards and varnished trim. If that happens, the surface must be stripped, and the varnish must be reapplied.

Varnish is very flammable, so direct fire damage warrants complete refinishing. In kitchen grease fires, for instance, refinishing an overhead cupboard door to match the rest of the cupboards is very difficult. If possible, an adjuster should try to have the affected cupboard door or surface replaced, then refinished to match the other cupboards as closely as possible. This method is costly because of the labor involved, but it might avoid the much higher cost of replacing all the undamaged cupboards. Adjusters should also consider an appearance loss allowance, if appropriate.

Shellac

Shellac is an alcohol solution of resin derived from tropical insects. It is an inexpensive and abrasion-resistant coating for bare or stained wood. It cannot be used over other coatings, however, because its alcohol base tends to dissolve the existing surface. It is easily damaged by water, which causes white spots to form, and by alcohol compounds, which dissolve shellac.

Stain

Like varnish, stain enhances the grain of wood by altering its color. It can only be applied to raw wood or wood that has been previously treated with only a sealer or bleach solution. After having been stained, the surface is usually varnished, oiled, or waxed for protection and easy cleaning. Any paint can be used over a surface of stain. If wax has been used over the stain, the wax must be removed before painting.

Damage to Exterior Paint

Because exterior paint is exposed to weather, it can be damaged in ways that interior surfaces cannot be. Wind-driven rain, dust, and debris can chip or pit surface paint and wear off its protective coating. Intense direct sunlight and heat and very cold temperatures and accumulations of ice and snow can peel and crack exterior paint and shorten its lifespan. Improper methods of construction, which prevent proper ventilation, can create a moisture build-up, causing wood siding to remain wet and paint to peel away from the surface. Problems such as these, caused by "normal" wear and tear, are not covered by insurance and should be handled through regular maintenance.

The two basic adjusting considerations in handling damage to exterior paint are (1) distinguishing normal wear and tear and deterioration from insurable damages and (2) determining an allowance for appearance. Physical damage caused by fire or exposure to heat from fire at an adjoining property, hailstone damage, strong winds that propel objects into the exterior finish, and direct impact by vehicles are some of the causes of exterior paint damage that insurance might cover.

The complete exterior must be treated as one unit. The adjuster must decide among painting only the damaged area, painting the entire side where the damage is present, or painting the entire building. Because paint can change color as it ages, new paint can rarely be perfectly matched to the old. Adjusters must carefully judge the situation after inspecting the property. Building interiors are segmented and generally a variety of different colors, but exteriors are usually one color and should present a consistent appearance.

Factors in Exterior Paint Estimating

The main considerations in estimating exterior painting are the same as in interior painting: the initial preparation, the type of surface involved, and the amount and cost of material and labor.

Preparation

Preparing exterior surfaces to be painted might include the removal and replacement of deteriorated wood siding. Adjusters should note areas that appear to be maintenance problems, take photographs to substantiate these findings, and communicate the problem to the insured and any contractor involved. No reputable contractor will paint a deteriorated exterior surface before replacing the rotted materials. Paint that is blistered, peeling, or cracked must be scraped, and the surface must be sanded and possibly filled with wood filler and then smoothed. Paint surfaces can be stripped to bare wood by heating the coating, but burning the paint might scorch the wood. Paint flakes off stucco or masonry for the same reasons that it peels from wood surfaces, but, in addition, masonry contains alkalis that affect the ability of the paint to adhere to the surface. The damaged surface might have to be sandblasted or cleared by chemical strippers. Staining can be a problem on exterior surfaces. Rust and stains must be covered or removed so that paint will properly adhere to the surface.

Surface

For metal surfaces, paint adheres best to the bare metal. Painting over a previously painted metal surface is acceptable if the original coating is still firmly bonded. Both aluminum and steel should be prime-coated before a final coat of paint is applied. Masonite siding and clapboard sidings are the smoothest surfaces for paint coverage. Aluminum and masonry need more preparation and expertise in treatment. As with interior painting, the smoother the surface is, the better the result and the higher the productivity will be.

Material

Materials for outside painting include alkyds, latex, epoxy, and oil. Because of weather exposures and the generally rougher surfaces to which exterior paints are applied, these paints contain additives that promote flexibility. Latex paint is the most versatile; it cleans in water, is the fastest drying, and allows water vapor to escape, reducing the chances of blistering. Latex might not, however, adhere over other types of paint. Although latex can be applied to masonry, an alkyd base or a rubber base coating is recommended for that type of surface. Oil-or alkyd-base metal paints are recommended for a direct application to metal siding.

Basic protection against moisture and expansion and flexibility characteristics needed for exterior finish materials are constantly being improved. An adjuster's knowledge of the proper use of these materials helps in assessing the reasons for preexisting conditions and enables the adjuster to make reasonable judgments regarding the distinction between direct physical damage and normal wear and tear.

Labor

By far the largest single factor to be considered in exterior paint estimating is the labor cost. Because of the effects of weather and the special preparation for exterior surfaces, proper labor estimating requires that the surface be inspected. In estimating labor costs, an adjuster should list each distinct operation separately. Normal unit prices per square foot do not usually include preparation or scaffolding. Operations vary so much by job that a single unit cost is unlikely to apply to any particular job.

Wallpapering

Wallpaper can be damaged by water, smoke, fire, or heat. Other types of losses to wallpaper are caused by vandalism, carelessness in moving furniture, or any striking or puncturing of the surface. Although these causes of loss affect wallpaper in different ways, the decision to repair a damaged section or to repaper a room is typically based on whether the existing paper can be matched. This section discusses the typical types of damage and repair options.

By far, water damage is the most common form of wallpaper damage. Water leakage from a shower, tub, or defective toilet seal in an upstairs bathroom can dilute the paste and cause the paper to loosen from the wall. In some cases, once the paper is dry, it can be carefully re-pasted with a small brush and laid back onto the wall. If the paper becomes stained or brittle, the only alternative is to replace the stained area. One advantage of papering is that it can often be repaired by applying a matching piece over the damaged area. The success of this approach depends on the experience of the paperhanger, the type of paper and adhesive used, and the pattern design.

When confronted with stained wallpaper, an adjuster should ask the homeowner whether matching paper is available. Because people generally buy more paper than they need, if the paper was installed within the past several years, a roll might be stored in the attic or basement.

If there is no extra paper, a match is unlikely because wallpaper, although manufactured in long rolls, is often made in different dye lots. For this reason, even if a pattern is available that matches the damaged pattern, the colors might be different. If a match cannot be made, the paper must be completely replaced. Therefore, although some wallpaper losses are small, others are very large.

Wallpaper does not need to be *on* fire to be damaged *by* fire. A nearby fire can generate enough heat to scorch wallpaper. Smoke can be washed from some vinyl or fabric wallpaper. Untreated common vinyl-coated or cloth-backed papers can be washed. Professionals should handle these tasks, though, because pattern inks might run or the paper can tear if handled too roughly. Professional cleaning is also required for oily soot damage. If not properly treated, soot will streak wallpaper, as it does a painted surface. Foil, flocked, and felt coverings are not cleanable, so if they are damaged by soot, they must be replaced.

Factors Affecting the Costs of Wallpaper Losses

The main factors to consider in estimating wallpapering losses are (1) preparation, (2) the size and shape of the surface to be covered, (3) the quality of material to be replaced, and (4) labor.

Preparation

Like paint, wallpaper requires a smooth surface. The best surface on which to apply paper is a bare wall. Undercoats of paper, especially if the seams are overlapped rather than butted, result in a poor appearance. If the damaged layer is to be covered, any loose material must be removed before the new covering is applied. More than three layers of paper are not recommended because the weight of the newest layer and the moisture of its adhesive might loosen the layers beneath it. Additional time must be allowed to wet down, heat, or steam-remove underlayers, to patch the bare surface, and, in some instances, to properly size the bare wall area for adhesion. **Sizing**, the application of a thin coat of paste onto a bare surface, enables the paste or glue on the back of the wallpaper to adhere more securely.

Surface Features

As with painting, wallpapering can be accomplished most quickly over a flat, smooth, continuous surface. Door openings, built-in shelving, windows, and other features slow the process of application, especially for patterned wallpaper, for which the lengths of paper must be carefully aligned. That alignment might involve as much as 15 to 20 percent waste, even in average-sized rooms. Areas above and below large windows, where the pattern must be aligned both vertically and horizontally, create additional waste and delay.

Materials

Wallcovering materials include such items as cork, carpet-like deep-pile material, fabric-backed vinyl, felt, and grass cloth. Handprinted wallpaper, leather, and wood veneer laminates are also used. However, the most common covering is machine-printed paper, either plastic-surfaced or vinyl with paper backing. The variation in materials creates wide variations in costs. As a result, adjusters must carefully identify the type of wallpaper in order to come up with an appropriate estimate. Following are three types of wallpaper:

- **Vinyl**—Vinyl wallcovering is basically an elastic film on a backing of paper or fabric. Vinyl paper does not breathe, as most other wallcoverings do, so the proper anti-moisture adhesive must be used to prevent mildew. Because fabric-backed vinyls are washable and durable, they are commonly used in the kitchens, bathrooms, and hall areas. The thickness and weight of the vinyl wall covering determine its ability to withstand grease, smoke, and dirt from contact with people's hands. Categories of vinyl range from decorative to industrial. When possible, adjusters should take a sample from the damaged area and secure an opinion from a knowledgeable local supplier as to material cost.

- **Fabric-backed foil**—Fabric-backed foils are installed in much the same way as vinyls, but more care is necessary to keep excess paste off the surface. If dried paste adheres to the foil facing, it can scratch it. Some foils have a plastic-coated covering that makes them more washable. Foils are difficult to work with, and their sheer surface magnifies any defects in the underlying wall surface. For this reason, lining paper is often used as a primer surface to reduce wall imperfections. Foil paper must be carefully applied so that the foil cover is not creased.

- **Flocked coverings**—Flocked wallcovering has part or all of the design made from short textile ends that are bonded to the wallcovering material. The textile material stands on end.

Coverage

Wall coverings are generally sold in a **standard double roll**, which covers seventy-two square feet, or in single rolls covering thirty-six square feet. Although rolls come in different widths, each single roll always covers thirty-six square feet, and each double roll always covers seventy-two square feet. Wallpaper designs include no pattern at all, random match patterns (which create an overall design effect, but which might not be the same design from roll to roll), straight-across matches, and a drop matches.

Waste

When estimating materials, adjusters can allow for the waste involved in a matching design by considering the area of coverage of a single roll to be thirty square feet and for a double roll to be sixty square feet. This calculation will be illustrated in the discussion of estimating below.

Labor

The experience of the paperhanger is the most important factor in estimating labor costs. Paperhangers can generally work alone. Their rate is typically about the same as the rates of painters. When checking estimates, adjusters should determine the trade cost averages for the particular area. An allowance should be made for difficult materials or work circumstances. The more intricate the pattern is, the more expertise will be required for applying the wallcovering.

As mentioned, wallcoverings should be applied to dry, flat, and clean surfaces. Removing existing paper that is plastic-coated, foil type, or not strippable requires that it be hand-sanded, then wet and scraped off. Spackling cracks, and gouges create porous surfaces that must be primed or sealed. Drywall is very porous and does not allow the proper application of wallpaper, so new drywall surfaces must be primed. In addition, the drywall would be damaged if the covering were ever stripped off. Sizing the surface to be covered creates a uniform and smooth surface to ensure good adhesion.

Estimating Wallpaper

Wallpaper estimates can be based on the net area method or unit cost method.

Net Area Method

Assume that a room to be papered is 18' x 20', has one door (3' x 7'), one window (4' x 5'), and a ceiling height of 8'. The wallpaper to be used is random match or small repeated pattern, so the anticipated average waste is between 15 and 20 percent.

Paper

If the amount of necessary materials is not estimated accurately, reorder at a later date might mean that the wallcovering is a different color or that the style is no longer available. As mentioned, wallpaper comes in different widths, but each double roll always covers seventy-two square feet, and each single roll always covers thirty-six square feet. The most common width is eighteen inches; this width comes in twenty-four-foot rolls.

To determine the amount of materials necessary, the adjuster should measure the perimeter of the room and multiply it by the height to determine the total wall area of the room. This calculation includes two areas that will not be covered, a door and a window. Just as in the net area method for estimating paint jobs, the openings should be deducted to arrive at the net area to be covered. Those calculations are as follows:

Perimeter (20' + 20' + 18' + 18')	76 feet
Wall height	x 8
Total wall area	608 square feet
Window (4' x 5')	20 square feet
Door (3' x 7')	21
Total openings area	41 square feet
Total wall area less openings area	608 square feet
	– 41
Net wall area	567 square feet

Assume that a single roll, allowing for 15 to 20 percent waste, will cover thirty square feet. This project will require 19 single rolls (567 ÷ 30 = 18.9, rounded to 19). If the wallpaper pattern is larger or less regular, more waste should be allowed, resulting in a need for additional material. However, a good average net area per single roll is thirty square feet; a good average for a double roll is sixty square feet.

Paste

To calculate the amount of paste needed, assume that one pound of paste is enough to apply ten single rolls. Therefore, two pounds would be needed for 19 single rolls (19 ÷ 10 = 1.9, rounded off to 2). The sizing material is a gelatin sealer, which is already added to the paste compound and need not be calculated separately.

Ceilings

If the ceiling is wallpapered, multiply the width times the length to determine the area. This area must be added to the wall surface area to determine total area to be papered. The room in this example would need 31 single rolls of wallpaper and 3 pounds of paste when the ceiling area is included, as the calculations below illustrate:

Ceiling (18' x 20')   = 360 square feet

Walls (net area)   567

                                  927 square feet

$$\frac{927 \text{ square feet}}{30 \text{ square feet of coverage per roll}} = 30.9 \text{ rolls of paper; rounded to } 31$$

If 10 rolls of paper can be applied with 1 pound of paste, then 3 pounds of paste are necessary (31 rolls of paper ÷ 10 rolls per pound of paste = 3.1 pounds, rounded to 3).

If the following prices are assumed, the estimate for materials can be completed as follows:

31 rolls @ $10 per roll   = $310

3 pounds of paste @ $1 per pound =   3

Total materials $313

Labor

The labor is based on the number of rolls of wallpaper to be applied. Exhibit 8-6 shows average rates of application per hour. The rate to overlap paper is faster than when the edges are butted. Working with high-grade paper or wall coverings, however, will reduce the number of single rolls that can be applied per hour.

The room in this example requires 19 rolls for the walls. The average labor factor is 3 single rolls per hour for butt joint, average grade material. Dividing 3 into 19 rolls shows that 6.33 hours of labor are required to hang 19 single rolls.

If the previous layer and several other layers must be removed, the labor hours estimate will change. As Exhibit 8-6 shows, the rate to remove paper is 100 square feet per hour. In the example, this rate adds 5.67 hours to the labor estimate. Total labor is then calculated as follows:

$$\text{Removing paper } \frac{567 \text{ sq. ft.}}{100 \text{ sq. ft./hr.}} = 5.67 \text{ hours}$$

$$\text{Applying paper } \frac{19 \text{ rolls}}{3 \text{ rolls per hour}} = 6.33 \text{ hours}$$

Labor total   12 hours

These figures do not assume extensive preparation of the bare walls or sizing.

Total Cost

The following breakdown shows the total estimated cost to remove the old paper and hang new paper on walls only (no ceiling) at the price of $10 per single roll with butted edges, no extreme pattern matching, and two openings:

Net area of walls: 567 square feet	
19 rolls @ $10 per single roll	$190
2 pounds paste @ $1 per pound	2
Labor to strip old and hang new paper	
plus border: 12 hours @ $20 per hour	240
Total cost	$432

As with paint estimating, the labor factor should include access time and any above-normal preparation of the surface. These extra items can be listed separately on an estimate sheet. Each additional allowance should be explained.

Estimates are subject to change since the damaged areas might need to be reinspected. The undersurface is normally not visible upon initial inspection. The area might need to be inspected again to determine whether the damage was caused by deterioration, which most policies do not cover.

Unit Cost Method

Because of the wide variation in the cost of material, estimating a single unit cost for some jobs is difficult, but applying a unit cost to separate rooms in the same house is possible. As shown in Exhibit 8-6, even the labor hours differ with the grade of wallcovering being applied. The unit cost for the room in the example would be the total estimated cost for the job divided by the total net square feet, as calculated below:

$$\text{Unit cost} = \frac{\$432}{567} = \$.76 \text{ per square foot}$$

Any unusual preparation or accessibility problems should be figured separately and added to the unit cost estimate.

Drywall

Common terms for **drywall** are "sheetrock," "wall board," "gypsum board," and "plaster board." It comes in four-foot widths and lengths of eight and twelve feet. Drywall is plaster material covered on both sides with a fiber paper bond. It is water-repellent and has many advantages over plaster, a building material common in old structures but rarely used now. For example, the cost of drywall is relatively low compared to plaster. Drywall can also have a finished design face instead of its paper bonding. Its use is limited to interior walls and ceilings. Paint and wallpaper are the most common coverings for drywall.

Exhibit 8-6
Wallpapering Time Estimates

Approximate Rate per Hour for Various Kinds of Paperhanging Work	
Kind of Work	**Quantity Per Hour**
Remove wallpaper—single layer	150 sq. ft.
Remove wallpaper—several layers	100 sq. ft.
Hang wallpaper—lap joint—cheap grade	4 single rolls
Hang wallpaper—butt joint—average grade	3 single rolls
Hang wallpaper—butt joint—high grade	2 single rolls
Hanging borders	30 yards
Flexwood	10 sq. ft.
Canvas	50 sq. ft.
Sizing plaster walls	400 sq. ft.

Adapted from Paul I. Thomas, *How to Estimate Building Losses and Construction Costs*, 1st ed. (Englewood Cliffs, NJ: Prentice Hall, 1960), p. 299.

Damage to and Repair of Drywall and Plaster

Fire can consume drywall, and heat can scorch it, especially on ceilings and upper wall areas. In addition to direct fire and heat damage, drywall can be punctured by vandalism or carelessness. Opening a door forcibly can cause the doorknob to puncture or dent the wall surface. Small amounts of water generally do not affect drywall, but when exposed to water for a longer period, it tends to absorb the water like an ink blotter, resulting in brownish stains. If allowed to dry properly, it can be sealed and covered by paint or paper as long as the bonding of the exterior paper is not damaged.

Drywall is a very repairable material. Even if punctured or pierced in some way, drywall is easily repaired by spot patching another piece to the damaged area or by filling any area less than six inches with spackle or joint compound material.

If a plaster wall or ceiling is damaged, it can be replaced with drywall instead of plaster; in fact, few contemporary workers can do plastering. If water damages a plaster ceiling, the "key" of the plaster might have been weakened.

The **key** is the plaster material that is forced through the original lathe, which in drying becomes a fastener for the plaster. If plaster is loose to the touch, it should be removed. For a sagging plaster ceiling, 1" x 2" strapping can be installed on the ceiling both to support the plaster and to provide a surface on which to install new ceiling tile. This technique eliminates the need to tear out the plaster ceiling. Even if the ceiling plaster appears tight, exposure to a large amount of water can cause loosening in the future. For water-damaged plaster ceilings, allowing for strapping and installation of ceiling tiles is necessary.

Drywall damages greater than six inches must be cut out. The drywall should be cut back with a utility knife to expose part of the vertical wall studs. Boards can be screwed to the vertical studs and the back of the existing drywall to provide a fastening surface for the new patch. After a patch of new drywall is screwed in place, it must be finished with drywall tape and joint compound.

Installation of Drywall

Drywall can be nailed or screwed onto wall and ceiling studs, or screwed onto metal stud framing. To minimize the finish work needed to fill in the seams where the panel sheets meet, drywall is normally installed lengthwise on the walls, not vertically. The ceilings should be done first so that the drywall that forms the walls butts under and supports the ceiling sheets. Nailing is recommended every six to eight inches vertically along the length of the stud on walls and every five to seven inches on ceiling sheets. The sides of the drywall are tapered to form a wide "V" shape where sheets butt together. This technique provides an area for joint compound and tape, which is used to smooth over and create a continuous wall or ceiling surface.

Tape and joint compound are used for inside joints. On outside corners, that is, where two walls meet at a right angle, metal strips are nailed in place over the corner, then covered by joint compound. This technique protects the outside edges from damage. After carpenters install the drywall, finish subcontractors or drywall specialists commonly do the tape and compounding. At least two and possibly three coats of joint compound are applied with at least a day allowed for each previous coat to dry.

Estimating Drywall

Drywall can be estimated with a gross area method or a unit cost method.

Calculating Area

The gross area of the room can be used to estimate the amount of drywall needed. Only openings larger than thirty-two square feet should be excluded.

Measuring in this way eliminates the need to apply a waste factor. Assume that a room measures 12' x 12'. It has a window (3' x 4') and a door (3' x 7') that are ignored. This room has gross area of walls of (12' + 12' + 12' + 12') x 8' = 384 square feet.

Materials

The three basic thicknesses for drywall are ⅜", ½", and ⅝". Prices vary by thickness. As mentioned, drywall comes in sheets four feet wide and eight and twelve feet long. For this job, 4' x 8' sheets are used. To find the amount of drywall needed for this job, divide the total area of the room by the area of one sheet of drywall:

Ceiling	144 square feet
Walls	384
Total area	528 square feet
Amount of drywall	528 ÷ 32 = 16.5, rounded to 17 sheets

Approximately 37 linear feet of perforated tape and 5 pounds of joint compound are required for every 100 square feet of drywall. Rather than price the materials for taping and jointing individually, adjusters can use a unit cost per square foot of drywall in calculating total materials cost:

17 sheets of drywall @ $8 per sheet	= $136.00
Tape and compound for 528 square feet	
@ $.07 per square foot	= 36.96
	$172.96

Labor

Labor is affected by the size of the job, by whether the drywall is installed horizontally or vertically, and by what will cover the drywall. In general, the larger the job is, the faster the rate of application is. The common rate for installing drywall in a large area is 1.5 hours per 100 square feet; in a medium-size area (1 to 3 rooms), 2.5 hours per 100 square feet; and in a small area where accessibility is a problem, 3.5 hours per 100 square feet. Taping and applying joint compound require 1.2 hours per 100 square feet. If the drywall is to be painted or wallpapered, it must be taped, and joint compound must be applied. However, tape and compound are not required on walls that are to be paneled or otherwise covered by decorator wood materials.

Total Cost

The room in this example is a medium-sized area. The calculations for labor are shown below:

528 square feet x 2.5 hours per 100 square feet =

5.28 x 2.5 hours	= 13.2 hours
5.28 x 1.2 hours (tape and compound)	= 6.3
Total labor time	= 19.5 hours
Labor 19.5 hours @ $20 per hour	= $390.00
Materials	172.96
Total estimated cost	$562.96

Unit Cost

Unit cost can be calculated by dividing the area into the total cost.

$$\frac{\$562.96}{528 \text{ square feet}} = \$1.06 \text{ per square foot}$$

That figure can be regarded as a valid unit cost for drywall in any medium-sized job.

Exterior Siding

The extent of and potential for damage to exterior siding are affected very much by the type of siding material. Wood shingles or shakes of redwood and western red cedar normally have an excellent moisture-resistant composition. Nevertheless, weather-related losses are the main cause of damage to such shingles. Over time, wind-driven rains can seep behind siding and cause deterioration. Hail can split wood shingles and puncture or dent aluminum or vinyl siding. Hail can cause a range of damage, from minor cosmetic damage to moderate and severe losses. The same force of impact that would dent aluminum would cause little if any damage to more pliable vinyl or even to wood clapboard surfaces. Siding losses related to vandalism involve spray paint damage or tearing of siding.

Although aluminum can be repainted, it will also need to be painted several years later. Even though it dulls over time, the original baked-on surface will not peel or crack, as will paint. Many siding losses, especially to aluminum siding, can be adjusted with an allowance for appearance. When in doubt, an adjuster should secure photographs of the damage, note the kind of siding involved, and try to arrange an inspection by an expert familiar with this kind of damage.

Spot repairs can be made to wood clapboard and vinyl/aluminum siding. Repair of wood siding is discussed in the next section.

Siding Materials

The major types of siding material are wood, exterior panels such as wood shakes, hardboard, aluminum, and vinyl. Masonry, stucco finishes, and composition asphalt coverings are also used.

Wood Siding

The most common types of wood siding are bevel design or dropsiding. Examples of both are shown in Exhibit 8-7, along with other types of siding. Wood siding is usually white pine, redwood, douglas fir, or red cedar. It is applied horizontally and readily accepts paint or stain. The corners can be finished with vertical trim boards or covered by metal corner caps. High-quality installations have mitered corners, which require more time.

Wood drop or bevel siding is applied over felt paper, which serves as a vapor barrier for the back of the siding. The siding is nailed directly onto the sheathing of the framed building. The siding material can range up to one inch thick and twelve inches wide and typically comes in lengths of eight to twenty feet.

Surface damage to wood siding can be filled and sanded, then painted. Broken boards, however, must be replaced. That replacement involves loosening the board strip above the damaged area, cutting the replacement boards to fit, and replacing all but the bottom board. The back lip of the bottom board must be cut away so that the board can be pressed against the siding and nailed in place. Wood siding can also be applied vertically.

Sheet Materials

Exterior sheet materials generally come in 4' x 8' panels, a variety of patterns, and several different colors. Exterior grades of particle board and plywood can be used when quality is not the primary concern. These materials can be easily painted and should have a good vapor barrier behind them. Batten strips should be nailed where the edges butt against one another to prevent leaking at the seams.

Wood Shingles

Wood shingles come in lengths of sixteen, eighteen, and twenty-four inches. Shingles are sold by the square, with four bundles per square. Four bundles cover 100 square feet with an exposure of five inches. (The *exposure* of a shingle is the amount that is exposed to the weather.) With a smaller exposure, such as four inches, the shingles cover less area.

Exhibit 8-7
Types of Siding

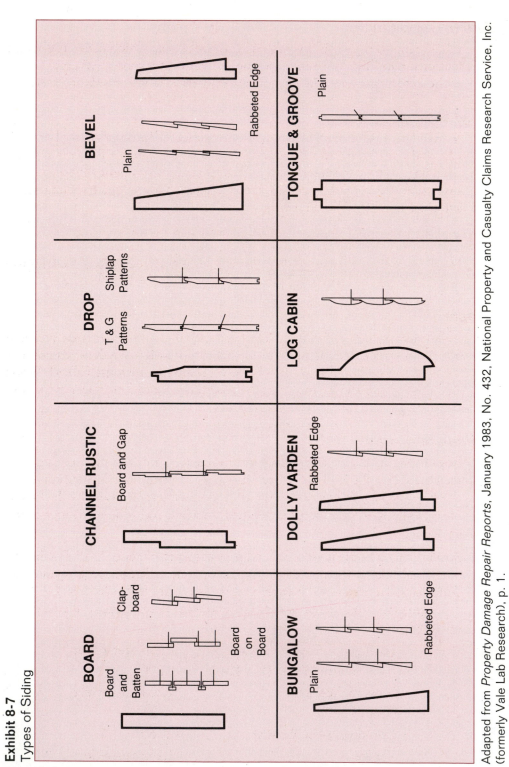

Adapted from *Property Damage Repair Reports*, January 1983, No. 432. National Property and Casualty Claims Research Service, Inc. (formerly Vale Lab Research), p. 1.

Aluminum Siding

Aluminum siding is sold in cartons of twelve sheets, which cover 100 square feet of surface. They are interlocking and have an exposure of eight or ten inches. For a slightly higher cost, they can be backed with insulating material.

Vinyl Siding

Vinyl siding might be an alternative to aluminum. The color of vinyl siding is part of the material and will not fade over time. It is pliable and not as prone to damage by hail or other minor impact. It can also be bought with or without insulation. Vinyl tends to stiffen in cold weather and can crack if bumped. Its surface is not adaptable to painting.

Estimating Siding

In estimating the amount and cost of siding, adjusters need to consider waste as well as materials and labor. Unit costs for siding can be calculated.

Waste

In estimating beveled siding, adjusters should use the net area and add 35 percent to account for mill waste and cutting. Exhibit 8-8 shows the various waste factors for different designs based on board foot measure (FBM). Wood siding is considered one inch thick. Thus, square foot measurements for one-inch-thick wood are equivalent to FBM.

Calculating Area

Regardless of the type of material used, the exterior of the structure must be measured, and the area of all openings must be deducted. To determine the exterior surface area of a house, multiply the perimeter measure by the height of the walls under the roofed eave, then calculate and add on the area of the gable ends.

Assume that a house is 40' x 26' and thus has a perimeter of 132'. The height of the walls under the roof eave is 8', so the surface area is 1,056 square feet. The triangular area of each gable end is 104 square feet, (26' x 8') ÷ 2. To determine the total *net* surface area, the adjuster must deduct the area of the openings:

Total exterior surface area	1,056 square feet
Total gable end area (2' x 104')	208
Gross surface area	1,264 square feet
Door (3' x 7')	– 21
3 windows (4' x 5' each)	– 60
Net area	1,183 square feet

Materials

The house in this example has 1" x 8" bevel siding. According to Exhibit 8-8, a 35 percent waste factor should be added for bevel siding of that size. Multiply the net area by 1.35 (1,183 x 1.35 = 1,597 FBM) to determine the amount of siding needed to cover the exterior walls and gable ends.

Before wood siding is installed, a vapor barrier of felt is installed over the wood sheathing material. Each roll of felt material covers approximately 400 square feet.

Exhibit 8-8
Waste Factors for Siding

Percentage of Milling and Cutting Waste Required per 1,000 FBM of Various Types of Wood Siding			
Type of Siding	**Nominal Size in Inches**	**Lap in Inches 1" Lap**	**Percentage of Waste**
Bevel siding	1 x 4	1	63
	1 x 6	1	45
	1 x 8	1¼	35
	1 x 10	1½	30
Rustic and drop siding	1 x 4	Matched	33
	1 x 6	Matched	25
	1 x 8	Matched	20
Vertical siding	1 x 6	Matched	20
	1 x 8	Matched	25
	1 x 10	Matched	15
†Batten siding	1 x 8	Rough	5
	1 x 10	Rough	5
	1 x 12	Rough	5
	1 x 8	Dressed	13
	1 x 10	Dressed	11
	1 x 12	Dressed	10
Plywood siding	All sizes	Sheets	5-10

†For 1" x 10" boards allow 1,334 lineal feet 1" x 2" joint strips for each 1,000 FBM of batten siding. Add 12 pounds 8d common nails.

Adapted from Paul Thomas, *How to Estimate Building Losses and Construction Costs,* 4th ed. (Englewood Cliffs, NJ: Prentice Hall, 1983), p. 249.

Labor

Labor for installing siding is based on 1,000 FBM of material. The first step in estimating labor is to determine the time needed to do the job. Exhibit 8-9 indicates the labor hours per FBM for different types of siding and nominal material sizes. Since this job require 1,597 FBM of material, 57.5 hours of labor will be necessary:

$$1{,}597 \text{ FBM} \times \frac{36 \text{ hrs.}}{1{,}000 \text{ FBM}} = 57.49 \text{ hrs., rounded to } 57.5$$

The second step is to determine the labor rate per hour in the locality. At $20 per hour, the labor cost is $1,150 ($20 per hour x 57.5 hours).

Exhibit 8-9
Siding Installation Time Estimates

Percentage of Milling and Cutting Waste Required per 1,000 FBM of Various Types of Wood Siding		
Type of Siding	**Nominal Size in Inches**	**Hours Labor per 1,000 FBM**
Bevel siding	1 x 4	40
(add 10% for	1 x 6	38
mitered corners)	1 x 8	36
	1 x 10	34
Rustic and	1 x 4	32
drop siding	1 x 6	30
	1 x 8	28
Vertical matched	1 x 4	40
siding	1 x 6	36
	1 x 8	32
†Batten siding	1 x 8	22
	1 x 10	20
	1 x 12	20
Plywood siding	1/4" thick	12 per 1,000 sq. ft.
	3/8" thick	14 per 1,000 sq. ft.
	7/8" thick	14 per 1,000 sq. ft.

†Allow 15 hours labor per 1,000 FBM of siding to apply joint strips when 1" by 10" boards are used.

Adapted from Paul Thomas, *How to Estimate Building Losses and Construction Costs*, 4th ed. (Englewood Cliffs, NJ: Prentice Hall, 1983), p. 249.

Total Cost

The total cost for material and labor to install 1" x 8" beveled siding is broken down as follows (the labor for the felt is included in the rate):

1,597 FBM @ $.155 per FBM	$ 247.54
Felt: 4 rolls @ 16 per roll	64.00
Labor: 1,597 @ 36 hours per FBM 1,000 = 57.5 hours	
57.5 hours @ $20 per hour	1,150.00
Total material and labor	$1,461.54

Additional factors that might need to be considered are removing damaged siding; erecting and disassembling scaffolding or staging; removing outside trim such as shutters, gutters, and headers; and applying stain, varnish, or paint.

Unit Cost

A unit cost per square foot is determined by dividing the total cost by the total board feet:

$$\text{Unit cost} = \frac{\$1,461.54}{1,597} = \$.915 \text{ per square foot}$$

This figure can be used as a basis for estimating the cost of other beveled wood 8" siding installations. No one unit cost applies to patch repair jobs, however. In siding as in other trades, smaller jobs make establishing a feasible unit cost more difficult.

Roofing

By far the most common residential roofing material is **asphalt** composition three-tab shingle. Estimates for these types of shingles are calculated on the basis of units equal to **one square**, or 100 square feet. Each square has three **bundles**. A 235# shingle weighs 235 pounds per square.

A bare roof consists of wooden boards, or decking, called **sheathing**, nailed onto roof rafters. (See Chapter 9 for further discussion of frame carpentry.) Roofing **felt paper** is laid onto the roof sheathing and stapled in place, and shingles are then nailed over the roof felt paper. Shingles are usually installed with a four-inch exposure, and the remainder of the shingle is covered by the rows of shingles above it. In shingling a roof, a roofer starts at the bottom (eave of the roof) with an edge "upside down" starter row, then lays the first row with the surface material showing. This technique prevents any leakage between the tabs of the first row of shingles. Subsequent rows of shingles are nailed in place, with each row overlapping about two-thirds of the previous row. Another double row is installed at the top (ridge), where shingles are cut and laid across the ridge joint to seal and join both sides of the roof surface at the top.

Wood shingles (which are sold four bundles to the square) are usually made from western red cedar, but they can also be made of redwood and cypress. They are normally sixteen inches long, with a five-inch exposure. The roofing felt, which serves as a moisture barrier, is not applied with wood shingles. Wood shingles must instead have both ventilation from the underside to properly dry out and space on either side for expansion.

Slate and *tiles* are laid over thirty-pound felt and are never applied over existing roof materials.

Rolled roofing paper of ninety-pound weight covers 100 square feet of area and is usually double-covered in areas of heavy snow accumulation. It is the least expensive roof covering and is used on flatter surfaces where shingling is not adequate to protect the interior from moisture of melting snow or ice.

Flashing is tin, aluminum, or copper sheet material that covers any break on the roof surface. It is applied around chimneys and around plumbing vent pipes, and can also be laid around the eave of the roof and where valleys are formed by intersecting roofs or dormers. Flashing is curled up along vertical surfaces and extends under the roof covering to seal any openings from moisture. Flashing on roofs extends up along the eave a distance of eighteen to twenty inches; when ice forms at the eave and then melts, the water does not run up under the shingle and damage the interior walls or ceilings.

Built-up roofs are common on flat roof surfaces. Although much more common on commercial structures, they are found on residences as well. In the installation of a built-up roof, the first step is to tack down a layer of red rosin sheeting over the roof board decking. This sheeting serves as a sealer or vapor barrier. A base covering of thirty-pound felt roofing paper is then applied and mopped with tar sealer. This process is repeated three times for a three-ply covering and five times for a five-ply roof. Crushed stone can then be put over the top layer. This type of roof is called a **tar and gravel roof surface**.

Damage to and Repair of Roofing

Strong winds (generally in excess of 40 m.p.h.), hail, and falling objects, such as tree limbs, are the usual insured causes of loss to roofs.

Exposure to heat from the sun and normal wear and tear exact a heavy toll on common roof coverings. The average life of an asphalt composition shingle roof is fifteen to twenty years. Worn granular surfaces, curling of the shingle ends, and leaks into the interior are signs of age and damage that accumulates over time. Insurance does not cover wear and tear, but it might cover a new roofing job as part of an insurable loss to a home with replacement cost coverage. Because of their composition, asphalt roof shingles might sustain several slight incidents of damage that go unnoticed. The first indications of leakage usually signal the need for a new covering.

Inspection of Roofs

When inspecting damages to an asphalt roof, adjusters should, if possible, climb onto the roof. Wind might have broken the shingles, but unless they are visibly torn, damage can only be observed by close inspection. Even if broken, the shingles will lay flat once the wind has subsided and will not appear to be damaged.

Roofs of slate, tile, fiber panels, or wood can be damaged if walked upon. Adjusters should go up on a ladder to get a good vantage point for inspection and should take photos from the edge of the roof.

No more than three layers of asphalt shingles are recommended. This amount is based on the capacity of the roof structure to bear the cumulative weight of the material. Some adjusters believe that if the roof already has three layers, an allowance should be made to remove only the top damaged layer. The second layer, though, will almost certainly be damaged while the top layer is being removed, resulting in a need to replace parts of the second layer. The care needed to minimize second-layer damage can make the job take longer, increasing the labor cost. Whether layers below the top should be removed therefore becomes a matter of judgment.

Spot Repairs

Both asphalt composition shingles and built-up roofing can be repaired on a spot basis.

Asphalt Composition Shingles

Individual shingles can be removed with a special tool. The nails of the next two layers are pulled up or cut off, exposing the entire shingle. The nails on the damaged shingle are then removed, and a new replacement shingle is inserted in place and nailed. The existing shingle or shingles above the new piece are renailed over that piece.

Shingles not only protect the interior, however, but also contribute to the exterior appearance. Matching older shingles can be a problem. Reroofing an entire side might be necessary if damages appear so extensive as to warrant replacement of 50 to 60 percent of scattered, missing, and broken shingles. The labor involved in patching such a large area will exceed the cost of replacing one whole side. The best way to estimate individual spot-patch repairs is by time and material. No unit price would accurately reflect such repairs.

Built-Up Roofing

Built-up roofing is repairable by patching. Tar- and gravel-surfaced roof covering is usually affected little by hail or strong winds, but damages might occur nonetheless. The damaged area can be cut out, and the layers or plies can be removed down to the decking. Patches cut to the opening are put in with alternating tar, as when the roof was originally constructed. The top patch should overlap all sides by about two inches. It is nailed to the decking and then tarred over. Gravel stones can then be replaced on the patch repair area.

Labor

Labor for roofing is affected by the experience of the workers, the slope of the roof itself, and the height of the area to be worked on. If the roof is too steep to be easily worked on, roof scaffolding brackets can be fastened under the shingle, and boards can be put across triangular brackets to provide a level standing and working area. Access scaffolding might have to be erected for high areas. Materials might have to be hoisted to the roof area. An allowance for these additional labor expenses is appropriate.

Roofing Estimates

Estimating for roof damages is based on net area, to which a waste factor is applied. Measurements can be made directly by someone on the roof, by counting rows of exposed roof shingle, or by mathematical computation. Measurements obtained directly should be accurate, but the roof must be sturdy enough for the adjuster to climb onto it. Counting rows of shingles is based on a standard exposure per row. For example, if each row is exposed four inches and thirty rows are showing, the distance from the eave of the roof to the ridge is 4" x 30 = 120" = 10 feet. The same distance can be determined if the geometry and measurements of a gable end are known.

Roof Area

Exhibit 8-10 illustrates the several common shapes of roofs. Determining the area of the most common, the gable roof, is explained in the equations that follow.

Exhibit 8-10
Common Roof Shapes

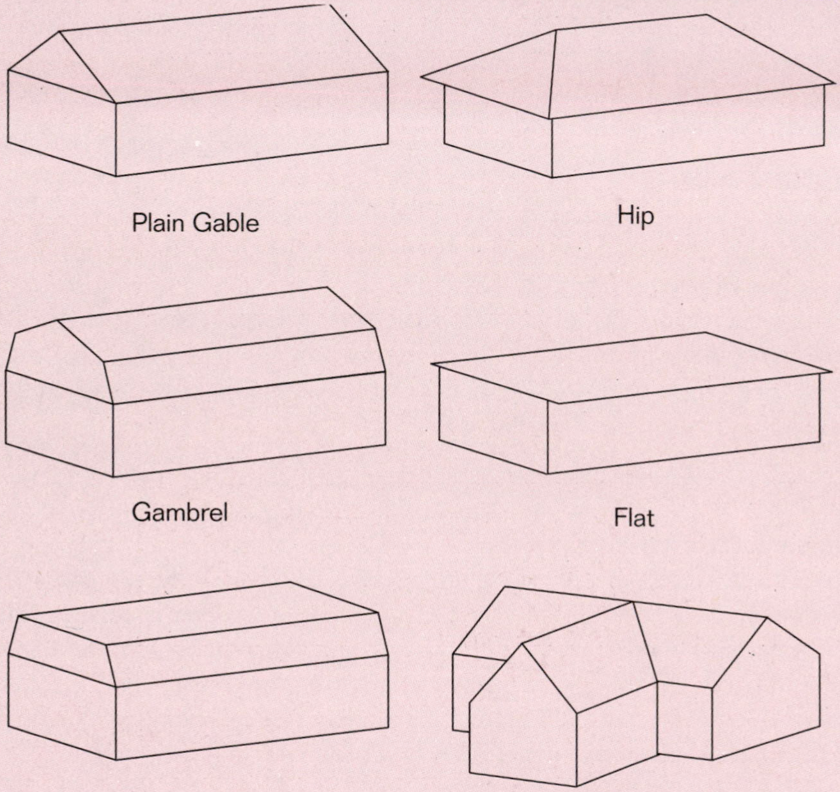

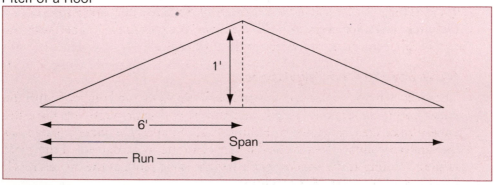

Plain Gable

Hip

Gambrel

Flat

Mansard

A variation of the plain gable is the intersection gable, which creates valleys at the intersections.

Exhibit 8-11
Pitch of a Roof

1'

6'

Span

Run

Exhibit 8-12
Roof Surface Areas

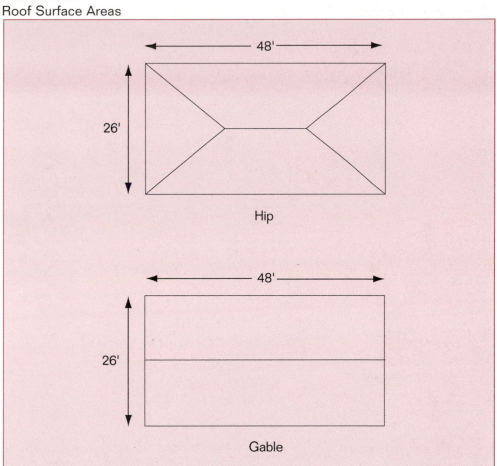

Pitch

A roof's **pitch** is the relationship of the **rise** in height of the roof angle to the span. In the example shown in Exhibit 8-11, for a rise of 1' and a span of 12', the pitch is $\frac{1}{12}$. For every foot (12") of span, the roof rises 1". The lower the number that the pitch is, the flatter the roof angle.

Gable and Hip Area Calculations

The most common roof shapes are **gable** and **hip**. Gable and hip roofs with the same outside dimensions (length and width) and same pitch will have the same surface area, as shown in Exhibit 8-12. Similarly, a window gable has the same roof surface area as the flat surface in the roof from which the gable juts out (as long as the window gable has the same pitch as the overall roof). Exhibit 8-13 illustrates this condition.

Exhibit 8-13
Window Gable

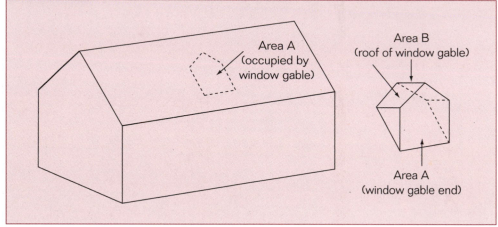

Rafter Length

The **rafter length** for a gable end can be calculated by using the following formula:

$$\text{Rafter length} = \sqrt{(\text{Run})^2 + (\text{Rise})^2}$$

This formula provides the length of the rafter in the example shown in Exhibit 8-14, as follows:

$$
\begin{aligned}
\text{Rafter length} &= \sqrt{13^2 + 8^2} \\
&= \sqrt{169 + 64} \\
&= \sqrt{233} \\
&= 15.26'
\end{aligned}
$$

The roof in the illustration has no overhang. If it did, the overhang should be measured and added to 15.26'. The roof might also extend beyond the gable-end walls.

A calculated rafter length can be rounded to the next half foot. For the roof surface in the example, a rafter length of 15'6" can be used.

Total Area

The area of this roof, which has no overhang, would be as follows:

Rafter length of 15'6"	15.5 feet
Length of roof	48 feet
Area of one side	744 square feet (48' x 15.5')
Total area (both sides)	1,488 square feet (744 square feet x 2)

Exhibit 8-14
Gable End Rafter Length

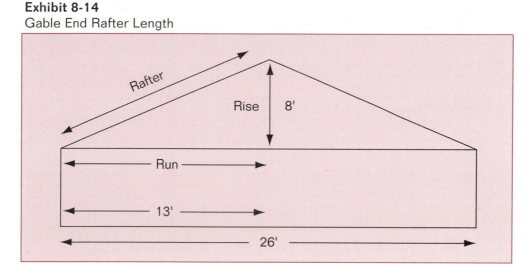

If the gable end overhangs, the extra length must be added to the overall length figure.

Material

In calculating the cost to remove damaged materials, adjusters should use the total area for removal labor. For calculating new felt and shingle materials, however, other factors might create a need for material beyond what the area alone indicates. For instance, in this case the eave edge is double-layered, and a cap layer is on the ridge to seal both sides of roofing. Waste would also result from fitting materials around roof openings, dormers, and valley areas. The most common way to account for waste is to use percentage allowances, such as those shown in Exhibit 8-15.

Exhibit 8-15
Approximate Percentage Allowances for Waste for Different Roofs

Roof Shape	Plain	Cut-up
Gable	10	15
Hip	15	20
Gambrel	10	20
Gothic	10	15
Mansard (sides)	10	15
Porches	10	—

Adapted from Paul Thomas, *How to Estimate Building Losses and Construction Costs*, 4th ed. (Englewood Cliffs, NJ: Prentice Hall, 1983), p. 282.

For the example based on Exhibits 8-12 and 8-14 (total area shown above), 10 percent waste would be appropriate:

1,488 square feet x 10% = 148.8, rounded to 149 waste allowance

1,488 + 149 = 1,637 square feet

Shingles

Asphalt shingles are bought by the bundle, with three bundles per square. To determine the amount of material needed for this gable roof, divide the total area including waste by 100 square feet (because 1 square = 100 square feet), and then round up to the next ⅓ square:

$$\frac{1,637}{100} = 16.37 \text{ squares}$$

Total shingles = 16 ⅔ squares = 50 bundles

Felt

The underlying felt covers approximately 400 square feet per roll. It comes in a roll 3 feet wide and 144 feet long, or 432 square feet. The felt must overlap, so some waste is inevitable. An allowance for waste is already considered if a 432-square-foot roll is used to cover 400 square feet of roof area. If any more than one roll of felt is necessary, then another whole roll must be purchased. For the roof in this example, four rolls would be needed:

$$\frac{1,488 \text{ square feet}}{400 \text{ square feet per roll}} = 3.72, \text{ rounded to 4 rolls}$$

Nails

A generally accepted allowance for roofing nails is two pounds per square.

Labor

The labor rate per hour reflects several considerations. Features that disrupt the surface such as dormers, several openings, and valleys with flashing slow productivity.

Exhibit 8-16 contains the generally accepted guidelines for roofing work. Like materials, labor is based on a per-square measurement. The labor for the roof in the example would be the following:

Removal of 14.9 square @ 1 hour per square	14.9 hours
Install 16.67 square @ 2 hours per square	33.3 hours
	48.2 hours
Labor @ $22 per hour	$1,060.40

The net area of the roof was used to determine the removal time because no waste removal is necessary. However, in the estimation of replacement time, a waste factor must be added because the roofer will handle all of the shingles, including the waste. Some estimators would not follow this practice, but would estimate labor without consideration for waste. This approach would result in an estimate of 29.8 hours labor, which is 3.5 hours and $77 less.

Exhibit 8-16
Roofing Time Estimates

		Hours of Labor per Square		
Type of Roofing	Pounds of Nails	Plain Roofs	Difficult or Cut-up Roofs	To Remove Old Roofing
Asphalt strip shingles	2	2	3	1
Asphalt individual shingles	4	4	6	1
Asbestos rectangular shingles	3	6	8	$1\frac{1}{2}$
Asbestos hexagonal shingles	3	4	6	$1\frac{1}{2}$
Spanish or mission tile		8	10	2
3/16" slate shingles	3	6	8	$1\frac{1}{2}$
Wood shingles	2	4	6	$1\frac{1}{2}$
Corrugated galvanized or aluminum on wood	2	$2\frac{1}{2}$	$3\frac{1}{2}$	1
Corrugated galvanized or aluminum on steel	2	6	8	1
3-ply built-up gravel roof	—	2	—	$1\frac{1}{2}$
4-ply built-up gravel roof	—	$2\frac{1}{2}$	—	$1\frac{1}{2}$
5-ply built-up gravel roof	—	3	—	$1\frac{1}{2}$
Roll roofing	—	$1\frac{1}{2}$	2	1

Approximate Hours of Labor to Remove and to Lay One Square of Roofing (including Underlayment of Saturated Felt Where Required)

Adapted from Paul Thomas, *How to Estimate Building Losses and Construction Costs*, 4th ed. (Englewood Cliffs, NJ: Prentice Hall, 1983), p. 292.

Total Estimate

The total estimate for this job is shown below:

	Material	Labor
Removal is 14.9 hours @ $22 per hour	—	$327.80
Install 16 ⅔ squares @ $35 per square	$583.33	
Labor is 33.3 hours @ $22 per hour		732.60
Nails for 16 ⅔ squares x 2 pounds per square = 33.3 pounds @ $1 per pound	33.30	included
Felt paper for 1,488 square feet/400 square feet per roll = 3.72 = 4 rolls @ $15 ea.	60.00	included
Total materials and labor	$676.63	$1,060.40
Total cost (material + labor)		$1,737.03

If the roof is cut up or if its height or access is a problem, the labor rate should be adjusted to allow more time per square. The labor to install individual shingles on several different areas of damaged roofing cuts productivity in half (four hours per square). Additional allowances for hauling debris, scaffolding, and a steep pitch might be necessary.

Unit Cost

The unit cost is determined by dividing the total cost of the job by the number of squares:

$$\frac{\$1,737.03}{14.88} = \$116.74$$

Since labor rates vary by area and additional factors might cause a job to be more expensive than an average job, adjusters should be wary about approaching every job on a unit-cost basis. For an average residential roofing loss, a breakdown of labor and materials helps to resolve discrepancies between the adjuster's estimate and the contractor's estimate.

Summary

The extent of damages to interior and exterior finish coverings largely depends on exposure to fire, heat, water, smoke, and weather. Any estimate of the cost to repair or replace damaged parts must take into account not only the extent of direct damage, but also factors of occupancy and accessibility and the type of material affected. When inspecting the damages, adjusters should consider the direct physical damage and any other factors that might affect cost, such as height, extensive ornamental work, minimal charges for minor repair, and local labor rates and practices. Profit and overhead, insurance costs, and supervision charges are involved whenever a general contractor hires subcontractors for interior decorating, exterior siding, or finish work for tape and joint compounding. Adjusters should accompany building experts to job sites to develop a working knowledge of the practices in the area.

Regardless of the kind of loss, adjusters should note the specifications of the materials damaged. When comparing any estimate differences with contractors, adjusters should find out whether the same quality materials are being considered.

Unit costs can be an efficient means to price work, but they are not always appropriate. Adjusters must consider the unique aspects of every project and understand what is included in the unit cost. Time and material estimates are best suited for most smaller residential losses.

Chapter 9

Residential Construction Losses and Estimates, Continued

This chapter continues the subject of residential construction methods and estimates with discussions of frame carpentry, finish carpentry, and mechanical systems.

Frame Carpentry

Frame carpentry, also called "rough carpentry," is the work done by a carpenter in erecting the basic shell of a house. About 80 percent of building construction involves a significant amount of carpentry work. For adjusters to be successful in estimating and evaluating property losses, they must have a working knowledge of how a home is constructed. Knowledge of frame carpentry is especially important because frame damage is not always visible after a loss. The easiest way to develop an understanding of frame carpentry is to study each of the basic elements of a house's shell separately, which the first part of this section does. This section then addresses how frame carpentry can be damaged, repaired, and estimated, and ends with a discussion of wood fences, which are often part of the property and prone to some kinds of loss.

Elements of Frame Carpentry

The two basic types of frame construction are platform (sometimes called "western") and balloon. **Platform construction**, illustrated in Exhibit 9-1, is the common method employed today. **Balloon construction**, illustrated in Exhibit 9-2, is seldom used in new homes because of the cost of the extra-long framing members. However, adjusters should be familiar with balloon construction because homes built before 1940 sometimes used this method of framing. These two types of frame construction are discussed below, followed by a description of the components that form the shell of a typical house.

Exhibit 9-1
Platform Frame Construction

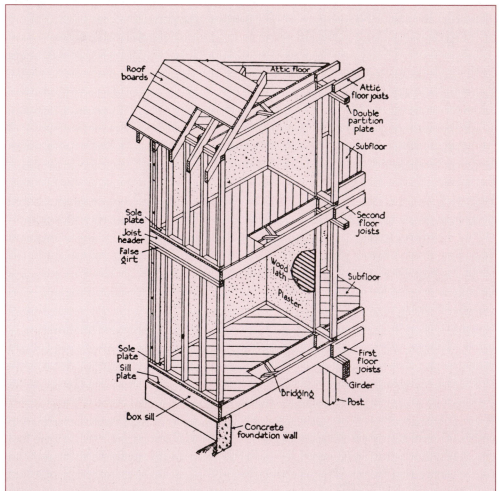

Exhibit 9-2
Balloon Frame Construction

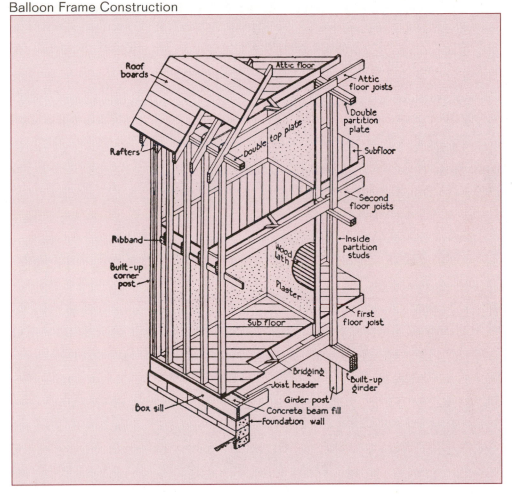

Platform Construction

In platform construction, each story of a house is built as a separate platform. The wall framing in platform construction is built above the subfloor and extends to all edges of the building. A common method of building these walls is to prefabricate full sections of walls and tilt them up and into place. This method is not always possible if only sections of a wall damaged by loss are replaced.

Exterior walls are usually built before interior walls. The **sole plates** are nailed to the floor joists and headers. Corners are strengthened with sheets of plywood, chipboard, or metal or wooden let-in braces. Door and window headers are fastened to adjoining studs, and corner studs are nailed together.

The interior walls in a house are located to serve both as bearing walls for the ceiling joists and as partition walls to divide rooms. **Studs** for these walls are almost always 2 x 4s. Interior walls are built the same as exterior walls, with a single bottom plate and double **top plates**. The upper top plate is used to tie together intersecting walls.

After all the walls have been erected, the carpenters add a second top plate, which overlaps corners and intersecting walls, thus tying everything together. Exhibit 9-3 shows the resulting framework.

Exhibit 9-3
Wall Framing Used With Platform Construction

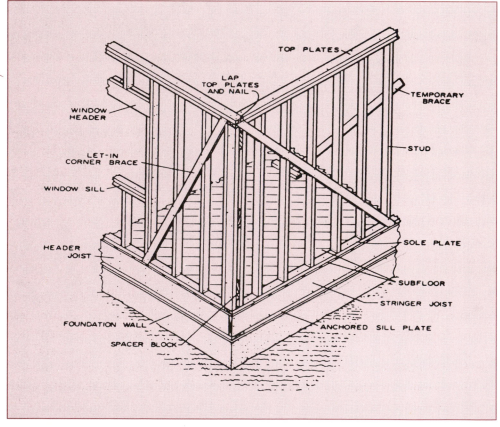

Balloon Construction

In balloon construction, the wall studs extend from the sill of the first floor to the top plate or end rafter of the second floor. In platform construction, the framed wall is complete for each floor. This is the major difference between balloon construction and platform construction. The construction of interior walls is the same for balloon framing as for platform framing.

Floor Framing

The **floor framing** of a wood-frame house consists of the **posts, beams, sill plates, joists**, and **subflooring**. Together, these form the level platform for the rest of the house. The posts and center beams support the inside ends of the joists. Wood or steel posts are generally used to support wood girders or steel beams. Exhibit 9-4 illustrates floor framing.

Posts and Girders

Wood and steel posts, girders, and beams are used in residential construction. The most common steel beam is the I-beam, which spans the full length of the house. When wood girders are used, they are generally built up, meaning that they are composed of two or more 2 x 10s or 2 x 12s nailed together. Some new homes are being constructed with plywood I-beams, which provide a great deal of support in light of their weight. As Exhibit 9-5 shows, the ends of the girders or beams are supported by notches in the foundation walls.

Wood Sill Construction

The type of wood sill construction depends on whether the framing is platform or balloon. Exhibit 9-6 shows that platform construction uses a box sill consisting of a two-inch sill anchored to the foundation wall, which provides support and fastening for the joists and box header at the end of the joists. In balloon-frame construction, the joists rest on the wood sill, but the studs also rest on the sill and are nailed to the floor joists and the sill.

Floor Joists

Wood floor joists are generally 2 x 8s, 2 x 10s, or 2 x 12s. They run perpendicular to the center beam and usually sit directly on it, with their ends slightly overlapping (see Exhibit 9-4). They can also be attached directly to a wooden girder or steel beam by joist hangers or a supporting ledger strip. They are usually spaced on sixteen-inch centers. Joists are attached to the sill, and the **header joist** is then attached to each **stringer joist**. Double joists are usually used under any area that will support additional weight, such as partition walls or bathtubs.

Bridging

Cross-bridging is placed between joists at various intervals to help transfer loads. Exhibit 9-7 shows the three types of **bridging** used in residential structures: solid board, wooden (usually using 1 x 2s or 1 x 3s), and metal. Metal is rapidly becoming the most popular bridging material because it is strong, lightweight, and easy to install.

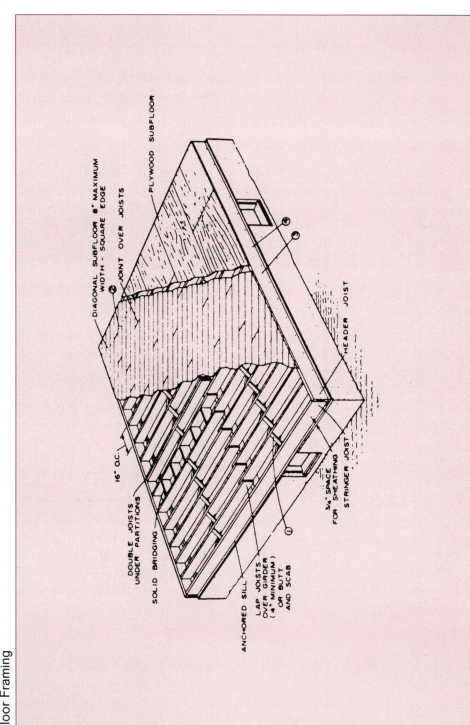

Exhibit 9-4
Floor Framing

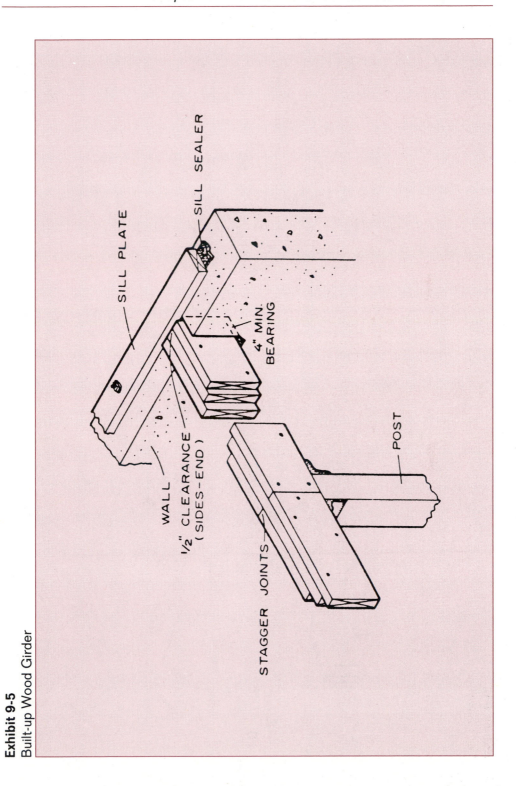

Exhibit 9-5
Built-up Wood Girder

Exhibit 9-6
Sill Construction

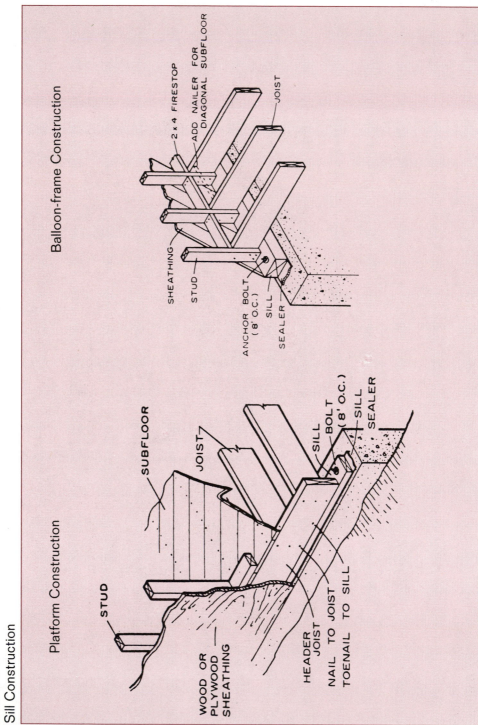

Exhibit 9-7
Types of Bridging

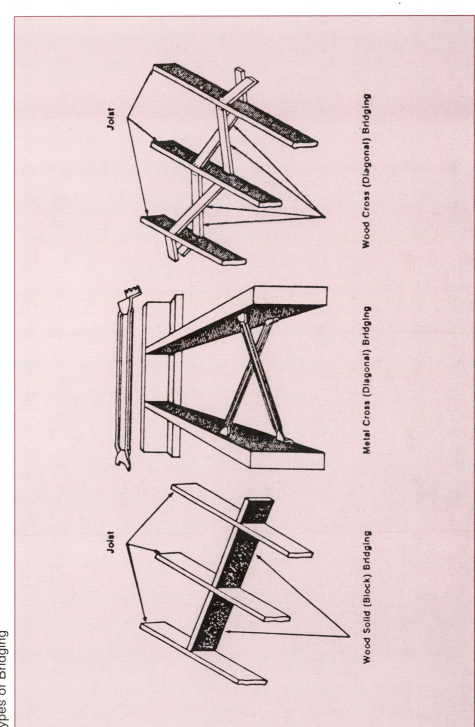

Joist

Wood Cross (Diagonal) Bridging

Metal Cross (Diagonal) Bridging

Joist

Wood Solid (Block) Bridging

Subflooring

Subflooring is used over the floor joists to provide a working platform and base for finish flooring. Plywood is by far the most common subflooring material. Depending on the strength needed, thicknesses from one-half inch to three-quarters of an inch are used. Plywood is installed with the grain direction running perpendicular to the joists and staggered so that end joints in adjacent panels line up over different joists. To avoid squeaky floors, carpenters both glue and nail most plywood subflooring. This practice varies, however, depending on the quality of construction.

Wall Framing

Wall framing includes the **studs**, **sole plates**, **top plates**, and **window and door headers** on interior and exterior walls. These walls support ceilings, upper floors, and the roof. The wall-framing members used in residential construction are generally 2 x 4 studs spaced sixteen inches on center. New construction often uses 2 x 6 studs spaced twenty-four inches on center to allow for thicker exterior wall insulation. Top plates and sole plates are also 2 x 4 or 2 x 6, depending on the studs used. Headers over doors and windows are doubled 2 x 6s or deeper members, depending on the span of the opening.

Window and Door Framing

As mentioned earlier, the members used to span over windows and doors are called "headers." Exhibit 9-8 illustrates a header supported at each end by the inner studs of a double stud joint at exterior walls and interior load-bearing walls.

Wall Sheathing

Wall sheathing, illustrated in Exhibit 9-9, is the outside covering installed over the studs, plates, and window and door headers. Various materials are used—half-inch plywood or chipboard is usually used in corners for reinforcement or when some form of continuous nailed exterior siding is planned. In some climates, plywood siding serves as both the sheathing and the exterior finish. With plywood, adding corner bracing to the walls is unnecessary.

Insulated sheathing, sometimes referred to as "blackboard," is composed of ground wood fibers supplemented by asphalt or other water-resistant products. It is not as structurally strong as plywood or chipboard, but it is less expensive and provides better insulation.

More and more new construction uses a rigid foam sheathing that has excellent insulating properties. It is generally one-inch thick and comes in 4' x 8'

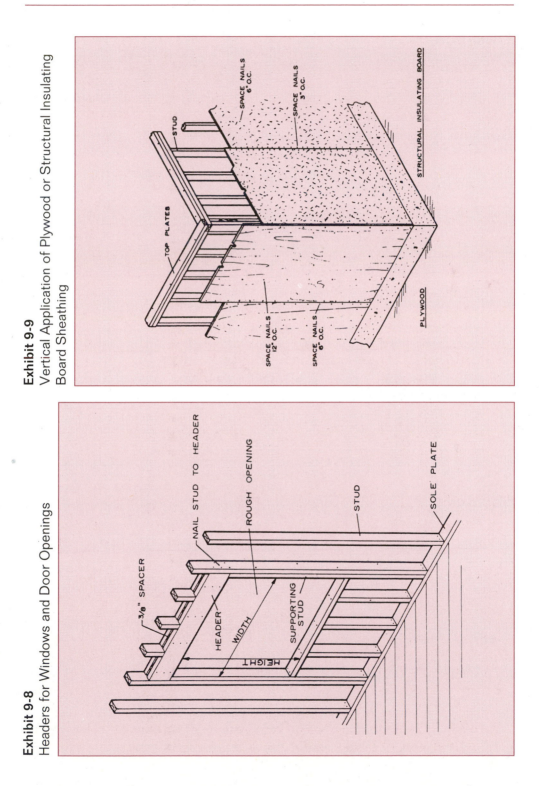

Exhibit 9-9

Vertical Application of Plywood or Structural Insulating Board Sheathing

Exhibit 9-8

Headers for Windows and Door Openings

Exhibit 9-10
Ceiling Joist Connections

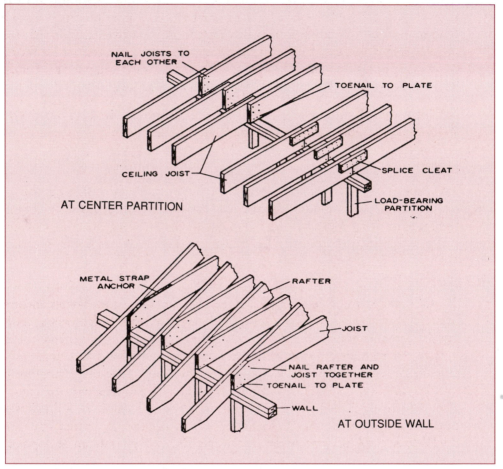

sheets. Because the foam lacks strength, metal let-in braces, plywood, or chipboard is used to strengthen the exterior wall corners. Foam sheathing costs about the same as plywood and is preferable in climates where insulation is important.

Ceiling Joists

After the exterior and interior walls have been constructed, ceiling joists can be nailed into place. Ceiling joists, illustrated in Exhibit 9-10, are normally placed across the width of the house. The sizes of the joists depend upon the span, the spacing between joists, and the load anticipated on the second floor or attic. Ceiling joists are used to attach the ceiling to the room below and act as floor joists for the floor above.

Rafters and Ridge Board

The type of rafter used in residential construction varies depending on the style of roof. In a gable roof, as shown in Exhibit 9-11, all rafters are the same length and run from a **ridge board** to the top plate of the exterior wall (or beyond, depending on the overhang). The ridge board is usually a 1 x 8 or a 2 x 8, which provides support and a nailing surface for the upper rafter ends. The rafters are notched out to fit snugly on the top plate.

In a hip roof, as shown in Exhibit 9-12, **hip rafters** run to the ridge board, and shorter **jack rafters** run from the top plate to the hip rafter.

Valleys

The **valley** is the internal angle formed by the junction of two sloping sides of a roof. Exhibit 9-13 shows the framing at a valley. The **valley rafter** runs from the top plate to the ridge and is often doubled to carry the roof load. Jack rafters extend from the valley rafter to the ridge.

Trusses

Trusses are becoming very popular in the construction of new homes and are often recommended by contractors in the repair of existing homes whose roof-framing members have suffered significant damage. They take the place of the joists and rafters and are installed without a ridge board. Most trusses are pre-engineered and assembled by a truss-fabricating plant, then delivered to the job site, where they are installed quickly, generally with the aid of a crane. They are usually placed on twenty-four-inch centers. Exhibit 9-14 illustrates the three kinds of trusses used most often in residential construction. They are the **W-type**, the **king-post**, and the **scissors**. The W-type is the most popular.

Adjusters must remember that the individual members of a truss can be replaced without replacing the entire truss. Replacing one or more members often becomes necessary when a rafter (known as a "rafter-cord") breaks as a result of either the weight of ice and snow or the impact of a fallen tree limb.

Roof Sheathing

Roof sheathing is the covering over rafters or trusses and usually consists of either half-inch plywood or seven-sixteenth-inch chipboard. Exhibit 9-15 illustrates roof sheathing. Many roofs still have solid board sheathing, although its use in new construction is limited to homes that will have wood shingles or shakes. With wood shingles or shakes, the solid board sheathing is laid with spaces between the boards, as shown in Exhibit 9-16. Plywood is also an option for wood shakes or shingles.

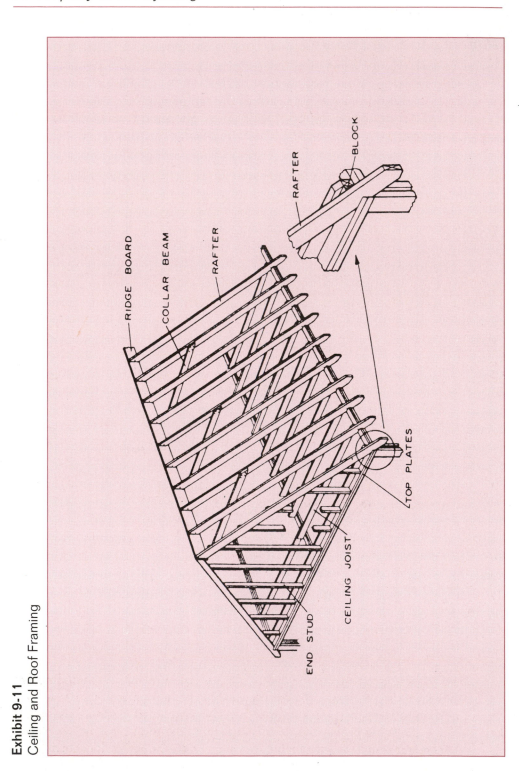

Exhibit 9-11
Ceiling and Roof Framing

Exhjibit 9-12
Detail of Corner of Hip Roof

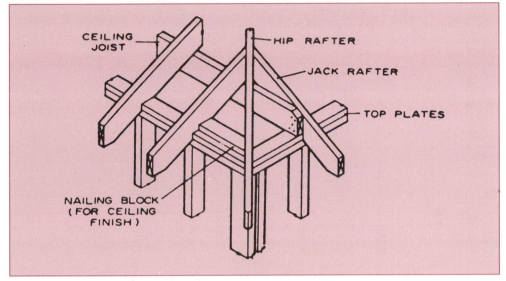

Exhibit 9-13
Framing at Valley

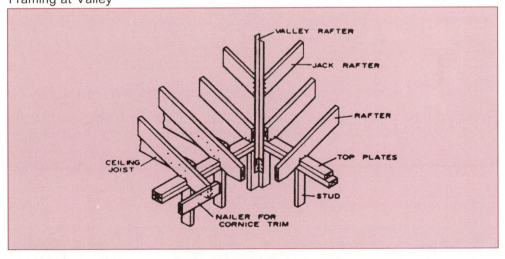

Damageability and Repair of Frame Carpentry

The frame of a house can be damaged by a variety of causes, including fire, smoke, windstorm, water, vandalism, earthquake, settlement, vehicle impact, and many other perils, some insured and others excluded. Serious losses might require replacing roof sections or completely reframing a room. Less severe losses might simply call for replacing a single rafter, stud, or floor joist.

Exhibit 9-14

Light Wood Trusses

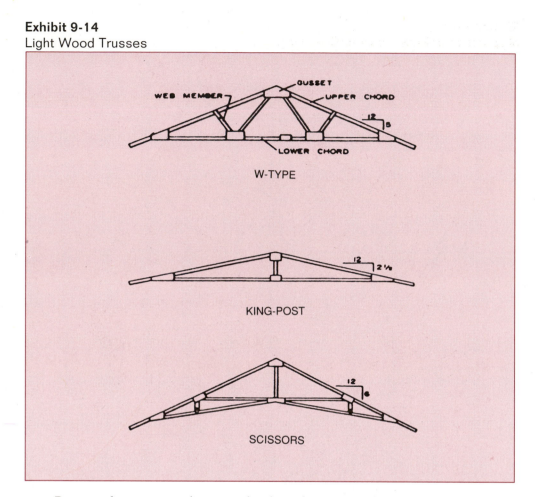

Because framing members are the first elements to be constructed when a house is built, removing and replacing undamaged items are often necessary to repair damaged structural members, such as when an attic fire severely chars roof rafters. Even if it is only slightly damaged, the finished roof surface and roof sheathing must be removed and replaced to replace the rafters.

In some cases involving cracked, split, or charred framing members, the damaged parts do not need to be removed. Instead, they can be reinforced by **splicing** (also called **sistering** or **scabbing**) new framing members alongside them. Framing members are almost always covered by finished materials, so the change created by splicing has no cosmetic effect. Structural members that are only slightly charred or stained by smoke can be spray sealed, painted, or covered by drywall. Most insureds simply want to be assured that the smell of smoke will not linger. Spray sealing is acceptable to most insureds and fire restoration contractors.

Exhibit 9-15
Application of Plywood Roof Sheathing

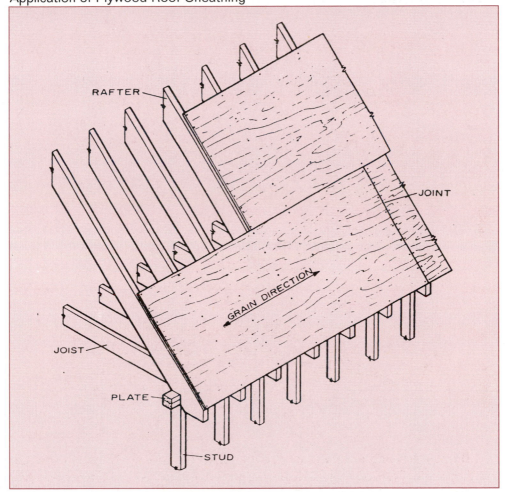

Estimating Frame Construction

Once the damaged area has been exposed and the demolition has been completed, estimating is similar to new construction. For example, if a tornado twists the roof framing from a house, once the demolition has been estimated, the adjuster only needs to determine the cost to frame a new roof using similar materials and construction methods.

Board Foot Calculations

Structural framing members such as joists, studs, rafters, headers, sills, and plates are sold by the board foot. Douglas fir is the most common material used

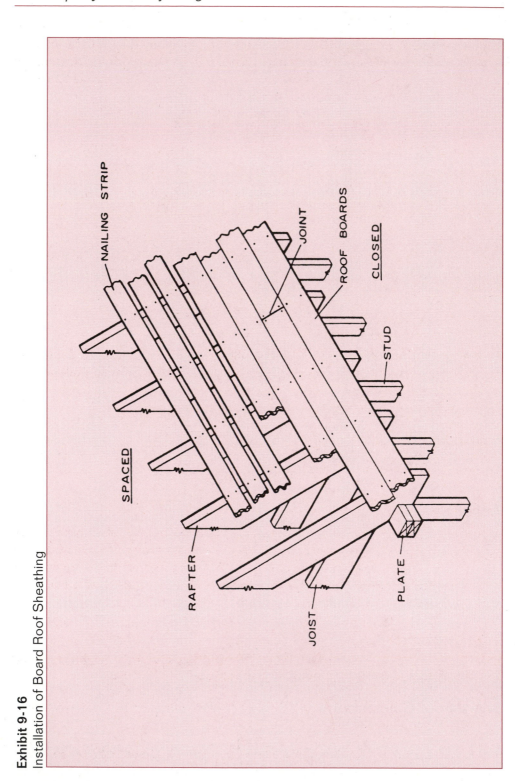

Exhibit 9-16
Installation of Board Roof Sheathing

for framing lumber, although southern pine or larch is also used in some locations. Estimating the materials needed involves determining the number of pieces, their nominal dimensions, and their length. The formula for calculating board feet was presented in Chapter 7.

Calculating Number of Pieces in a Section

The following formula is used to calculate the number of pieces (such as joists, rafters, or trusses) when counting the pieces is not possible:

$$\frac{\text{Length of section (in feet) (measured perpendicular to framing pieces)} \times 12}{\text{On-center spacing (in inches)}} + 1$$

For example, if a foundation measures 16' x 24', and the joists are spaced 16" on center, the number of 16' joists that are needed is calculated as follows:

$$\frac{24' \times 12}{16"} + 1 = 19 \text{ joists}$$

The Board Foot Formula

The next step is to determine the number of board feet of joists. If 2 x 10s are used, the number of board feet is found by using the formula presented in Chapter 7:

$$\text{Board feet} = \frac{\text{Number of pieces} \times \text{Length} \times \text{Dimensions}}{12}$$

$$\frac{19 \times 16 \times (2' \times 10")}{12} = 507 \text{ Board feet}$$

Labor

Framing construction labor tables usually quote the number of hours necessary for a particular operation per 1,000 board feet. Dividing 507 by 1,000 and multiplying by the house quoted for 1,000 board feet yields the number of hours for this job. The table in Exhibit 9-17 can be used as a guide for estimating labor for frame construction.

Total Estimate

The cost of tearing out and replacing the joists in this example can be calculated given the information that follows.

If 2 x 10s 16' long cost $450 per 1,000 board feet, and the carpenter's labor rate is $20 per hour, then:

$$\text{Tear-out} \quad 507 \text{ board feet} \times \frac{8 \text{ hours}}{1,000 \text{ bd. ft.}} = 4.1 \text{ hours} \times \$20 = \$82$$

$$\text{Materials} \quad 507 \text{ board feet x} \quad \frac{\$450}{1,000 \text{ bd. ft.}} = \$228$$

$$\text{Labor} \quad 507 \text{ board feet x} \quad \frac{22 \text{ hours}}{1,000 \text{ bd. ft.}} = 11.2 \text{ hours x } \$20 = \$224$$

Total cost $534

Profit and overhead should then be added.

Exhibit 9-17
Framing Lumber Time Estimates (in Hours)

Item Description	Installation Labor	Demolition Labor
	Per 1,000 Board Feet	Per 1,000 Board Feet
Sills and plates	20	8
Studs	25	8
Joists	22	8
Rafters (gable)	30	8
Rafters (hip)	33	8
	Per 1,000 Square Feet	Per 1,000 Square Feet
Sheathing boards (gable)	20	8
Sheathing boards (hip)	22	8
Sheathing plywood (gable)	16	10
Sheathing plywood (hip)	18	10
Trusses	.5 to 1, each	.25 each

Wood Fences

Estimating losses to wood fences requires a careful survey of how the fence was built, what materials were used, and whether it was put together on site or factory-built in sections and installed on site.

Materials and Construction

The materials used for wood fences are usually redwood, pine, and treated pine. Since many fences are stained or painted, identifying the wood is not always easy. Adjusters must sometimes take a sample from a damaged section to a local lumber yard for identification.

Most fences today are factory-built in eight-foot sections and range in height from three-and-a-half to six feet, depending on style. Because they sit in the ground, the posts are usually 4 x 4 stock and are generally treated lumber. Older fence posts, not made with treated lumber, show early effects of weather and rot, which makes the fence more susceptible to destruction by wind.

The best method for installing fence posts is to concrete them into holes dug just below the frost line. The sections are then attached to the posts with either galvanized nails or screws. Each pre-built section usually contains one post. Separate corner and gate posts and hardware must be priced separately.

Damageability and Repair

The most frequent type of claim related to wooden fences results from loss by windstorm or tornado. Wooden fences can be blown down in even a mild windstorm. Other causes of loss include fire, vehicle impact, and rot, but most policies exclude rot as a cause of loss. Fences damaged by wind often show considerable damage from rot and must be depreciated, but only after the adjuster has inspected the fence carefully and discussed the case with his or her supervisor.

Most fences can be spot repaired, with only those boards, posts, or sections involved in the loss replaced. Standard carpenter labor rates should apply, although companies specializing in fencing often do this work. Posts often need to be torn out, which can be expensive if they are imbedded in concrete.

Finish Carpentry

Finish carpentry is the work done by a carpenter to complete, or "finish off," the interior of a house after the frame has been erected. It includes the installation of wood floors, windows, doors, cabinets, counter tops, interior wood trim, stairs, and exterior wood trim.

Finish Wood Floors

The term **finish flooring** refers to the material used as the top layer or final wearing surface of a floor. A wide selection of wood materials can be used for flooring. Hardwoods and softwoods are available as strip flooring in a variety of widths and thicknesses and as random-width planks and block flooring. Because each kind comes in different grades, adjusters should be certain of the kind, size, and quality of the flooring material.

Softwood finish flooring costs less than hardwood types. However, it is also less dense and less wear-resistant, and it shows surface scratches and abrasions more readily. On an actual cash value estimate, a softwood floor would be subject to more depreciation than would a hardwood floor. Hardwood and softwood flooring is available in both prefinished and unfinished styles.

Types of Flooring

The most common types of flooring are strip, plank, and block or parquet. Exhibit 9-18 shows types of strip flooring and wood-block flooring.

Strip Flooring

Strip flooring is among the more popular styles of wood flooring. It is available in various sizes, but the most common is $^{25}/_{32}$" x 2¼". It comes in random lengths, from two feet to more than sixteen feet. It is tongue and grooved and generally applied over a plywood subfloor, although it can be installed over concrete if sleepers (1" x 2" wood strips) are used. The most common materials used for strip flooring are red oak, white oak, maple, and yellow pine.

Plank Flooring

Plank flooring is a type of strip flooring, but it often comes in two or more widths. It is usually prefinished, which raises the price of material considerably but reduces installation time.

Block or Parquet Flooring

Block or **parquet** is one of the more expensive types of wood flooring and is available in a variety of patterns, thicknesses, and sizes ranging from four-inch to twelve-inch squares. It is usually applied with adhesive over wood subflooring or concrete.

Damageability and Repair Methods

Wood floors burn and can be severely damaged by fire and smoke. Water from firefighting activities, broken pipes, or overflows can also ruin wood floors as the wood fibers absorb the water and expand. Water must therefore be wiped from a wood floor as soon as possible. Occasionally, if the water has not soaked too long, the flooring can shrink back to its normal size, resulting in a minimal loss. If the flooring in a room is ruined, it must be replaced with similar kind and quality. In a partial loss, replacing only the damaged areas and then sanding and refinishing the entire room are possible.

Estimating Wood Flooring

Chapter 7 explained milling and cutting waste, which are important factors in estimating wood flooring. Lumber yards and suppliers sometimes, but not

Exhibit 9-18
Strip and Wood Block Flooring

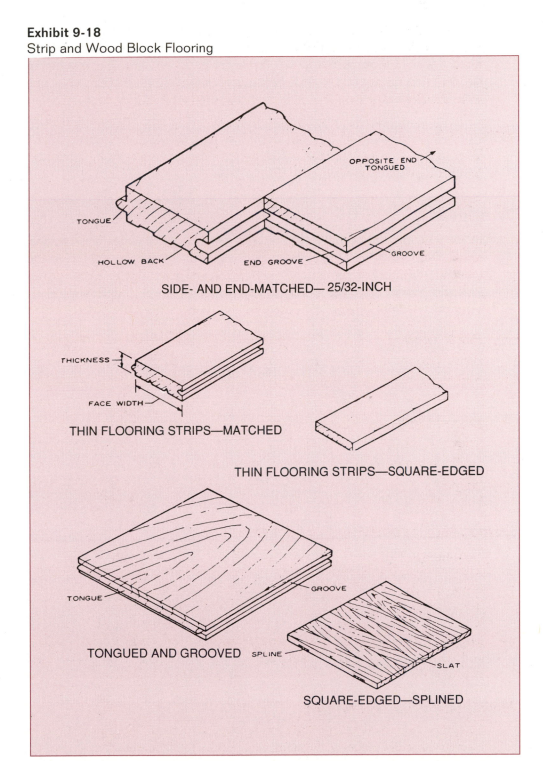

OPPOSITE END
TONGUED

TONGUE

HOLLOW BACK   END GROOVE   GROOVE

SIDE- AND END-MATCHED— 25/32-INCH

THICKNESS

FACE WIDTH

THIN FLOORING STRIPS—MATCHED

THIN FLOORING STRIPS—SQUARE-EDGED

TONGUE   GROOVE

TONGUED AND GROOVED   SPLINE

SLAT

SQUARE-EDGED—SPLINED

always, account for milling waste when they quote the price of wood flooring. Adjusters must recognize this difference when estimating losses involving wood floors. Milling waste can range from 30 to 50 percent or more on strip flooring, depending on the width. Five percent is usually a sufficient allowance for cutting waste.

Once the milling waste problem has been resolved, determining the number of square feet of flooring needed to restore the loss is simple. If the flooring is unfinished, time must be added for finishing the wood floor, which usually involves sanding and varnishing. A unit cost is used for this operation.

Windows

In the past, window building required the special skills of a master carpenter. Today, most windows are fully assembled at the factory and are shipped to the job site to be installed. Exhibit 9-19 shows the parts of a window, including the **sash** and **interior trim**. Although windows are factory-assembled, many manufacturers sell replacement parts, especially sashes that hold the glass.

Types of Windows

Proper estimating requires identifying the type of window. The most common styles are double hung, casement, sliding, jalousie, awning, and stationary.

Double Hung

Double-hung windows are probably the most common. They consist of an upper sash and lower sash that slide up and down in separate grooves in the side jambs. The sashes can be divided into several different lights (pieces of window glass) by small wood members called muntins. The screens are located on the outside. The hardware for double-hung windows includes sash locks and sometimes sash lifts.

Casement

Casement windows have a side-hinged sash and are usually designed to swing outward. The screens are located on the inside. Hardware consists of a rotary closing operator and a sash lock.

Sliding

Sliding windows look like casement windows. In construction, though, the sash slides horizontally in pairs in separate tracks or guides located on the upper and lower jambs. The screens are located on the outside. The hardware is usually simple, consisting of a sliding handle and a lock.

Exhibit 9-19
Parts of a Window

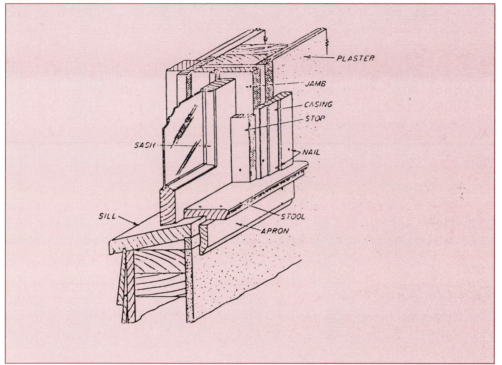

Jalousie

Jalousie windows consist of several sashes that pivot on pins located on the side jambs. The screens are located on the inside. The hardware includes a rotary operator, which can be closed tightly to prevent the window from being opened from the outside.

Awning

Awning windows consist of a frame in which one or more sashes are installed. The sash swings outward at the bottom. A similar type of window is called a **hopper,** in which the top of the sash swings outward. The screens for both types are located on the inside. The hardware includes a crank or swing arm along with hinges, pivots, and a lock.

Stationary

Stationary windows have a sash that is permanently fixed in the frames. They can be used alone or in combination with double-hung or casement windows located on either side.

Estimating Windows

The key to estimating windows is to identify the type and size of window and, if possible, the manufacturer. Windows can vary greatly in cost depending on the manufacturer and material, which can be wood, vinyl-clad wood, steel, or aluminum. The sash might be a single thickness or insulated glass, which consists of two or more sheets of glass with factory-sealed edges and a space between the sheets. Insulated glass is better able to prevent both the loss of heat in winter and air conditioning in summer, is more expensive, and can often be used without a storm window.

Once the material cost is established, the labor time for tear-out and replacement is generally standard. The table in Exhibit 9-20 can be used as a guide for estimating labor.

Exhibit 9-20

Window Installation Time Estimates (in Hours)

Item Description	Installation Labor	Demolition Labor
Double hung	2	0.5
Casement	2	0.5
Awning	2	0.5
Large stationary	3-4	1.0
Storm windows	.5	0.5
Sash only		
Double hung	1.5	Included
Casement	1.5	Included

Doors

The two types of doors commonly found in residential construction are exterior and interior. The parts that make up a door are the **jambs**, the **door**, the **door stop, casings**, and hardware including **hinges** and **locksets**. The parts can be purchased separately, but many doors come as complete units. Most interior door units are pre-hung (assembled at the factory) and are easy to install.

As shown in Exhibit 9-21, exterior doors come in many styles. The panel type consists of stiles (solid vertical members), rails (solid cross members), and filler panels. Exterior flush doors are usually solid-core to provide more insulation and to prevent warping. Many new homes are being built with decorative steel doors, which are foam-filled for even greater insulation. Most exterior doors now also come complete and ready to install, except that they are not pre-drilled for the locksets.

The two most common types of interior doors are also flush and panel. Flush interior doors are usually made with a hollow core framework of plywood, hardboard, or even cardboard. Flush interior doors are available in several different woods, including oak, birch, and mahogany. Closets often have wood or metal doors, which slide on tracks or come as folding units. Exhibit 9-22 shows some types of interior doors.

Exhibit 9-21
Exterior Doors

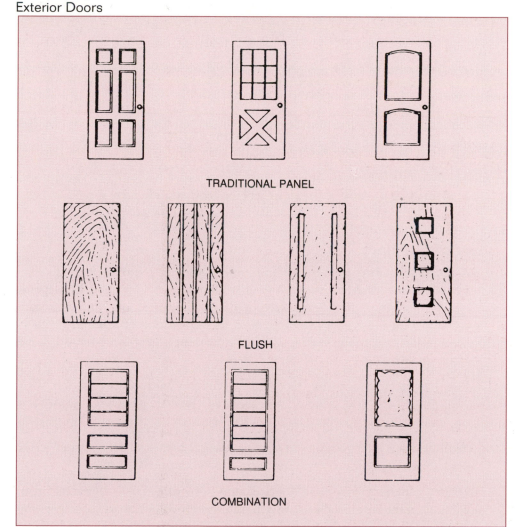

TRADITIONAL PANEL

FLUSH

COMBINATION

Like windows, doors come in a variety of styles, so adjusters must be able to describe the kind of material the door is made of and its size, style, thickness, and type of casings. The hardware varies depending on type, material, and manufacturer. Often, as in a burglary loss, only a part of the door unit needs to be replaced. At other times, the complete unit must be replaced. The table in Exhibit 9-23 shows the average time needed to install and remove different kinds of doors.

Assume that a burglar, in an attempt to gain entry, damages a front door and frame beyond repair. The door is a pre-hung panel door. The door unit costs $250. The carpenter's labor rate is $20 per hour. The estimate for the job would be prepared as follows:

Demolition	1 hour x $20/hour	= $ 20
Material cost	1 door unit, complete	= $250
Installation labor	3 hours x $20/hour	= $ 60
Reinstall lockset and deadbolt	.5 hour each x $20/hour	= $ 20
Total cost		$350

Profit and overhead should be added to this total.

Kitchen Cabinets

In estimating the cost to repair or replace cabinets, adjusters should consider the cabinet type, quality, type of damage, and methods of repair.

Types of Cabinets

Kitchen cabinets can often account for a sizable portion of a claim. The key to estimating cabinets is identifying their quality. Cost usually depends on the quality of materials used for doors, drawer fronts, and hardware. Exhibit 9-24 illustrates the three basic classifications of kitchen cabinets: base, wall, and utility cabinets. Over the years, their sizes have become standardized.

Base cabinets rest on the floor and are covered with a counter top. They contain drawers and usually have shelves. They are generally twenty-four inches deep to allow for a twenty-five-inch counter top to overlap by one inch.

Wall cabinets are about half as deep as base cabinets and are attached to the wall above the counter top. They have shelves but no drawers.

Utility cabinets come in a variety of sizes. One of the most common utility cabinets is the broom cabinet, which runs from the floor nearly to the ceiling.

Exhibit 9-22
Interior Doors

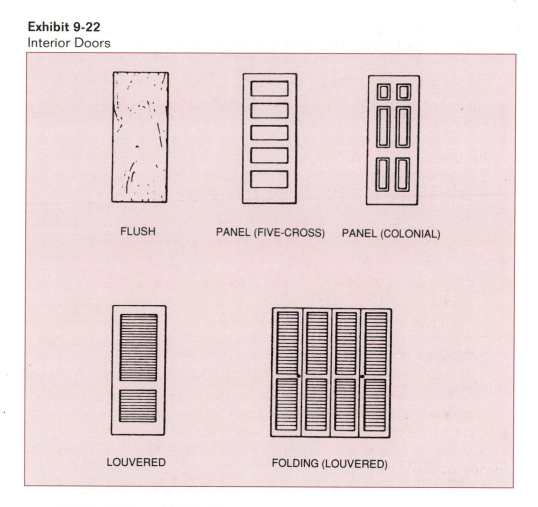

FLUSH   PANEL (FIVE-CROSS)   PANEL (COLONIAL)

LOUVERED   FOLDING (LOUVERED)

Identifying Cabinet Quality

This section provides some guidelines for identifying the quality of cabinets by examining economy-quality, average-quality, and premium-quality cabinets.

Economy

Economy-quality cabinets often have a photographic wood grain finish rather than real wood for doors and drawer fronts. The doors are usually flush-mounted and lack a more appealing recessed edge. The shelves are usually particle board or hardboard. The front frames are generally pine. Economy-quality cabinets sometimes have no back and are attached to the wall by a 1" strip on the inside top and bottom. These cabinets only come in stock sizes. Drawer guides are usually plastic, and the drawers might not be removable.

Exhibit 9-23
Door Installation Time Estimates (in Hours)

Item Description	Installation Labor	Demolition Labor
Exterior Pre-Hung		
Solid core flush	3	1.0
Panel	3	1.0
Steel foam filled	2.5	1.0
Interior Pre-Hung		
Flush	1-1.5	0.5
Panel	1-1.5	0.5
Louver	1-1.5	0.5
Interior Unassembled		
Flush	2.5	0.5
Panel	3	0.5
Louver	3	0.5x 4"

Average

Average-quality cabinets are the most common. The doors and drawer fronts are usually half-inch solid wood or raised panel. The front frames of cabinets are usually three-quarter-inch solid wood with a natural finish. The shelves and the rest of the cabinet are usually particle board or plywood. The shelves are often fixed in place. Like economy-quality cabinets, these cabinets are only available in stock sizes. The drawer guides are metal with nylon rollers, and the drawers are usually removable.

Premium

Premium-quality cabinets are usually found in more expensive homes. They are often custom-made and can be ordered in special sizes. The doors are usually solid hardwood or raised panel. The front frames of cabinets are solid hardwood like birch, maple, or oak, and are at least three-quarters of an inch thick. The shelves are usually plywood and adjustable on metal strips. Although very little particle board is used in the construction of premium-quality cabinets, it is usually faced with some other material when it is used.

Damageability and Repair Methods

Fire, smoke, water, and vandalism are the most common perils causing damage to cabinetry. Kitchen grease fires might be the single most common cause of loss. Methods of repair vary depending on the scope of damage, the quality of

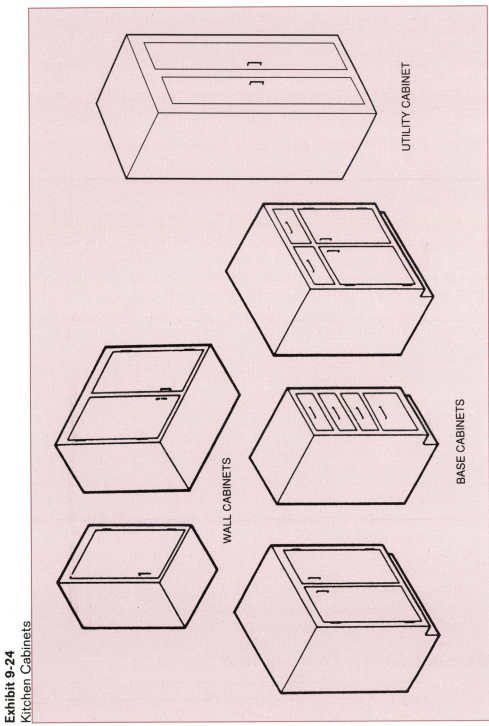

Exhibit 9-24
Kitchen Cabinets

UTILITY CABINET

WALL CABINETS

BASE CABINETS

the cabinets, and the attitude of the insured. If all of an insured's cabinets are destroyed, the adjuster's job is simply to scope the damage to determine the replacement cost. However, if only one or two cabinets are involved in a loss, the adjuster would have several options.

If the cabinets are economy or average quality, the manufacturer might still make the same style, so exact replacements would be easy to obtain. If the cabinets are custom-made, a cabinetmaker might be able to duplicate the cabinets, but stripping and refinishing all of the undamaged cabinets might be necessary to match the new ones. Another approach is to replace the damaged cabinets with new cabinets and only replace the doors and drawer fronts of the undamaged cabinets.

Because of the high cost of cabinetry, the repair options available to adjusters are numerous; the cost to replace more expensive items is usually much higher than the cost to repair them. Some imagination is often required to arrive at the best method for handling the loss. The final choice must be acceptable both to the insured and to the insurance company.

Estimating Kitchen Cabinets

Cabinets are usually estimated on the basis of cost per linear foot. Because of the differences in cabinet quality, doors, drawer fronts, and hardware, adjusters should consult a lumber yard, supplier, or cabinetmaker to establish material costs. Generally, the cost quoted for base units will differ from the cost quoted for wall units, and special cabinets might be individually priced. Cabinetmakers might quote the price installed. The adjuster should take a sample with permission from the insured, such as a drawer front, when seeking prices.

Regardless of cabinet quality, the labor to tear out and replace cabinets is usually standard. Most labor guides indicate .25 hours per linear foot for demolition and a range of between .25 and .5 hours per linear foot to install either base or wall cabinets.

Counter Tops

Base cabinets are generally covered with a counter top made from ceramic tile or Formica. Formica counter tops can be assembled on site using flat stock Formica; they also come preformed with rounded edges and a backsplash. The Formica is laid over a three-quarter-inch-high density particle board using contact cement.

Counter tops usually come in twenty-five-inch widths so that they overlap the base cabinets by one inch, giving a more finished appearance and protecting the cabinet surface from spills. They are usually priced on a cost-per-linear-foot basis.

Interior Trim

Interior trim consists principally of **base moldings, baseboards, ceiling moldings, picture moldings, chair rails**, and **door** and **window trim**. They add a decorative and finished appearance to interior walls, floors, and ceilings, and are available in hardwoods, softwoods, and prefinished plastic. The hardwoods include birch, maple, and oak. The softwood is usually ponderosa pine and is sometimes available prefinished.

Base molding can be made up of one, two, or three separate members. The main baseboard is between two and eight inches high and up to three-quarters of an inch thick. Large and ornate base molding is often constructed of hardwood in older houses. Exhibit 9-25 illustrates types of base molding.

Ceiling moldings are usually of a cove or picture type and are almost always one member. Chair rails are one-, two-, or three-member moldings that are

Exhibit 9-25
Base Molding

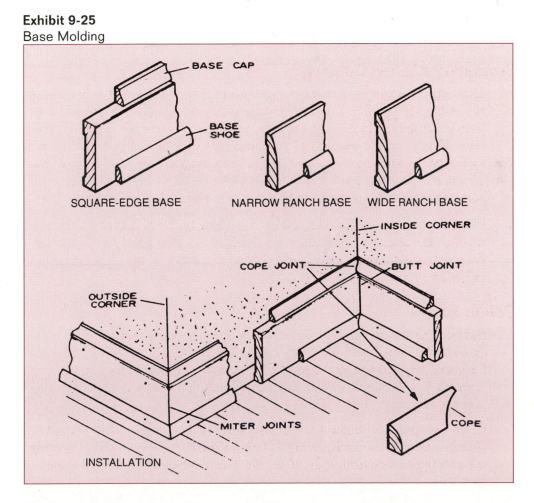

SQUARE-EDGE BASE   NARROW RANCH BASE   WIDE RANCH BASE

BASE CAP

BASE SHOE

INSIDE CORNER

COPE JOINT

BUTT JOINT

OUTSIDE CORNER

MITER JOINTS

COPE

INSTALLATION

applied around the perimeter of the room at chair-back height. Door and window trim (or "casings," as they are commonly known) is generally made of the same material and is usually included in the estimate along with the windows or doors. Exhibit 9-26 illustrates ceiling moldings.

Exhibit 9-26
Ceiling Moldings

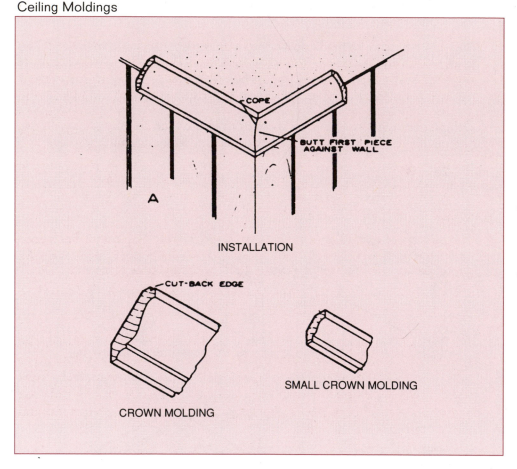

Estimating Interior Trim

Interior trim is estimated by the linear foot. Adjusters must determine the style and type of wood as part of the scope. If the trim is popular, a lumber yard or supplier can give a material price per foot. Especially on older or more expensive houses, obtaining a bid to have the moldings specially milled to match the existing molding is sometimes necessary. A sample is needed for an accurate estimate. Tables are available to help adjusters calculate labor costs. These tables are usually based on hours per 100 linear feet.

Exterior Wood Trim

Exterior trim is usually considered the part of the exterior finish that is not the wall covering. Included are window trim, door trim, cornice moldings, facia boards, soffits, water table, drip cap, corner boards, and rake edge or gable end trim. The woods used for trim are fir, pine, cedar, cypress, and redwood. Cedar, cypress, and redwood offer excellent resistance to moisture and are more expensive than the other woods.

Window and door trim might come with the window and door units, or it can be purchased separately. As the name suggests, it is applied to the exterior of the windows and doors to seal the opening, provide decoration, and prevent water from dripping onto the glass as it runs down the siding. The exterior trim member that prevents the water from dripping on the glass or against the foundation is called a **drip cap**. The **water table** is the baseboard where exterior siding begins. It is located at the base of the building where the foundation ends and the wall framing begins. **Corner boards** are attached to the outside and inside corners of the house to produce a sealed and finished appearance.

Cornices

The **cornice** of a building is the projection at the roof line that forms a connection between the roof and the sidewalls. On gable roofs, it appears on the rake edge of the house; on hip roofs, it is found on all four sides. The three types of cornices common in residential construction are box, open, and closed.

Box Cornice

The **box cornice** is the most common and can be either wide or narrow. The narrow box cornice, shown in Exhibit 9-27, consists of soffit board nailed to the underside of the rafters, a facia board nailed to the rafter ends, and a frieze board placed underneath the soffit and attached to the side wall. A wide box cornice is similar except that lookouts might be attached to the rafter ends and sidewalls to support the soffit.

Open Cornice

The **open cornice** is structurally similar to the wide box cornice without lookouts, except the soffit is eliminated. This type of cornice can be used in post and beam construction or where cost considerations are important, as in garages, sheds, or cottages.

Closed Cornice

The **closed cornice** shown in Exhibit 9-28 has no overhang because the rafters are cut off flush with the exterior sheathing. A frieze board and crown molding are used to end the siding at the top of the wall.

Exhibit 9-27
Narrow Box Cornice

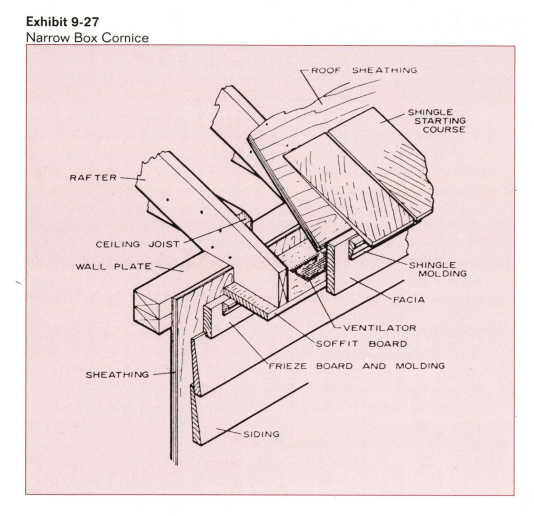

Mechanical Systems

Several building trades are more specialized than carpentry, including plumbing, heating and cooling, and electrical work. The purpose of this section is not to teach the detailed methods of estimating claims involving mechanical systems, but rather to stress that adjusters should have a working knowledge of the vocabulary and elements of those systems and be able to evaluate the estimates prepared by subcontractors specializing in those trades. Although estimates are not always easy to obtain, adjusters should insist that these estimates be broken down into specifications, labor, and materials so that an analysis is possible.

Exhibit 9-28
Closed Cornice

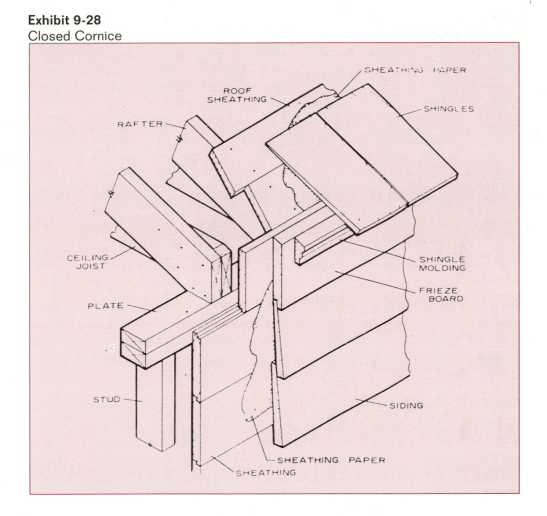

The labor rates paid to these specialists run much higher than those which carpenters and other laborers command. A rule of thumb for approaching costs in these trades is that rates can be expected to be one-and-a-half times the labor rate that carpenters charge.

Plumbing

The plumbing systems in residential construction use four distinct networks of pipes. The first two networks are made up of the pipes that carry hot and cold water to faucets and appliances, as illustrated in Exhibit 9-29. The third is the system of drain pipes that carry away waste water (illustrated in Exhibit 9-30), and the fourth is a ventilation system that allows for the equalization of air

Exhibit 9-29
Water Supply Pipes

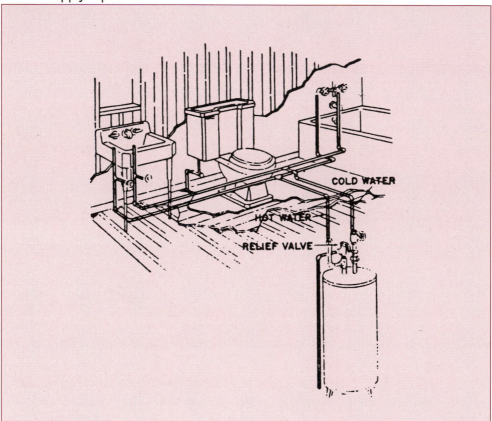

pressure needed for the drain system to function properly. All plumbing systems work similarly, but the materials in different systems might differ considerably.

Plumbing work is broken down into rough plumbing and finish plumbing. **Rough plumbing** involves placing pipes and drains within walls and under floors. **Finish plumbing** involves the installation and repair of fixtures.

Water Supply

Galvanized steel piping, rigid and flexible copper tubing, and polyvinyl chloride (PVC) piping are the most common materials in use today. Galvanized steel piping comes in various inside diameters, but one-half inch and three-quarters of an inch are most common in houses. The ends are threaded, usually at the job site, so that the pipes can be joined to prevent leaks. Various elbows, tees, and angles are available to complete the system.

Exhibit 9-30
Drain Pipes

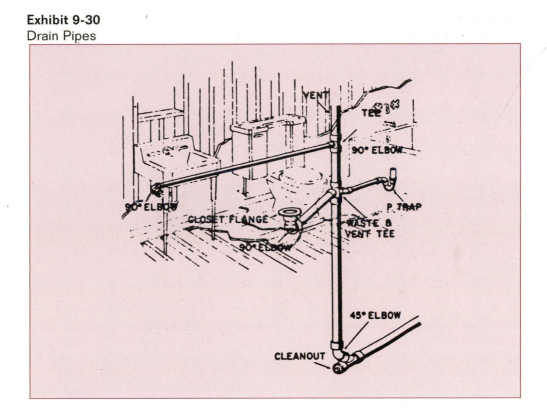

Copper tubing is the preferred and most common material used today. Joints are made through a process known as **sweating** in which the point of connection between two pipes is heated and solder is applied and allowed to flow into the joint, thus sealing it. Because no threading is necessary, copper tubing is less time-consuming to install than galvanized pipe. As with galvanized pipe, one-half inch and three-quarters of an inch are the most common sizes in residential plumbing.

Although not allowed by many building codes, plastic piping is gaining popularity because it is both less expensive and easier to install than either galvanized pipe or copper tubing. Plastic pipe is rigid and is joined by a cement designed specifically for this purpose. It can be joined to existing galvanized or copper systems.

Drain/Waste/Vent Systems

In the past, cast iron was usually used for piping in these systems. The most common material used today is a plastic compound, acrilonitrile-butadiene-styrene (ABS). PVC might also be used in the drain and waste systems.

Plumbing Fixtures

The presence of hot tubs and whirlpools, in addition to the more common **plumbing fixtures** such as sinks, bathtubs, toilets, and faucets, has changed the task of estimating plumbing losses. Adjusters must identify the quality of plumbing fixtures involved in the loss because prices vary considerably depending on brand, material, finish, and installation.

Damageability and Repair Methods

The most common losses affecting plumbing are fire damage and water damage, primarily from leakage and freezing. Galvanized pipe can usually withstand considerable heat without being significantly damaged. Copper tubing can withstand less heat because the copper and especially the solder melt at lower temperatures. Plastic pipes also melt at relatively low temperatures. Smoke from a fire is usually acidic and can etch the finish on plumbing fixtures unless cleaned shortly after the fire. The porcelain finish on fixtures such as sinks and bathtubs is porous, and hot smoke can stain it permanently. Porcelain can be reapplied to bathtubs, but the cost of the procedure cannot usually be justified for sinks, which are far less expensive to replace.

Most residential insurance policies do not cover the cost to repair leaking pipes, although the resulting water damage is often covered, as is the cost to locate the leaks. Freezing damage, covered by most policies, is common in many climates. Both leakage and freezing losses can involve cutting into walls, floors, or ceilings to locate the damaged plumbing.

Most plumbing losses should be inspected by a qualified plumber. A pressure test is usually performed on extensive losses to help pinpoint the damage. Appliances should also be inspected and tested to determine whether repair is feasible.

Heating and Cooling Systems

Each of the many available heating and cooling systems works according to similar principles. For example, with heating systems, each must transfer energy from a fuel source to either water or air, circulate the warm water or air throughout the house, allowing the heat to dissipate, and then return the water or air to the energy source to be reheated.

All heating systems have a thermostat that controls temperature. The thermostat sends an electric signal to the furnace telling the fuel valve to open up when the air temperature in the house falls to a certain point. Either an electric ignitor similar to a spark plug or a pilot light ignites the fuel.

Adjusters need to understand how the various types of heating systems work in order to analyze, evaluate, and negotiate losses involving these systems.

Warm-Air Heating

The most common methods for warm-air central heating are forced air and radiant systems. Each uses a furnace fueled by oil, gas, or coal. Some allow wood to be used alone or in conjunction with other fuels.

Exhibit 9-31 illustrates a forced warm-air heating system. Forced warm-air systems have a blower at the cool-air entrance to the furnace to suck in the cool air while it blows out the warm air. The air flows through a system of warm-air ducts, and it exits through registers located in each room. Cool air is drawn through cold-air returns into ducts to be returned to the furnace. The cool air passes through a filter, which removes dust and other particles, and then flows through a heat exchanger that sits above the furnace's burners. Once heated, it enters the plenum, a chamber attached to the furnace where the duct runs begin.

Radiant heating systems have ducts or tubes, rather than registers, contained within the floors or ceilings. When heated by the ducts or tubes, these surfaces warm the air around them. The furnace and controls work like a forced warm-air system, although they are more difficult to access for repairs.

Steam and Hot-Water Heating Systems

Both steam and hot-water heating systems use a boiler rather than a furnace. The boiler is usually fired by oil or gas. In a steam system, the water in the boiler is converted to steam and circulated to radiators through pipes. The steam condenses in the radiators as it dissipates the heat and is then returned to the boiler either through the same pipes or in separate pipes connected to the opposite end of the radiators.

Exhibit 9-32 illustrates a hot-water heating system. Hot-water systems circulate heated water rather than steam; otherwise, they work the same as steam systems. Hot water can also be used with copper tubing in a radiant heating system.

Electric Heating

Electric heaters burn no fuel, require no vents, and are quiet, durable, and easy to maintain. The simplest and most common electric system is the baseboard heater, which is available in a variety of sizes. It contains a series of fins, which are heated by electric coils. Warm air rises and gradually heats the air. One of

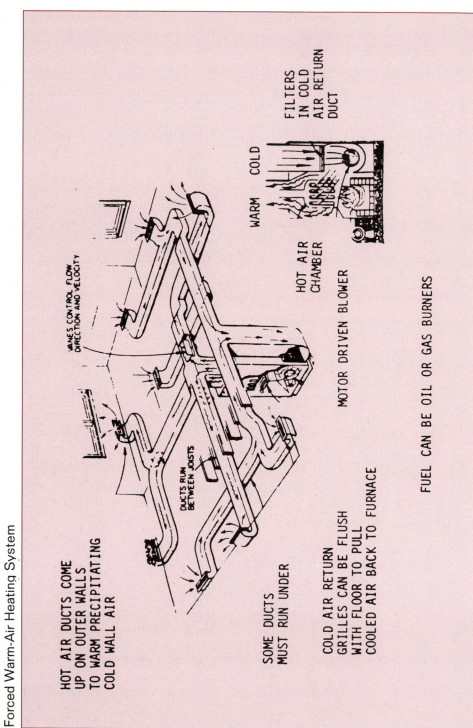

Exhibit 9-31
Forced Warm-Air Heating System

Exhibit 9-32
Forced Hot-Water Heating System (One-Pipe Distribution)

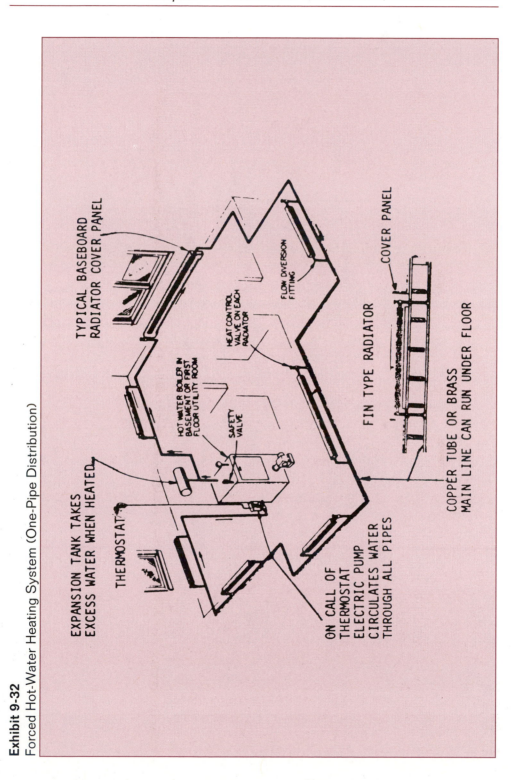

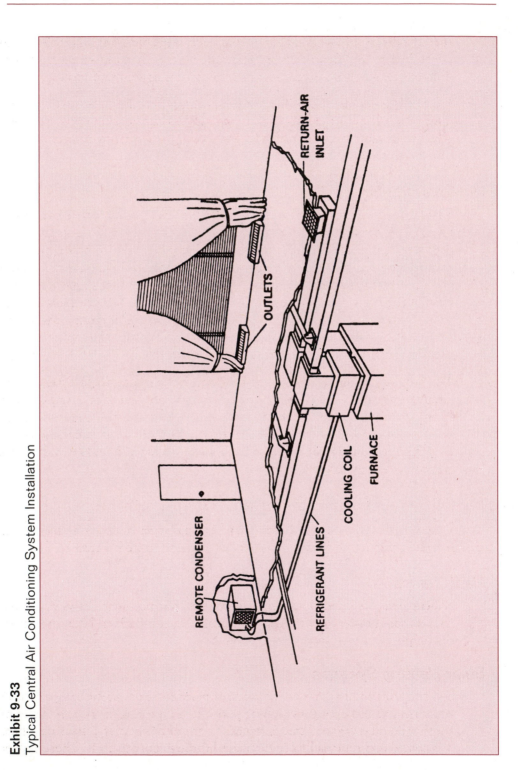

Exhibit 9-33
Typical Central Air Conditioning System Installation

the advantages of electric heat is that each baseboard heating unit can be controlled by a different thermostat, allowing each room to be heated to different temperatures and allowing individual units to be shut off.

Electric heaters can also be installed on walls or in ceilings. Some come with fans, which allow for greater air circulation. Electric heating units are generally installed by electric contractors, rather than by contractors specializing in heating and air conditioning.

Air Conditioning

Residences are generally air conditioned either by a central system or by room air conditioners installed in windows or in wall pockets. This section only discusses central air conditioning systems because losses involving room air conditioners are less complicated to evaluate. Exhibit 9-33 illustrates a **central air conditioning system**. A typical system includes a condensing unit located outside the house, evaporator coils placed within the furnace plenum, and refrigerant tubing connecting the two. For the purpose of circulating air, air conditioning systems are usually used in conjunction with a forced air furnace, thereby using the furnace's blower and duct system.

The furnace blower draws in warm air through the return ducts, filters it, and circulates it through the evaporator coils in the plenum to the supply ducts. Humidity removed in the cooling process runs down the coil and into a drain line running to a floor drain. A separate 240-volt circuit supplies the power that the compressor motor and fan in the condensing unit need. A thermostat controls the compressor and blower.

Miscellaneous Heating and Cooling Systems

Adjusters should be aware of several additional types of heating and cooling systems, including heat pumps, solar systems, and space heaters.

Heat Pumps

A **heat pump** is basically an air conditioner that not only draws heat from indoors and transfers it outdoors, but can also reverse itself and draw heat from the outdoors to the interior of the house.

Solar Heating Systems

Solar systems are used for a wide range of purposes, from preheating water for water heaters to heating swimming pools. In a typical solar system, water or another liquid is pumped through tubes to one or more solar collectors, where it is heated and returned to be circulated through copper coils. These copper coils might be located within a water heater or in a special solar tank. Because of the variety of solar collection systems, adjusters should consult with the original contractor or supplier when adjusting losses involving one of these systems.

Space Heaters

Individual room space heaters are generally fired by natural or propane gas and can be freestanding, mounted to walls, or hung from ceilings. They usually require a vent to the exterior both to draw in fresh air and to exhaust fumes. Many different types of space heaters are available, so adjusters should consult with experts such as dealers and jobbers when estimating losses involving these units.

Damageability

Forced air heating systems generally run for years with little trouble. Normal maintenance includes periodically changing the filters, lubricating the bearings, and cleaning. Fire is the most common cause of loss to these systems. When the smoke is heavy, the furnace often draws it in through the return ducts. Heat exchangers can crack when cold water is sprayed on them during firefighting activities.

Furnace puff-back is caused by the sudden ignition of unconsumed fuel. As a result, heavy soot can be spread throughout the house, especially if the house contains an oil-fired furnace. A cracked heat exchanger can also cause soot deposits, but less gradually than a puff-back.

Steam and hot water systems are more likely to break down simply because they are more complicated than forced air systems and have more parts. The most common claims for these heating systems are for freezing, which can crack radiators and boilers. These losses can be extensive because of the resulting water damage. Pressure tests are required to determine the extent of damage.

Claims for losses related to air conditioning are most often associated with the compressor, a hard-working unit subject to heavy wear. Lightning and power surge are the most typical causes of air conditioning failure. Adjusters should have experts check these units before committing to coverage.

Electrical Systems

Although residential electrical systems might appear complicated, the methods used in wiring homes are generally straightforward and follow strict guidelines. The National Electrical Code establishes those methods, and most local codes and electrical contractors follow them.

Entrance of Electrical Service

The wires that transmit electricity from the power company to residences are either above or below ground. Most homes use a weatherhead, which receives the wires from the utility pole. Many newer homes have an underground cable running through a pipe called a "conduit." In both cases, the wiring passes through the electric meter before running into the service panel.

The electric meter fits into a space called the "meter socket." The meter registers the amount of electricity that is consumed by the use of dials, which the utility company's meter reader checks.

Service Panel

After passing through the meter, the wires enter one of two types of service panels, a **circuit-breaker** or a **fuse box**. The circuit-breaker panel and fuse box serve two purposes. First, they distribute electricity into several branch circuits. Second, they act as a safety device by breaking the circuit if an overload occurs, preventing the wiring from overheating and causing a fire.

These panels are rated by amperage. Adjusters need to identify the service panel rating when scoping the loss because it significantly affects the cost of the loss. The amperage of service is also often upgraded after a loss. The 60-amp fused service was standard before the invention and increased use of many modern electrical appliances. Today, new homes usually contain a 200-amp service using circuit breakers.

Branch Circuits

Branch circuits are made up of wires running from the service panel to the outlets, switches, and fixtures located throughout the house. They can generally supply different amounts of electricity depending on their amperage, which varies by the size of the wire.

With the exception of heavy-duty appliances, which should have their own circuits, most residential branch circuits serve eight to ten outlets each. The National Electrical Code recommends one 20-amp circuit for every 500 square feet of living area for lighting. Appliances such as air conditioners, electric ranges, electric water heaters, and electric dryers often have their own 220-volt circuit as opposed to the 110-volt circuits used for lighting and general usage.

Types and Methods of Wiring

The types and methods of wiring have a considerable effect on the cost of materials and amount of labor required for repairs. Following are the most common types of wiring used in residential construction:

- Rigid conduit
- Thin-wall conduit
- Nonmetallic sheathed cable
- Armored cable

Rigid Conduit

Rigid conduit is similar to water piping and is usually used outside or underground. It comes in ten-foot lengths and various inside diameters. The pipe is threaded for coupling and connecting to boxes. Conduit systems are installed before the wiring is threaded through them.

Thin-Wall Conduit

Thin-wall conduit is similar to rigid conduit in many ways. It is available in ten-foot lengths and the same inside diameters. However, because it can be easily cut and bent and because it has compression fittings rather then threaded ones, thin-wall conduit is far more popular than rigid conduit for residential electrical applications. Another name for thin-wall conduit is "electrical metallic tubing" (EMT).

Nonmetallic Sheathed Cable

This is one of the most popular methods of electrical wiring. It is both less expensive than conduit and less time-consuming to install. Unlike the conduit systems, in which wires are run after the tubing has been installed, **nonmetallic sheathed cable** is made up of individual plastic-coated wires and a bare ground wire all wrapped in a flame-retardant, water-resistant plastic sheath. Connections must be made in metal or plastic junction boxes. Adjusters should be aware that many local building codes prohibit the use of nonmetallic sheathed cable in some types of residential construction.

Armored Cable

Commonly called "BX cable," armored cable is not used as often as it once was because of the popularity of nonmetallic sheathed cable. Armored cable consists of two or more insulated wires encased in a spiral steel sheath. Like the other forms of wiring described, BX has special connectors and fittings.

Damageability

Residential electric systems can be damaged by a variety of causes, but fire, lightning, and power surges are the most common. The extent of damage varies by type of electric wiring. Plastic sheathed cable can withstand less heat than can metal conduit. Building inspectors often require the complete rewiring after a loss when it is not necessary. As indicated in Chapter 7, adjusters should consider employing an electrical engineer or qualified contractor to obtain an expert opinion, thus resolving disputes and satisfying the building inspector.

Summary

To adjust residential losses, adjusters must have a working knowledge of frame carpentry, finish carpentry, and mechanical systems, the three topics that this chapter discussed. Frame carpentry is the work that a carpenter does in erecting the basic shell of a house. That shell includes the floor, the walls, and the ceiling. The floor framing of a house consists of the posts, beams, sill plates, joists, and subflooring. The wall framing includes the studs, sole plates, top plates, and window and door headers. Ceilings are made up of ceiling joists, rafters and ridge board, trusses, and roof sheathing.

A variety of causes can damage the frame of a house, including fire, smoke, windstorm, water, vandalism, earthquake, settlement, and vehicle impact. The framing members are the first elements to be constructed when a house is built, so removing and replacing undamaged parts of the frame are often necessary to repair the damaged parts. In some cases, the damaged parts can be reinforced rather than removed. Estimating frame losses is similar to new construction.

When a wood fence is damaged, estimating the loss requires a survey of how the fence was built, what materials were used, and whether it was built on-site or factory-built in sections. Most fences are factory-built in eight-foot sections that range in height from three-and-a-half to six feet, and they are made out of redwood, pine, and treated pine. Damaged fences can usually be spot repaired.

Finish carpentry is the work that carpenters do when they "finish off" the interior of a house. It includes the installation of wood floors, windows, doors, cabinets, counter tops, interior wood trim, exterior wood trim, and stairs.

Finish flooring is the material used as the top layer of a floor. Both hardwoods and softwoods are used for finish flooring; softwood floors are subject to more depreciation than hardwood floors. The most common types of flooring are strip, plank, and block or parquet. Fire, smoke, and water can all severely damage all types of wood floors.

The most common styles of windows are double hung, casement, sliding, jalousie, awning, and stationary. Most windows are assembled at factories and shipped to job sites to be installed. Many manufacturers sell replacement parts for windows.

The parts that make up both interior and exterior doors are the door itself and the jambs, door stop, casings, hinges, and locksets. Although the parts can be bought separately, most doors are assembled at the factory. Exterior doors come in three styles: traditional panel, flush, and a combination of the two. Interior doors also come in flush and panel styles.

The key to estimating losses to kitchen cabinets is identifying their quality. The three classifications of kitchen cabinets are base, wall, and utility cabinets. This chapter described the differences among cabinets of economy quality, average quality, and premium quality. Repairing cabinets is usually less expensive than replacing them, so adjusters should try to find methods of repair that are acceptable to both the insurance company and the insured. Base cabinets general have counter tops of ceramic tile or Formica.

Interior trim consists of base moldings, baseboards, ceiling moldings, picture moldings, chair rails, and door and window trim. These items are decorative, and interior trim is estimated by the lineal foot. Exterior trim includes window trim, door trim, cornice moldings, facia boards, soffits, water table, drip cap, corner boards, and rake edge or gable end trim. Fir, pine, cedar, cypress and redwood are all used for exterior trim. The last three types of wood are exceptionally water-resistant and are therefore more expensive.

This chapter ended with discussions of plumbing, heating and cooling, and electrical systems. The two types of plumbing are rough plumbing (which involves the pipes and drains within walls and under floors) and finish plumbing (which involves the installation and repairs of fixtures). The plumbing systems in residential construction use four types of pipe networks: two networks that carry hot and cold water to faucets and appliances, a system of drain pipes that carry away waste water, and a ventilation system that equalizes air pressure.

Heating and cooling systems come in many varieties. All heating systems work according to the same principles: they transfer energy from a fuel source to either water or air, circulate the water or air, and then return it to the energy source to be reheated. The most common methods for warm-air central heating are forced air and radiant systems, which use furnaces fueled by oil, gas, or coal. Steam and hot-air heating systems use boilers rather than furnaces. Electric heaters need no fuel, and they are usually installed by electric contractors rather than by heating and air conditioning contractors.

The two most common types of air conditioning are central systems and room air conditioners. Central systems are usually used in conjunction with a forced air furnace's blower and duct system.

Most electrical systems adhere to strict rules promulgated by the National Electrical Code. The types and methods of wiring that a system uses affects the cost of materials and the amount of labor required for repairs. The four most common types of wiring are rigid conduit, thin-wall conduit, nonmetellaic sheathed cable, and armored cable. Nonmetallic sheathed cable is probably the most common type used today.

Chapter 10

Merchandise Losses

Mercantile claims present adjusters with different policy terms, definitions, conditions, and limitations. This chapter explains the basic coverage, accounting procedures, methods of determining value and damage, and other normal adjustment practices involved in claims for merchandise.

Merchandise includes manufactured, processed, or sale goods and is found in many different locations and conditions. Any piece of merchandise begins as raw material or a combination of raw materials in a manufacturing or processing plant, progresses through the manufacturing operation as goods in process, and emerges as finished goods. The terms "raw materials," "goods in process," and "finished goods" are found in various commercial policies. Merchandise is sometimes referred to as "stock" or "goods" in this chapter.

Some finished goods become the first step in another manufacturing process. Other finished goods are sent in transit to the premises of the manufacturer's customers, such as distributors or retailers. Separate insurance policies cover merchandise in each stage: during manufacture, in transit, and at the retail level. This chapter addresses merchandise claims in this last stage. At the retail level, the adjuster determines the insured value of the merchandise. This determination involves examining the insured's books and records. Merchandise losses frequently involve salvage. Reporting form coverage is common for merchandise, and adjusting merchandise losses requires unique considerations.

Insured Value of Merchandise

In a retail establishment, merchandise is damaged most often by fire, smoke, water, actions of firefighters, flood, sprinkler leakage, leaking roofs, collapse, or windstorm. Damage to merchandise can be either total or partial. A total loss does not necessarily mean destruction. Merchandise can be damaged to an extent that it cannot be sold by the insured and is therefore treated as a total loss in the adjustment even though it has some remaining salvage value.

Smoke, heat, water, or odor can inflict partial damage. Many items in a retail establishment are packaged in such a way that smoke or water does not penetrate to the merchandise itself. In this case, a cleaning allowance is an appropriate settlement of the claim. **Hard goods**, such as glass, metal, and china, can often be cleaned after exposure to smoke or water. **Soft goods**, such as apparel, linens, and other items made of fabric, however, are not truly restored by cleaning. Because the insured is in the business of selling new merchandise, not cleaned or laundered merchandise, adjusters must work with insureds to adjust losses involving goods that cannot be cleaned appropriately. In adjusting a merchandise loss, the adjuster considers coverage, insurable interest, and valuation issues.

Coverage

Adjusters encounter merchandise claims for retail goods under two general types of commercial property policies: the building and personal property coverage (BPP) form and the business owners policies (BOP).

The BPP

The BPP extends coverage for personal property to "furniture and fixtures, machinery and equipment, stock, meaning merchandise held in storage or for sale. . .and supplies used in packing or shipping." Coverage can be on an "all-risks" or specified perils basis. Stock valuation is typically at actual cash value, but the policy can be modified to provide replacement cost coverage. For stock the merchant has sold but not delivered, the BPP provides reimbursement of "selling price less discounts and expenses you otherwise would have had." Coverage on personal property of others is included, but with strict limitations. A coinsurance clause usually applies.

The BOP

Many insurers use a package property insurance policy known as **business owners policies** (BOP). Stock coverage under the BOP is similar to the coverage in the BPP. Although the BOP definition of business personal property is not as detailed as the BPP's, it extends to all likely exposures, including owned property, property of others, and improvements and betterments. The two kinds of business owners policies are (1) the standard BOP, which covers specified perils and values stock at replacement cost and (2) the special BOP, which provides "all-risks" coverage and also values stock at replacement cost.

All BOPs incorporate a seasonal automatic increase clause, which automatically increases business personal property coverage by 25 percent, providing for seasonal variations. This seasonal increase is effective only if insureds carry insurance equal to at least 100 percent of their average monthly value during the twelve months preceding a loss. BOPs do not contain a coinsurance clause.

Coverage Review

The most important first step for the adjuster on any mercantile claim is to review the applicable policy thoroughly. The adjuster cannot rely on coverage information recalled from previous claims. Policies can differ in many ways, including such areas as a coinsurance clause, the coinsurance percentage, the deductible, and the difference between standard and reporting form coverages. An adjuster handling numerous homeowners claims might eventually memorize general coverage provisions, but adjusters cannot memorize the many variations in commercial policies.

Insurable Interest

The intent of commercial property policies is to cover only the named insured's interest in the property. The BPP states that its coverage extends to "your business personal property." The BOP covers "business personal property owned by the insured." Both the BPP and the BOP contain identical language: "We will not pay you more than your financial interest in the Covered Property."

Certain property not owned by the insured is automatically covered under commercial property policies. The BPP describes this property as personal property of others in the insured's care, custody, or control and located in or on the described building. The BOP is more explicit, describing the covered property of others as property held by the insured and belonging to others, but not exceeding the amount for which the insured is legally liable, including the labor value, materials, and charges furnished, performed, or incurred by the insured. The property coverage of others in the BPP differs from that in the BOP. Under the BPP, coverage exists regardless of the insured's legal liability for the damage. For example, if an act of God destroyed the insured's property as well as property of others contained there, the insured would not be legally liable to the other owners, but the BPP would cover such losses. The BOP would not. Despite the difference in wording in these policies, the coverage is similar with respect to the types of property to which it extends. Merchandise such as layaways and items in the insured's custody for alterations or repairs are covered.

In adjusting a retail store loss, the adjuster must separate the claim from any merchandise not owned by the insured, such as merchandise in leased departments. In larger stores, this merchandise usually includes jewelry, cameras, and shoes. In smaller stores, items such as sales displays of hosiery and watches are generally not the property of the insured merchant, although the insured might be responsible for them under contract. If the insured claims legal responsibility, the adjuster should examine the contract between the insured and the manufacturer or distributor.

Valuation

Commercial property policies normally insure retail merchandise for replacement cost or actual cash value (ACV). A policy might also base valuation on the selling price.

Replacement Cost

Replacement cost is the cost to the insured of buying stock from its suppliers, less any trade discounts or allowances, plus incoming freight, and, possibly, the cost of receiving, opening, tagging, marking, and arranging the goods in the insured's premises. These additional costs reflect the different (usually greater) value the merchandise has on the merchant's premises ready for sale to the public as compared to the value it has in the supplier's warehouse or factory. Determining replacement cost is not difficult if the adjuster has access to the insured's books and to records such as invoices.

Freight

Incoming **freight charges** are the amounts that insureds pay to have goods shipped to their premises from suppliers. Any freight paid by the insured's suppliers is not counted.

Trade Discounts and Allowances

Trade discounts and allowances are reductions in the stated purchase price that suppliers grant the insured for purchasing in volume or for paying in a timely manner. Discounts and allowances represent reductions in the effective price paid by the insured for its merchandise, and they reduce the cost value of the insured's inventory.

Handling Costs

Handling costs incurred on the insured's premises are not always accounted for in the value of merchandise, but they represent a real cost and real value. These costs reflect the difference in value to the insured between goods on a receiving dock and those ready for sale to the public. If handling costs are identified in the insured's accounting records, they can be included for adjustment purposes in the value of goods. Insureds, however, do not always want these costs counted. These costs increase the insured's stock value for settlement purposes but also increase it for coinsurance purposes. Higher value does not necessarily translate into a higher settlement if a coinsurance penalty is incurred. Handling costs should be treated the same for loss settlement and coinsurance purposes.

Actual Cash Value

Calculating the actual cash value of merchandise is more difficult than calculating replacement cost because no policy defines the term "actual cash value." Actual cash value can equal replacement cost when there is no depreciation, markdown, or other loss of value. If so, determining actual cash value requires examining the insured's purchase records item by item in the same way that replacement cost is determined.

Causes of Depreciation

Any retail stock of merchandise can suffer a reduction in value and selling price because of depreciation even if it never leaves the merchant's premises. The possible causes of depreciation are innumerable, but the principal causes are physical damage and obsolescence. Physical damage can be caused by careless handling, dust, fading, moisture or humidity, missing parts, varmints, excessive heat, freezing, and thawing. Obsolescence means that the item has lost value because it is out of fashion, past its marked shelf life, a fad, or a seasonal item; because it shows evidence of slow turnover; or because it was offered in an incomplete size, color, or pattern range. The adjuster must inspect the goods to determine whether any physical damage to merchandise existed before the loss.

Market Value

In California, courts have ruled that actual cash value equals market value. The market is where the insured merchant obtains its stocks of merchandise. The insured is a buyer in the wholesale market. The insured's costs reflect the value of goods in this market, including incoming freight and handling costs, less trade discounts. Unless unusual circumstances are present, the insured's costs can be interpreted as an accurate reflection of market value in a given wholesale market. Any loss of value to the merchandise once it is on the insured's premises is not easy to detect. Goods are seldom resold on the wholesale market. The adjuster must judge whether goods on the insured's premises would sell as prime merchandise on the wholesale market. If not, some reduction in actual cash value is appropriate. Markdowns at retail strongly suggest that goods have lost value to the merchant and would likewise have less value at the wholesale level.

Markdowns

Most retail accounting systems operate on the premise that when the merchant reduces the selling price of a piece of merchandise because the item is not moving, is approaching the end of its season, or has become shop-worn, the original cost value of the item automatically drops by the same percentage by which the merchant has reduced the selling price. For example, if the retail price of an item is reduced 40 percent, from $100 to $60, then its cost value must likewise be reduced by 40 percent. If the original cost value was $50, it would drop (for ACV purposes) to $30 (40 percent less). Examples of this phenomenon are calendars and date books. These items rapidly lose value after January of every year. A retailer suffers a loss in March that would have certainly reduced the retail price of its remaining calendars and date books by then. In determining the ACV of that loss, the adjuster would value any damaged date books and calendars not according to their cost value when purchased, but on the basis of the marked-down price. Because these items are nearly worthless to the merchant in March, regardless of what was paid for them, their ACV will be extremely low.

Adjusters might find that merchants resist this method of determining value. If the adjuster can show that he or she is using the same method as the insured's own accounting system for valuing merchandise, the argument for using such value determination would be strengthened. All retail merchants mark down merchandise at some time. If the insured's inventory system reveals that end-of-year inventory values are always devalued, then the merchant clearly subscribes to the retail method of accounting and inventory valuation. The **retail method of accounting** assumes a consistent profit percentage, so that goods marked down at retail also lose value as assets on the business's books. This system should be included in ACV determination.

An adjuster cannot automatically assume that all marked-down items have been reduced in price because of depreciation or obsolescence. Grocery markets commonly have weekly promotions during which certain popular items are marked down as loss leaders. At the end of the promotion, the unsold items are marked back up to their normal prices. This practice is also common in other retail establishments such as shoe stores, clothing stores, drugstores, and record stores. If a loss occurs during the promotion, the adjuster cannot realistically argue that an item only temporarily marked down for a sales promotion has actually been reduced in value and that its ACV should be reduced accordingly.

Selling Price

Adjusters sometimes (though infrequently) encounter policies that give merchants selling price coverage on their merchandise. The selling price is the tagged price on the merchandise at the time of the loss, whether it is the originally marked selling price or a marked-down price. Almost all value calculations begin with the selling price marked on each piece of merchandise at the time of the loss.

Layaways

Layaways are treated differently from merchandise held for sale. A layaway should be valued at the selling price, whether it has been completely paid for or not. Layaways are valued on the assumption that once the item has been put aside for a customer, the sale has been made, and a profit has been realized. This standard for layaway values must be used whenever total valuation of the insured's stock of merchandise is relevant, such as when a coinsurance clause applies. The insured's inventory figure ordinarily does not include layaways since they are considered to have been sold.

Universal Pricing Code

The **universal pricing code** (UPC) is the small box of bars of various width appearing on an item of merchandise. As the item is scanned at the checkout counter, the UPC registers an electronic entry in inventory records and prints a price on the register tape. This method of checking out merchandise eliminates the need for a price tag on each item. It complicates the process of determining retail inventory values, however, because the absence of a price on each item makes verifying the price on the date of loss more difficult. The approach used in conducting a partial or total physical inventory with the UPC system must be different from the one used when each item is tagged with a price. Fortunately, computerized inventory systems using UPCs should have detailed histories of retail price changes and physical inventory counts.

Books and Records

If merchandise has been partly or completely destroyed, its total value must be established. Merchandise has suffered a total loss if it has been destroyed, as by fire, or has been so badly damaged that the insured cannot be expected to try to sell it at a reduced price.

Merchandise damaged beyond recognition, called **out-of-sight merchandise**, poses a problem for adjusters since it cannot be inventoried or identified. One precaution an adjuster should take when a loss involves out-of-sight merchandise is to determine by measurement that the quantity of merchandise claimed could have fit into the space in which it was supposed to have been stored or located. If a physical inventory is impractical because some merchandise has been destroyed or damaged beyond recognition, the only way to establish acceptable values is by using the insured's books and records.

Types of Financial Records

The fundamental financial records of any business are its income statement and its balance sheet.

Income Statement

The **income statement** is also called the *profit and loss statement* or *financial statement*. It is an account of the operations of the business, from gross revenue to net profit before taxes, over a defined period of time.

At a minimum, an income statement is prepared at the end of the insured's fiscal year. Income statements are commonly prepared monthly so that merchants have the opportunity to follow trends in the business. Year-end statements furnish adjusters with valuable reference material for handling property claims. They disclose the cost of goods sold and other merchandise-related costs that adjusters can use to value stock. They are also invaluable for handling attendant loss of earnings claims.

Balance Sheet

A **balance sheet** provides values on a stated date of all assets and liabilities. It is especially important for the property claim adjuster because it includes among the assets a physical inventory figure. A balance sheet is usually prepared only at the end of the fiscal year, and it furnishes an inventory figure for that date. This figure represents an actual physical inventory at values determined by the insured and the insured's accountant. To bring that inventory figure up to the date of loss, an adjuster must examine purchase and sales records since that physical inventory.

Determining Book Value

The value of an inventory that is lost out-of-sight can be determined by using the information contained in most businesses' books and records. The basic method is straightforward. The inventory was accurately known the last time a physical count was made, usually at the end of the year or at the end of the business's fiscal year. Since then, the business has added to its inventory by making purchases from its suppliers. Suppose a retailer selling men's suits had 500 suits in inventory on December 31 and purchased 900 suits between December 31 and the date of loss. This retailer had a total of 1,400 (500 + 900) suits that it could have sold between December 31 and the date of loss.

The number of suits sold between December 31 and the date of loss is subtracted from the total number of suits that could have been sold. The remaining number is inventory unsold. In the example, suppose that 950 suits were sold between December 31 and the date of loss. The total remaining in inventory would be as follows:

1,400 (500 + 900)	(What could have been sold)
− 900	(What was sold)
450	(What remains in inventory)

This formula applies whenever determining the amount of inventory that has been lost out-of-sight or beyond recognition is necessary. The following summarizes the method for determining book value:

    Amount in last physical inventory

  + Amount added to inventory between last physical inventory
     and date of loss

  = Amount that could have been sold

  − Amount that was sold between last physical inventory and date of loss

  = Amount remaining in inventory on date of loss

The above method was presented in terms of the number of physical units. To determine the true book value of inventory, dollar amounts must be used in the formula. All businesses maintain their accounting records in dollars; not all of them maintain records in physical units. The issue in a claims adjustment is the dollar value of lost inventory; an insurer would not be obligated to replace 450 suits, but the insured value of those suits. If the insured value of the suits is $100 per suit, the book value of inventory would be calculated as follows:

$ 50,000	(500 suits x $100 each)	(Value of beginning inventory)
+ 90,000	(900 suits x $100 each)	(Value of additions to inventory)
= $140,000	(1,400 suits x $100 each)	(Value of amount that could have been sold)
− 95,000	(950 suits x $100 each)	(Value of amount that was sold)
= $ 45,000	(450 suits x $100 each)	(Value of amount remaining in inventory on date of loss)

In the above analysis, the dollar figure for the amount of suits sold cannot be directly obtained from most businesses' records. Although all businesses can provide a dollar figure for the number of items sold, sales figures are kept in terms of retail prices or values. To determine the book value of inventory accurately, this amount must be reduced from the retail value to the cost to the business of obtaining the suits. In the above analysis, $100 is the cost to the suit retailer of obtaining suits from its suppliers. This cost must be used for the following two reasons:

1. Sales figures and purchase figures are otherwise not comparable. Purchases to inventory worth $1,000 are not the same as retail sales of $1,000. Assume, for example, that the retail store actually sells the suits for $200. *Purchases* of $1,000 represents *ten suits,* but *sales* of $1,000 represents only *five suits.*

2. Generally, the insured value of stock with a business is the cost to the business of replacing the stock, not its selling price.

Determining Cost of Goods Sold

The historical relationship between the cost and the selling price of goods determines the **cost of goods sold**. This relationship is determined by examining a business's complete records for a year, or several years, in which no loss occurred.

Cost of Goods Formula

The cost of goods sold during a year is determined as follows:

Beginning inventory
+   Additions to inventory
=   Amount that could have been sold during the year
−   End inventory (amount not sold during the year)
=   Cost of goods sold

In the above example, assume that in the year *before* the loss, the suit retailer began with an inventory of $52,500 and made purchases to inventory of $110,000. The cost of goods sold for this retailer was as follows:

$ 52,500   (Beginning inventory)
+   110,000   (Additions to inventory)
=   162,000   (Amount available for sale)
−   50,000   (End inventory on 12/31, as mentioned above)
= $112,500   (Cost of goods sold)

The $112,500 can be compared to the retail sales figure to determine the historical relationship between these two figures. If retail sales were $225,000, then retail sales are twice the cost of goods sold, because $25,000 ÷ 112,500 = 2. This represents a 100 percent markup, as when a business buys a suit for $100 and sells it to the public for $200. Markups by retail businesses can be any amount, but between 50 percent and 200 percent is common.

The Cost-to-Sales Ratio

In this example, the **cost-to-sales ratio** is one-half ($112,500 ÷ $225,000), or 50 percent. In the year of a loss, a business is not likely to have a figure for cost of goods sold, and such a figure cannot be determined without an accurate ending inventory figure. When the inventory is lost out-of-sight, determining an accurate ending inventory figure is not possible. However, the business should know its historic cost-to-sales ratio and its retail sales figures for the year of the loss. The business has retail sales figures from the date of the last physical inventory to the date of loss. The cost-to-sales ratio multiplied by the retail sales figure results is the cost of goods sold. For example, if retail sales were $84,000 and the cost-to-sales ratio is 50 percent, the cost of goods sold is $84,000 x 50%, or $42,000.

Summary of Book Value Method

After a loss occurs, a business can provide the figure for its sales since its last physical inventory. The adjuster or an accountant working for the adjuster can determine the cost-to-sales ratio from historical data. These two figures (the sales since the last inventory and the cost-to-sales ratio) determine the cost of goods sold during the year of the loss. This cost of goods sold figure can be inserted into the following formula:

         Beginning inventory

   +   Purchases to inventory

   =   Amount that could have been sold

   –   Cost of goods sold

   =   Value of inventory remaining on date of loss

The value of the inventory on the date of loss is the amount of the loss on which a settlement is based when the inventory is destroyed or lost out-of-sight. A more elaborate example of the calculation of book inventory appears in Exhibit 10-1 and Exhibit 10-2.

Exhibit 10-1

Income Statement for Period 1/1 through 12/31

Good Times Merchandise Co., Inc.

Gross Sales		$240,000.00
Less:		
Returns and allowances	$2,500.00	
Discounts	2,800.00	
Bad debts	700.00	6,000.00
Net Sales		$234,000.00
Determination of Cost of Goods Sold		
Inventory 1/1	$ 50,000.00	
Purchases	144,000.00	
Incoming freight	3,000.00	
	$197,000.00	
Less discounts received and returns	3,000.00	
Merchandise available for sale	$194,000.00	
Less ending inventory	46,000.00	$148,000.00
Cost of Goods Sold	$148,000.00	
Gross Profit on Sales		
{36.75% of net sales, $234,000.00} = $86,000.00		$ 86,000.00
Expenses		
Payroll and taxes	$35,100.00	
Rent	18,000.00	
Advertising	2,000.00	
Utilities	6,000.00	
Supplies	2,000.00	
Telephone	1,000.00	
Depreciation	9,000.00	
Insurance	2,500.00	
Taxes and Licenses	900.00	
Miscellaneous	500.00	$ 77,000.00
Net Income		$ 9,000.00

Exhibit 10-2
Calculation of Book Inventory
Good Times Merchandise Co., Inc. Total Fire—12/20

Last physical inventory 12/31		$ 50,000.00
Net purchases		140,000.00
Available for sale		$190,000.00
Less Cost of Goods Sold:		
Net Sales, same period	$215,000.00	
Less gross profit % (36.75) from Income Statement (Exhibit 1) or tax return	79,012.50	135,987.50
Indicated Inventory 12/20		$ 54,012.50

Note: Insured's perpetual inventory records indicate stock on hand as of 12/20 to be $54,500. Shrinkage for 51 weeks could account for the difference. The book inventory figure should prevail.

Adjustment Difficulties With Book Inventory

The value of merchandise losses can in theory be determined from the insured's books and records, but practical difficulties can arise when adjusting a particular loss. These include the destruction of records, the phenomenon of shrinkage, and differences between perpetual and physical inventories.

Destruction of Records

The destruction of the insured's records at the time of the loss would make the adjuster's task difficult, but not impossible. If the insured has an outside accounting or bookkeeping service, year-end records will be available. If sales records have been destroyed, the sales history can be reconstructed by referring to bank statements and to state sales-tax records. Purchase information can also be developed by referring to bank records and by requesting information from all known suppliers. Tax returns are, in effect, profit and loss statements. They cover all salient points, including a total inventory figure. With the insured's permission, previous state and federal income tax returns can be obtained from the IRS and state tax department.

Shrinkage

The adjuster must also consider the phenomenon of **shrinkage**. All businesses suffer a reduction in stock on hand caused by theft, breakage, other mishaps, and unrecorded sales. This reduction, known as "shrinkage," can be represented by a dollar figure. The total amount of shrinkage increases with the length of time that has passed since the last physical inventory. Although shrinkage is not generally a large figure, it can amount to as much as 4 percent of sales. Exhibit 10-2 shows shrinkage of about 3 percent. A deduction for estimated shrinkage can be included in the book value of inventory on hand, when it has been a regular pattern in past physical inventories.

Perpetual Inventories

Insureds often present a **perpetual inventory** record. The insured might tell the adjuster that the perpetual inventory eliminates the need for all the accounting work of producing a book inventory or the time and effort involved in a physical inventory. The insured might be completely sincere in believing that the perpetual inventory record is accurate, but that sincerity does not guarantee its accuracy.

The accuracy of a perpetual inventory depends on the accuracy and adequacy of the method of entering information into the inventory record keeping. This information consists of a record of each purchase of merchandise and a record of each sale of merchandise, at cost. Over time, errors of omission and commission occur, and normal shrinkage will not have been deducted. By the end of a fiscal year, a perpetual inventory figure will almost never be equivalent to the results of the physical inventory taken on that date.

For this reason, adjusters should not depend on the accuracy of a perpetual inventory figure because a computer printout is only as accurate as the method of entering information into the computer. People enter this information, and people make mistakes. If using a computer printout in a book inventory calculation becomes necessary, a CPA should test the accuracy of the insured's method of making computer entries.

Salvage

Adjusters often use the services of an outside expert called a "salvor" on claims involving merchandise. **Salvors** are experts in preserving and realizing the value remaining in partially damaged merchandise. Leading examples of salvors currently providing nationwide service are M.F. Bank and Company of Minneapolis and George M. Ruddy and Company of Piscataway, New Jersey and New York City.

Services of Salvors

If an adjuster anticipates that a salvage company will be needed, he or she should call in the salvage company at the beginning of the adjustment process.

A salvor can assist the adjuster in surveying the loss scene and can offer immediate advice on protecting remaining merchandise, minimizing further damage, and determining the feasibility of a physical inventory. A salvor can talk professionally with the insured about the insured's line of business. A salvor works with the insured's employees in separating damaged and undamaged goods, conducting a physical inventory, and checking invoices. A salvor can also offer the adjuster confidential and professional advice on the degree of damage to merchandise.

Role of Salvor in Settlement

One of the most important decisions that an adjuster must make on a merchandise loss is the manner of settlement. The adjuster can choose to do any of the following:

1. Pay the insured the full value of the merchandise and take the salvage for the account of the insurer

2. Have the salvage sold on account of the insured and pay the insured the difference between the salvage proceeds and the insured value of the merchandise

3. Agree with the insured on the percentage of damage to the merchandise, paying the insured for that percentage of value and leaving the merchandise with the insured for disposal

The salvor can provide invaluable advice on the likely outcome of these three choices. Even with the third option, in which the salvor does not sell the merchandise, the salvor's advice can be crucial.

Sale of Salvage

The insurer will take over some merchandise to sell during the adjustment process because the insured will have no way to dispose of it in the retail market. The salvor can arrange for packing and shipping the merchandise or for an on-site, complete disposal of the merchandise in an as-is, where-is condition. A salvor knows the best people to contact if a sale is held and can ensure that the best possible price is obtained for the merchandise taken over by the insurer. The salvor is the adjuster's most important colleague in any sizable or complex merchandise claim adjustment.

In merchandise claims, certain types of stock must be treated differently from ordinary stock. Examples are prescription drugs, for which there is practically no market, no matter how lightly they are damaged; alcoholic beverages, which can be disposed of only through licensed dealers; and highly perishable edibles, which should not be disposed of without the authority of local health and food inspectors. Salvors can assist adjusters in helping to realize some kind of return in disposing of this type of merchandise.

When necessary, the salvor must communicate with a health and food inspector. The salvor has the expertise to discuss in a professional manner the possible disposition of damaged edibles. For example, almost all granulated sugar can be re-refined at a reasonable cost, regardless of how it has been damaged. Contaminated salt and items not fit for human consumption but acceptable as animal feed also have markets. Salvors know of markets for merchandise of all kinds, and their advice should be closely heeded.

The Adjuster's Role

All insurance companies have a list of approved experts of all kinds, including salvors. An independent adjuster should not choose a salvor without first consulting the insurer, preferably by telephone. Staff adjusters should refer to their employer's list of recommended experts when choosing a salvor.

An adjuster who has engaged the services of a salvor should never expect the salvor to substitute as an adjuster. The salvor should never argue any point with the insured. Professional salvors never try to intercede in any dispute between the adjuster and the insured or the insured's representative. The adjuster must always maintain control of the adjustment process and should never rely on others to negotiate with the insured.

Acting Without Salvor Assistance

Adjusters must be able to make on-the-spot field decisions during the adjustment of a merchandise loss. When certain types of merchandise become wet, they must be dried out to prevent mildew or staining damage. In such a case, an adjuster must work immediately with the insured to arrest the moisture damage. If an adjuster waits and submits a report asking for instructions, the merchandise affected by water might become worthless. Adjusters should realize when field decisions must be made and when the insurer must be consulted for instructions.

Salvage Contracts

Damaged merchandise is still owned by the insured and cannot be taken without permission. Salvors operate in a professional and legal manner and never remove merchandise from an insured's premises until a proper contract has been executed by the insurer and the insured. An example of such a contract appears in Exhibit 10-3.

Exhibit 10-3

Agreement for the Removal of Stock

M. F. BANK & COMPANY, INC.

**AGREEMENT FOR THE REMOVAL OF STOCK
FOR BETTER PROTECTION AND DISPOSITION**

Insured: _____   Stock: _____
_____   _____
Insurance Company: _____   Location of Stock: _____
_____   _____
Date of Loss: _____   MFB Stock No.: _____

BACKGROUND:

The Stock may have been damaged by fire, smoke or other casualty, and it is to the benefit of all who may have an interest in the Stock that the Stock be handled with as little delay as possible and without waiting to determine the respective interests, rights or liabilities under policies purporting to insure the Stock.

AGREEMENT:

1. M. F. Bank & Company, Inc. ("MFB") is hereby retained to take possession of the Stock and to place the Stock in the best possible order for sale and to sell the Stock in the interest of whom it may concern. The proceeds of any sale of the Stock, less MFB's commissions and expenses, as set forth below, will be held by MFB in trust until the loss is adjusted and will then be turned over to such party(ies) as may be entitled to receive those proceeds.

2. As compensation for its services, MFB will receive an amount equal to (a)_____ % of the gross proceeds of any sale of the Stock, plus (b) all costs and expenses (including labor costs) incurred by MFB in connection with the removal, handling, maintenance and sale of the Stock. MFB may retain such amount from the gross proceeds of any sale of the Stock.

3. If MFB at any time determines that the cost of the removal, handling and maintenance of the Stock exceeds the estimated salvage value of the Stock (less MFB's expenses and commissions, as set forth above), the responsibility of MFB for continued custody of the Stock may be terminated.

4. The Insurance Company and the Insured will hold MFB harmless from and against any claim made by any person or entity, other than the Insurance Company or the Insured, who or which may claim an interest in the Stock.

5. This Agreement is the entire agreement between the parties hereto and may only be changed in writing.

Date: _____, 199___

M. F. BANK & COMPANY, INC.   **INSURANCE COMPANY**

By: _____   By: _____
   Its: _____   Its: _____

                                              INSURED

                                              By: _____
                                                 Its: _____

Salvage Fees

The salvor's fees and commissions come out of the sale proceeds. The settlement with the insured is based on *net* proceeds. The salvor's fees and commissions become part of the loss indemnified by the insurer.

Insured's Liability to Salvor

The insured is never directly liable for the salvor's fees, except possibly in one circumstance. The insured might want to use the salvor to separate, inventory, and protect the merchandise even though the insured ultimately retains the goods. This might happen when the insured's premises are in a physical condition that threatens the merchandise. Ordinarily in this situation the policy covers the reasonable cost of removal for protection. An adjuster might disagree with the need for removal and might resist approving the expense. Since the insured owns the property, the insured is free to contract directly with the salvor. Although the insured would undoubtedly submit the salvage fees as part of its claim, the insured would bear the initial liability to the salvor. This situation is undesirable and should be avoided if possible. The salvor's expert advice should be sought to resolve any dispute between the adjuster and the insured over whether property needs to be removed. If the salvor believes it should be, the adjuster should approve the expense. If the salvor thinks the property is safe on the insured's premises, the insurance company bears the risk of the salvor's being wrong.

Sale Before Settlement

When goods must be sold quickly, as in the case of perishables, the adjuster and the insured do not have to settle the claim before the salvor can take over the goods. As long as the adjuster and insured agree that the goods must be sold, they can execute a contract to that effect with the salvor. The salvor will sell the goods on "account of whom it may concern."

Salvage Proceeds

Various ways of accounting for proceeds are described below.

- Sale on Account of Insurer

The adjuster and insured agree on the full insured value of the merchandise. The insurer pays the insured this full amount and takes the salvage for its own account:

Agreed full value of stock	$100,000
Insurer pays insured	$100,000
Net proceeds from salvage sale paid to insurer	$ 35,000
Insurer's net payment	$ 65,000

- Sale on Account of Insured

The salvage sale is used to determine amount of loss:

Agreed full value of stock	$100,000
Net proceeds from salvage sale paid to insured	$ 35,000
Therefore, insurer pays insured	$ 65,000
Total payments to insured	$100,000

- Sale on Account of Whom It May Concern

The salvage sale is made before agreement on value of stock:

Net proceeds from salvage sale held by salvor pending agreement	$ 35,000
Agreed full value of stock	$100,000
Net proceeds paid to insured	$ 35,000
Insurer pays insured	$ 65,000

- Sale in Which Insured Coinsures

If the insured has inadequate limits of coverage and is required to bear a coinsurance penalty, the insured will share in the net proceeds of the salvage sale in the same percentage as the loss. Assume a 25 percent coinsurance penalty:

Agreed full value of stock	$100,000
In light of coinsurance, insurer would pay no more than	$ 75,000
In light of coinsurance, insured might have to bear up to	$ 25,000
Net proceeds of salvage sale	$ 35,000
Shared 75% with insurer	$ 26,250
Shared 25% with insured	$ 8,750
Insurer pays ($75,000 – $26,250) to insured	$ 48,750
Insured bears ($25,000 – $8,750) of loss	$ 16,250

Reporting Form Policies

The **reporting form** is a type of coverage for merchandise associated with risks in which the value of covered merchandise fluctuates by season or by month. The reporting form is used for such risks because it is designed to respond to what can be extreme fluctuations in the value of merchandise. Reporting form coverage is offered as an endorsement to a commercial policy. It affects the policy only by the method of determining compliance with policy conditions, such as the coinsurance clause. The value reporting form can cover at one or many locations and even covers property at newly acquired and incidental locations. The form incorporates a declarations page, which describes all locations at which coverage is to be provided and also establishes different limits at different locations.

A reporting form is designed to provide maximum dollar coverage when it is needed. For a merchant with a seasonal business, carrying commercial insurance throughout the year with a coinsurance clause based on the maximum possible value on hand at peak season would be very expensive. With reporting form insurance, merchants can obtain coverage equal to full value, or the face amount of policy, no matter how much the inventory fluctuates.

Operation of Reporting Forms

Reporting form coverage has certain conditions. First, a provisional amount of insurance is designated when the policy is written. This provisional amount has little effect on any claim adjustments and is provided mainly for initial premium calculations. Once reporting form insurance is in effect, the insured must report total values on hand at each of the designated reporting times during the term of the policy. The reporting period is usually a calendar month, but it can be on a quarterly or even semiannual basis. The value report must be submitted to the company through the producer within thirty days of the end of any designated reporting period. Any submitted report is binding upon the insured and cannot be changed or corrected after a loss has occurred.

Reporting Full Values

The reporting form accomplishes its purpose by replacing the coinsurance clause with what is called a **full reporting clause.** Although the intent of reporting form coverage is for an insured to report full value at every insured location within thirty days of the designated reporting date, the form does not explicitly require the full value to be reported. Instead, the full reporting clause allows the insured to coinsure the losses when values have been underreported. The full reporting clause replaces the coinsurance clause with the following:

> If your last report of values before loss or damage for a location where loss or damage occurs shows less than the full value of the Covered Property at that location on the report dates, we will not pay a greater proportion of loss, prior to the application of the deductible, than:
>
> (1) The values you reported for the location where the loss or damage occurred, divided by
>
> (2) The value of the Covered Property at that location on the report dates.

An adjuster should not regard an insured who has underreported values as willfully dishonest. Some insureds deliberately underreport by a certain amount, acknowledging that they will be in the position of a coinsurer in the event of a loss. The insured's premiums are reduced, and if no loss occurs during the term of the policy, the insured has saved insurance expense.

Timeliness of Reports

Other restrictive conditions in the value reporting form address the insured's failure to submit reports on time. If an insured fails to make a report on a stipulated reporting date, thirty days after the end of the designated reporting period, the coverage at any insured location will be limited to the amount of the last report made for that location, no matter how long before the date of loss it was made. If the insured is late in making a first report of value and a loss occurs before any report has been made, the coverage at any given location is limited to 75 percent of the amount the insurer would have otherwise paid. That is not 75 percent of the amount of insurance shown for that location; it is 75 percent of what an adjusted claim would have been.

Specific Insurance

Another possible complication in adjusting a claim under a reporting form policy concerns the existence of what is referred to in the reporting form as **specific insurance**. Specific insurance is other insurance covering the same insured and at least some of the same property that the reporting form covers at the described location. The claim payable under the specific insurance, whether collectible or not, and after the deductible has been applied, must be calculated according to the terms of the specific insurance. The reporting form coverage applies to the balance of the claim. Specific insurance should be reported to the reporting form insurer along with each value report. This is often not done, so the adjuster must determine the existence of any specific insurance.

Determination of Values for Last Report Date

In all losses involving reporting forms, the adjuster must determine inventory values for the last report date. Exhibit 10-4 illustrates this procedure.

Checking Reported Values

In the process of adjusting a claim under reporting form coverage, certain values must be checked and verified. The value of all stock on the date of loss is not important except for a total loss. The value figure that must be verified is the value of the stock on the date of the insured's last report of values. The adjuster should check these values against a copy of the last report received by the insurer or the producer.

Exhibit 10-4
Procedure for Determining Inventory Values for Last Report Date

Date of Loss 10/1
Demonstration of Value Calculation for Last Reported Date
Under Reporting Form Policy

Last report of value, for 7/1/9X	$173,000.00
Last physical inventory as of 1/1/9X	$160,000.00
Add net purchases—1/1 to 7/1	70,000.00
Available for sale	$230,000.00
Deduct net sales, at cost, same period	60,000.00
Indicated inventory 7/1	$170,000.00

Variation
Reverse Book Inventory Calculation

Complete physical inventory for 10/1 (Date of Loss)	$150,000.00
Deduct net purchases 10/1 back to 7/1	8,000.00
	$142,000.00
Add net sales, at cost, same period	28,000.00
Indicated value as of 7/1	$170,000.00

Both methods indicate that the insured fully reported values for the last report date, 7/1. The reported amount, $173,000, exceeds the actual amount.

The adjuster must determine book inventory, perhaps with the assistance of an accountant. This calculation was demonstrated in Exhibit 10-2. Exhibit 10-4 shows that a book inventory calculation can be worked either backward or forward. If establishing a precise total inventory value figure for the date of loss is possible, a reverse book inventory figure to a previous report date should be more accurate than one obtained by working forward from a past physical inventory figure, especially if the figure is from the distant past. The actual value of the inventory on the date of the last report should be no more than the value reported. If the established value of the inventory on the last report date exceeds the amount stated in the report, the insured must coinsure the loss.

Often the reported value does not include items such as incoming freight, the cost of handling and tagging merchandise after its receipt, and trade discounts. These items should be included when they are identifiable in the insured's accounting records. The adjuster must ascertain whether the value that he or she calculated, as of the date of the last received report, is determined on the same basis as that the insured used in making the report. The calculation of value for claim purposes must be made on the same basis.

In calculating a book inventory figure, sales, whenever entered into a calculation, must be entered at *cost*, not at *selling price*. In an actual case involving a claim under reporting form coverage, the insured had been calculating value on hand on the date of each value report by taking the value figure from the previous report, adding purchases at cost, and subtracting sales at *selling price*. Since the policy had been in effect for several months, the insured had been understating his values by an increasing amount with each report and would soon have been reporting no value at all had the mistake not been discovered.

Reporting forms might also cover furniture, fixtures, machines, and other personal property (even though their primary purpose is to cover stocks of merchandise). The reporting form is used to insure stock that might vary in total value each month. The insured is required to submit regular reports of values. The balance of nonstock items of personal property does not usually change much from month to month. Thus, the insured might overlook additions to personal property other than stock. The adjusters must carefully evaluate the nonstock portion of the values because new equipment purchased in the past few years might have been omitted from the monthly reports of values.

The Value Reporting Form Illustrated

Exhibits 10-5 through 10-10 illustrate solutions to various problems arising under claims involving reporting form coverage, with and without specific insurance. In these illustrations, assume under the reporting form that (1) the limit indicated is either the original provisional amount of insurance or the amount of the last report of value received by the insurer before the date of loss and (2) the insured is not delinquent in reporting.

Exhibit 10-5
Proper Reporting—No Specific Insurance

Bad Times Mercantile Co., Inc.	
Date of Loss 10/1	
Coverage: no specific insurance	
Stock reporting form	$175,000 limit (provisional)
Last report of value, for 7/31, new limit	$173,000
Actual value as of 7/31	$170,000
Agreed loss	$26,000
Insured recovers entire loss	$26,000

Exhibit 10-6
Proper Reporting—Specific Insurance Applicable

Bad Times Mercantile Co., Inc.
Date of Loss 10/1

Coverage: $ 25,000—specific insurance on stock, 80% coinsurance
            $175,000—reporting form limit

Last report of values, for 7/31, to reporting form insurer

Total value, new limit	$173,000
Specific insurance	25,000
Actual value, 7/31	170,000
Actual value, 10/1	180,000
Agreed loss	26,000

Specific insurance pays:

$$\frac{\$25,000}{\$144,000 \ (80\% \ of \ \$180,000)} \times \$26,000 = \qquad \$ \ \ 4,514$$

Reporting form insurance pays balance of loss	$ 21,486
Insured collects entire loss	$ 26,000

Exhibit 10-7
Values Underreported—No Specific Insurance

Bad Times Mercantile Co., Inc.
Date of Loss 10/1

Coverage: reporting form only—$200,000 limit

Last report of value for 7/31	$150,000
Actual value, 7/31	170,000
Agreed loss	26,000

Insurance pays:

$$\frac{\$150,000}{\$170,000} \times \$26,000 = \qquad \$ \ \ 22,942$$

Insured shares loss	$ 3,058

Exhibit 10-8
Values Properly Reported—Existing Specific Insurance Not Reported

Bad Times Mercantile Co., Inc.	
Date of Loss 10/1	
Coverage: $ 25,000—specific insurance, 80% coinsurance	
$175,000—reporting form limit	
Last report of values for 7/31 (no report of specific insurance)	$173,000
Actual value, 7/31	170,000
Actual value, 10/1	180,000
Agreed loss	26,000
Although not reported, the existence of specific insurance is developed.	
Specific insurance pays, as in Exhibit 10-6	$ 4,514
Reporting form insurer pays	21,486
Insured collects entire loss	$26,000

Exhibit 10-9
Values Underreported—Specific Insurance Applicable

Bad Times Mercantile Co., Inc.	
Date of Loss 10/1	
Coverage: $ 25,000—specific insurance on stock, 80% coinsurance	
$175,000—reporting form limit	
Last report of value for 7/31	$150,000
Actual value 7/31 established	170,000
Actual value 10/1 established	180,000
Agreed loss	26,000
Specific insurance pays, as in Exhibit 10-6	$ 4,514
Reporting form insurer pays:	
$\dfrac{\$150,000}{\$170,000} \times \$21,486 =$	18,958
Insured collects	$ 23,472
Insured shares loss	$ 2,528

Exhibit 10-10
Values Properly Reported—Specific Insurance Not Collectible

Bad Times Mercantile Co., Inc.
Date of Loss 10/1

Coverage: $175,000 limit reporting form	
Last report of value for 7/31, to reporting form insurer	$173,000
Specific insurance reported	25,000
Actual value, 7/31	170,000
Actual value, 10/1	180,000
Agreed loss	26,000

Specific insurance not collectible, thus:

Reporting form pays only the excess of what should have been paid by the specific insurance.

Specific insurance should pay, as in Exhibit 10-6	$ 4,514
Reporting form insurance pays excess of $26,000 over $4,514	$ 21,486
Insured collects	$ 21,486

Loss Adjustment

Adjusters should always prepare a file and follow standard procedures for all large merchandise losses. Percentage damage settlements frequently arise with merchandise losses, and considerable negotiation might be required. Small losses do not require as elaborate procedures.

Preparation of File for Adjustment

To build an acceptable and reliable file, the adjuster must prepare to do everything in an orderly and complete manner. An adjuster should use a mental or preferably a written checklist from the first visit to the insured's premises. Such a checklist should include at least the following steps, not necessarily in order of importance:

1. Introduce and establish a satisfactory relationship with the insured.
2. Inspect the entire premises, including merchandise that is not involved.
3. Decide whether to use a salvor. If a salvor is to be used, the insured should be told because the salvor will probably arrive while the adjuster is not present.

4. Take snapshots if possible.

5. Inquire about the existence and availability of books and records and other insurance.

6. Identify the insured's independent accounting firm or bookkeeping firm.

7. Discuss with the insured immediate steps to minimize damage, including board-up and general security.

8. Obtain the insured's explanation of the cause and origin of the loss. Inquire about whether a fire department investigator has already been to the scene.

9. Provide the insured with a general description of the normal procedure to follow during the adjustment process.

10. Be prepared to answer the insured's questions in a competent but cautious manner. Anticipate many questions.

11. Investigate thoroughly any possibilities of subrogation on arrival at the scene of the loss. This is possibly the most important step for an adjuster. In many claims, the adjuster discovers that the damage resulted from a malfunction in a piece of equipment or from the negligence of some third party. Evidence in proof of subrogation possibilities can disappear rapidly, especially if the person who furnished or installed equipment or the person whose negligent act caused the damage realizes the exposure to a possible subrogation action. The adjuster must determine by questioning both the insured and any possible investigative authority whether subrogation possibilities exist.

Procedure—Large Loss

When damage to merchandise is severe and widespread but not total, the first visit by the adjuster involves a general inspection of the premises, taking photos, and guiding the insured, who has probably suffered his or her first major insured loss. On this visit, the adjuster must establish a rapport with the insured and develop mutual trust and confidence.

Preliminary Survey

The adjuster's inspection of the premises and the damaged merchandise should reveal whether a complete physical inventory is practical or even possible. Even when an appreciable amount of merchandise has been damaged beyond identification, a physical inventory of remaining merchandise can help provide an estimate of the out-of-sight loss (by subtracting the inventory of remaining merchandise from book inventory) as well as information on pre-loss obsolescence or other loss of value.

The adjuster should use the first visit to gain a preliminary idea of the scope of damage and of the total value involved (perhaps a statement from the insured will suffice) and to assure the insured that he or she will be treated fairly and reasonably throughout the adjustment.

Discussions With the Insured

During the first visit to the insured, the adjuster must establish general procedures that will be followed during the entire adjustment process. The adjuster must notify the insured of the insured's duties in the event of loss as outlined in the policy. The adjuster should not, on the first visit, try to describe to the insured every aspect of an adjustment. The adjuster should also refrain from confusing the insured, who is probably already upset, with discussions of the coinsurance clause, the application of books and records information to the loss, or other matters that can best be discussed during subsequent visits.

Also important during the adjuster's first visit is a thorough, but courteous questioning of the insured about the conduct of the business before the loss. The insured knows more about its business than does the adjuster. By questioning the insured about its marketing and merchandising methods, the adjuster can gain insight into how this particular business operates and can develop some ideas of how to prepare the claim file. Most insureds are eager to answer such questions and to demonstrate their own expertise regarding the conduct of the business.

If a great deal of lightly damaged merchandise remains on the premises, during the first visit the adjuster should determine the insured's attitude about a fire sale after the adjustment is complete. The insured's answer to a question about a fire sale will guide the adjuster in how to conduct the adjustment.

The adjuster should be prepared to answer questions that the insured is likely to ask concerning board-up and protection of the premises, expenses that must be incurred immediately to minimize damage, and possibly the use of a public adjuster. In larger cities, public adjusters often contact insureds after a serious fire, even before the company adjuster arrives on the scene. An insured who has never heard of public adjusters might be confused. The company adjuster should be prepared to answer questions about the activities of public adjusters but should refrain from making derogatory remarks about them. The adjuster representing the insurer should assure the insured that the claim will be fairly and properly adjusted.

Exercise and Nonwaiver of Rights

During the first visit, the adjuster should exercise the insurer's right of access to all books and records of the insured's business. If an outside accountant possesses the records, the adjuster should get permission to contact the accountant directly to obtain the necessary information.

The adjuster should be cautious during this first visit not to make any commitments, such as the following, that waive policy conditions:

1. Giving permission to move merchandise before it has been inventoried
2. Approving expense that later proves not to be covered under the policy
3. Approving expense that, although possibly covered, might not be justified by the circumstances
4. Making a decision on the property adjustment that might be prejudicial to adjusting the business interruption claim or that might inadvertently increase the business interruption claim

The insured's first impression of the adjuster is extremely important. The adjuster should reflect an attitude of professionalism and competence and should proceed with authority and with prudence.

Percentage Damage Settlements

Merchandise damaged but still salable at retail level will almost certainly be worth more to the insured than to anyone else. If the insured is considering retaining the merchandise for a fire sale, the merchandise would only have to be moved within the store and repriced. Such expense will be much less than the cost of having an outside purchaser pack the merchandise, move it to another location possibly hundreds of miles away, unpack it, classify it, and reprice it. Generally, if a salvor estimates the net salvage return on merchandise after being taken over by the insurer to be 40 percent of cost, then the merchandise is likely to be worth more, perhaps between 50 and 60 percent of cost, to the merchant who retains it.

Mutual Advantage of Percentage Damage Settlements

If, in the merchant's opinion, the stock has lost *at least* 40 percent of its value, the merchant could sell it for no more than 60 percent of its value. To the insurer, the stock has lost *no more* than 60 percent of its value. The insurer could reimburse the merchant 100 percent and take the stock for salvage. Since salvage is expected to yield 40 percent of value, it has suffered *no more* than a 60 percent loss. Settlement should be made at a loss figure between 40 percent (the least the merchant will accept) and 60 percent (the most the insurer will pay).

If both parties have accurately assessed the situation, any amount between 40 percent and 60 percent will be fair to *both* parties. For example, assume a settlement at 50 percent. The insured receives 50 percent from the insurer and retains the stock, which the insured still believes has 60 percent of its value. The insurer would be satisfied to pay 50 percent since the only alternative would be to pay the insured 100 percent and take the stock as salvage, for a net loss of 60 percent. Sixty percent is the maximum, or **break point**, that an insurer should pay if the merchandise is left with the insured. Beyond 60 percent, the insurer would be better off paying the insured the full value of the merchandise and taking the salvage for itself.

Use of Salvors in Percentage Damage Settlements

After a salvor is hired and has initially inspected the damaged merchandise, the adjuster and salvor meet. The salvor's advice should guide but not control the adjuster. The salvor offers opinions on the degree of damage and possible net salvage return and advises the adjuster on what the break point is likely to be.

If a large percentage of the insured's stock has been lightly or moderately damaged, the salvor might divide the stock into lots. The salvor can then assign a possible damage allowance percentage to each lot. Seldom is an entire stock subject to the same degree or percentage of damage.

In a fire sale promotion, markdowns on merchandise damaged to any degree must be substantial. Damaged merchandise marked down only 10 percent will not move. Insureds know this and will likely argue for the greatest possible damage percentage. In this situation, the adjuster must usually rely heavily on the advice and recommendations of the salvor. If the insured can handle the damaged merchandise, the best adjustment will probably result by agreeing on the percentage of damage by lots and leaving the merchandise with the insured. This kind of adjustment might be advantageous to both the insured and the insurer. Even with discount, the merchant might not be able to sell damaged merchandise, as in the case of high-fashion ladies' apparel. Most purchasers of high-fashion dresses and gowns are not tempted by a fire sale.

Brands and Labels Clause

Certain policy conditions are sometimes added by endorsement, which makes the ultimate salvage value of merchandise much less than might normally be expected. A **brands and labels clause** requires the manufacturer's label to be removed from all merchandise taken in salvage by the insurance company. When the label is popular or prestigious, its removal certainly reduces the value of the salvage to the insurer. The insured who keeps merchandise on a percentage-of-damage settlement need not remove labels. This increases the attraction of such settlements.

Negotiation

The adjuster's negotiation skills are especially important when adjusting serious merchandise damage claims. The adjuster's negotiating ability determines whether a satisfactory adjustment is possible. When the discussion focuses on damage allowances, the adjuster should inform the insured that a negotiated settlement of the damage allowance will be considered. During the process of negotiating an adjustment, the adjuster should maintain a confident but flexible attitude, depending on the insured's attitude. If the insured is inflexible about a percentage of damage allowance, the adjuster has the right to take over the damaged merchandise for salvage disposal. With the break point in mind, the adjuster will at some point realize that paying the insured the full insured value and taking the salvage for the insurer's account is cheaper than paying the percentage that the insured is demanding.

In negotiating a settlement for partial damage to merchandise, the adjuster is dealing in an area in which the insured is much more knowledgeable. The subject under discussion is the insured's own merchandise and the insured's ability as a merchandiser. An adjuster should be the expert on fire sales and is responsible for bringing the adjustment to a conclusion that is fair to both the insurer and the insured.

Small Losses

The preceding discussion outlined procedures and considerations for adjusters handling large, complicated merchandise claims. Most merchandise claims, however, are relatively small and uncomplicated. For such routine losses, following all of the preceding procedures is contrary to the insured's and the insurer's interests. Adjusters should not overlook smaller merchandise claims. The adjuster should establish to the best of his or her ability, without bringing in outside salvors or accountants, the accurate measure of the insured's actual loss, and then apply policy conditions to readily conclude the matter.

Adjusters should handle every merchandise loss with at least one visit to the insured's premises. The adjuster should not instruct the insured to prepare its own claim and call the adjuster when it is ready. On all merchandise losses, the adjuster should work with the insured to establish the facts of the loss and fair and accurate figures, not leaving the determination of loss and damage to the insured. Otherwise, the insured would apply his or her own ideas of value and damage to the claim. No matter how incorrect the insured's conclusions later seem to be to the adjuster, changing the insured's mind would be extremely difficult.

Summary

Merchandise is personal property held by a merchant for sale. It is also known as "stock" or "inventory." A merchant's stock is insured under commercial property insurance policies whether the merchant owns the property or merely holds it on consignment. Merchandise is usually valued for claim settlements at actual cash value. To determine actual cash value, adjusters must review records from the insured's suppliers and adjust the cost for freight, handling, and trade discounts. Settling losses to merchandise requires adjusters to follow procedures and make considerations not present in other claims.

Adjusters must consult policyholders' books and records to resolve merchandise claims. Every business should periodically create income statements and balance sheets. An adjuster is not expected to have the expertise of a professional accountant, but must be able to follow accounting statements. Adjusters can use the information in accounting statements to reconstruct the value of an inventory destroyed or otherwise lost out-of-sight.

Merchandise losses are the most frequent circumstances in which adjusters use professional salvors. Salvors perform a variety of services, including protection, removal, inventorying, and sale of merchandise involved in a loss. Most important, salvors provide invaluable advice to adjusters on how a loss can be settled to everyone's satisfaction. Adjusters must be familiar with salvage operations and salvage contract provisions and must be scrupulous in accounting for salvage sale proceeds.

Reporting form policies sometimes apply to merchandise losses. These policies were designed so that merchants could adequately insure inventories that fluctuate widely in value. They require the merchant periodically to submit reports of value to the insurer. A merchant who complies with this requirement should have adequate insurance coverage for any merchandise loss. Adjusters must understand what to do when merchants are late with their reports or underreport inventory values. In either of these circumstances, the merchant will coinsure the loss.

When negotiating merchandise losses, adjusters should have a clear understanding of (1) when to pay the policyholder a percentage of the inventory value for settlement and leave the damaged goods with the merchant for a fire sale and (2) when the insurer would be better off to pay the merchant full value and to take the remaining stock for salvage sale. Adjusters should also develop judgment about the degree of effort appropriate to settling small losses versus settling large losses.

Chapter 11

Time Element Losses

So far, this text has considered only claims for damage or destruction of property. The financial consequences of damaged or destroyed property, however, can extend beyond repair or replacement of the property in question. Damage or destruction of property can cause the policyholder to suffer loss of income or increased expenses. Most property insurance policies do not cover loss of income and increased expenses. Such policies generally cover only the cost to repair or replace or the actual cash value of damaged or destroyed property. Nevertheless, a policyholder who suffers loss of income or increased expenses has suffered a real loss.

Loss of income and increased expense are called **time element losses** because they occur over time. Adjusters handling these losses must understand their nature and duration. For businesses and other organizations, time element losses can include loss of income, increased expenses, or both. For homeowners, time element losses consist of increased living expenses. Insurance covering time element losses generally extends only to losses occurring during the repair or replacement of damaged property.

This chapter begins by describing time element exposures faced by organizations. Both for-profit businesses and other organizations can experience time element losses as a result of damage or destruction of property. The Business Income Coverage (BIC) Form applies to a wide variety of time element losses experienced by organizations. Homeowners policies provide coverage for time element losses for individuals.

165

What Happens to an Organization After a Loss?

After losses involving physical damage to or destruction of tangible property, adjusters should indemnify policyholders for the damage or destruction according to the terms of the insurance policy. Once the policyholder receives payment, he or she can repair or replace the property in question. Organizations, however, can suffer losses that go beyond damage or destruction of tangible property. For example, the damage or destruction of tangible property might interfere with an organization's operations. That interference could cause loss of revenue or increased expenses, both of which are harmful to organizations. Such loss of revenue or increased expenses are called **business interruption losses**. Because business interruption losses are purely financial losses, they are more difficult to understand than physical damage or destruction.

To evaluate business interruption losses, adjusters must understand the basics of accounting and the financial records of organizations that suffer direct physical losses. Business interruption losses can be detected and proven only with financial records. Adjusters need not be expert accountants, but they must be comfortable enough with financial and accounting principles to grasp the nature of business interruption losses and to follow the reports produced by expert accountants.

Basic Accounting for Organizations

The basic elements of accounting are essentially the same for all organizations, regardless of whether the organization is a for-profit business, a nonprofit organization, a corporation, a partnership, a sole proprietorship, a large manufacturer, or a small retailer. The two basic financial statements for any organization are the balance sheet and the income statement. This chapter is primarily concerned with the financial consequences of a loss affecting the income statement. The important elements of the income statement are revenue and expenses. The operations of an organization generate revenue, usually from sales, and incur expenses in creating such revenue. Revenue should exceed expenses for any organization that wishes to continue its operations. If expenses exceeded revenue, the organization would eventually run out of money and be forced to close.

Balance Sheet

An organization's balance sheet answers the question, "Where do we stand?" It is a snapshot of the organization at one moment in time. The **balance sheet** is a simultaneous listing of everything the organization owns and everything it owes. What it owns are called **assets** and what it owes are called **liabilities**. Exhibit 11-1 shows a simple balance sheet.

Exhibit 11-1
A Simple Balance Sheet

ABC Inc. Balance Sheet December 31, 1994				
Assets		**Liabilities**		
Cash	$ 75,000	Accounts Payable	$ 50,000
Accounts Receivable	100,000	Bank loan	150,000
Inventory	325,000	Mortgage	800,000
Plant and equipment	1,500,000	Total	1,000,000
Real estate	1,000,000		
		Owners' Equity	2,000,000
	$ 3,000,000		$ 3,000,000

For a for-profit business, the difference between assets and liabilities is called **owners' equity** or **net worth**. Owners' equity is shown on the liabilities side of the balance sheet because a business does not own its net worth. It "owes" its net worth to its owners. Owners' equity (net worth) is *always* the difference between assets and liabilities. Owners' equity is therefore calculated as follows:

$$\begin{array}{r} \text{Assets} \\ - \text{Liabilities} \\ \hline \text{Owners' equity (net worth)} \end{array}$$

For example, the owners' equity for ABC, shown in Exhibit 11-1, was calculated as $3,000,000 (assets) − $1,000,000 (liabilities) = $2,000,000 (owners' equity). Owners' equity (net worth) is negative whenever liabilities exceed assets. A business with negative owners' equity (net worth) is eligible for bankruptcy. Because of how owners' equity (net worth) is calculated, the balance sheet always balances—hence the name "balance sheet."

The Income Statement

For an organization, the income statement answers the question, "How did we do during. . . ?" for some past time period, such as a year, month, or quarter (three months). Whereas the balance sheet is a snapshot of the organization at a given moment, the **income statement** describes the organization's experience over time. Exhibit 11-2 shows an income statement for a year for ABC.

Exhibit 11-2
A Simple Income Statement

ABC, Inc. Income Statement January 1, 1994, to December 31, 1994	
Revenue	
Sales	$ 1,500,000
Expenses	
Cost of goods sold	$ 700,000
Employee wages	300,000
Depreciation	100,000
Interest	100,000
Utilities	50,000
	1,250,000
Net Income	$ 250,000

Almost all organizations prepare annual income statements. Some organizations have a fiscal year different from the January-December calendar year. They keep financial records and usually pay taxes based on some other 365-day period of their choice. For example, a university or college might have a fiscal year of August 1 to July 31 that corresponds to the academic year.

An income statement lists money received by an organization in its ordinary operations and money spent by the organization to conduct those operations. The money received is called **revenue**. The money spent is called **expenses**. Every organization wants its revenue to exceed its expenses. In this respect, organizations are like people. A person cannot spend more than his or her income unless he or she borrows the money or depletes savings. Neither an organization nor a person can borrow or deplete savings for long. The major elements of the income statement are revenue, expenses, cost of goods sold, and net income, as explained below.

Revenue

The money generated by an organization's operations is its revenue. For a for-profit business, revenue usually comes from sales of its products or services. For a nonprofit organization, revenue might come from dues, memberships, contributions, or sales. A business' revenue depends on the number of sales it makes and the prices it can charge, both of which are affected by competitive pressures. Most businesses have some products that generate increasing revenue and other products that produce decreasing revenue. Most businesses also have seasonal, annual, and overall trends in their revenue. Any organization can experience a change in revenue without a corresponding change in expenses.

Only money generated by the organization's *operations* is counted as revenue. Operations do not include the purchase or sale of major assets, investment activities, or other unrelated receipts and expenditures. Thus, for example, if a manufacturing business sold a piece of real estate, the money it received would not be part of its revenue. The proceeds from the real estate sale would appear on the manufacturer's balance sheet, but not on its income statement. Likewise, when a business settles an insurance claim, the money it receives from the insurance company is not revenue. For accounting purposes, settlement of an insurance claim substitutes one asset, cash, for another asset, "insurance claim receivable," on the business' balance sheet. This transaction is explained further below.

Expenses

All organizations incur expenses in generating their revenue. The nature of these expenses depends on the nature of the organization. Almost all organizations have payroll expense for employee services. Most organizations have expenses for utilities, such as gas and electricity; for professional services, such as accountants and lawyers; and for insurance, including health, workers compensation, auto, and property.

A key distinction among businesses is between those which sell services and those which sell goods. Service businesses, such as barbers, dry cleaners, landscapers, realtors, insurance agencies, physicians, and accountants, do not sell any significant tangible product. Thus, these businesses do not manufacture or purchase tangible goods for resale, and their income statements will not show any corresponding expense. Some businesses, such as auto repairers, building contractors, and restaurants, sell significant goods in addition to services. These businesses incur some expense in acquiring the materials they resell. Other businesses, such as supermarkets, department stores, and manufacturers, are in business primarily to sell goods, although they also try to distinguish their service from that of competitors. These businesses have significant expenses for the cost to acquire or manufacture the goods they sell. The expense item "cost of goods sold" is treated further in the next section.

The difference between a business' revenue and its cost of goods sold is its **gross margin**, or **gross profit**. For example, in Exhibit 11-2 ABC had gross margin or gross profit of $800,000, calculated as $1,500,000 (revenue) – $700,000 (cost of goods sold) = $800,000. A business must cover all other expenses and hopes to earn net income out of its gross profit. Gross profit is sometimes called mark-up, but this term can be misleading in that "mark-up" implies that a business controls it. Gross profit comes from revenues, which depend on quantity of sales and prices, both of which are subject to competitive market pressures.

Similar to the treatment of revenues, not all money spent by a business is counted as expense. Expenses must be incurred in the business' ordinary *operations* to be recorded as accounting expenses. For example, if a manufacturing business bought a piece of real estate, the money spent on the purchase would not be an expense item on the manufacturer's income statement. The purchase would only appear on the manufacturer's balance sheet, as a reduction of one asset, cash, and an increase in another asset, real estate. Exhibit 11-3 shows the effect on ABC's balance sheet of the purchase of a piece of real estate for $1 million.

Exhibit 11-3
Effect of a Real Estate Purchase on the Balance Sheet

ABC Inc.
Balance Sheet Before Real Estate Purchase

Assets		Liabilities	
Cash	$ 1,075,000	Accounts payable	$ 50,000
Accounts receivable	100,000	Bank loan	150,000
Inventory	325,000	Mortgages	1,800,000
Plant and equipment	1,500,000		
Real estate	1,000,000	Owners' Equity	2,000,000
	$ 4,000,000		$ 4,000,000

Balance Sheet After Real Estate Purchase

Assets		Liabilities	
Cash	$ 75,000	Accounts payable	$ 50,000
Accounts receivable	100,000	Bank loan	150,000
Inventory	325,000	Mortgages	1,800,000
Plant and equipment	1,500,000		
Real estate	2,000,000	Owners' Equity	2,000,000
	$ 4,000,000		$ 4,000,000

Cost of Goods Sold

The **cost of goods sold** is an ordinary expense for businesses, but an expense that deserves special note. Unlike other expenses, the cost of goods sold corresponds directly to sales. When sales go up, so does the cost of goods sold. When sales go down, so does the cost of goods sold. This pattern is true even though sales is a revenue item on business income statements and cost of goods sold is an expense item.

This direct correspondence is caused by the method of accounting for cost of goods sold. The accounting item "cost of goods sold" is incurred when sales are made, not when the merchandise being sold was actually bought or manufactured by the business. For example, a retailer that specializes in selling ski equipment might have peak sales during December, January, and February, but it might acquire the merchandise it sells earlier, such as in September, October, or November. This merchant will, for accounting purposes, incur "cost of goods sold" as it makes sales to its customers, even though it might have actually bought and paid for the goods months earlier. Indeed, if skiing suddenly became unpopular and the merchant sold nothing to its customers, it would incur zero "cost of goods sold," even though it had already paid for its inventory.

Net Income

The difference between revenue and expenses is called **net income**. Net income is often expressed as the following formula:

$$\begin{array}{r} \text{Revenue} \\ - \text{Expenses} \\ \hline \text{Net Income} \end{array}$$

Thus, in Exhibit 11-2, ABC's net income was computed as $1,500,000 (revenue) − $1,250,000 (expenses) = $250,000 (net income). Net income is colloquially known as the "bottom line" because net income appears as the bottom item in a listing of revenue and expenses.

Net income can be negative whenever expenses exceed revenue. Negative net income is known as a **loss**. Positive net income for a for-profit business is often called **profit**. The ability to earn net income is essential to a business' continuation. Indeed, many say that the purpose of a business is to earn profit. Anything that decreases revenue or increases expenses threatens a business' profit and its future.

For nonprofit organizations, the difference between revenue and expenses might be called by a different name, such as "contribution to surplus" or "excess of revenue over expenses." Nevertheless, just like for-profit businesses, nonprofit organizations must have revenue greater than expenses.

"Net income" is the most precise term to use for the difference between revenue and expenses. Two less precise terms are "profit" and "income." "Profit" is sometimes used to mean gross profit, or margin. "Income" is sometimes used to mean net income, but it can also refer to gross revenue or to taxable income, two different and distinct concepts. This chapter uses "net income" to mean the difference between revenue and expenses for all organizations, whether for-profit or not-for-profit.

Effects of a Loss

All losses that are the subject of insurance claims are troublesome, but some are so disruptive that they affect revenues, expenses, and net income. Thus, risk managers for organizations recognize that insurance for direct physical losses alone might not be sufficient. Business interruption losses can threaten an organization's well-being as much as or more than direct physical losses. Adjusters who handle claims for business interruption losses must evaluate the effect of direct physical losses on revenue, expenses, and net income for organizations.

Effects of Property Losses on the Balance Sheet

Direct damage to or destruction of physical property is the subject of most property insurance claims. For an organization, such losses affect the assets on the balance sheet. Direct losses do not affect the income statement unless they disrupt revenue or expenses. Such disruptions are called business interruption losses.

Typical assets for any organization include "cash," "inventory," and "real estate and improvements." These are the items affected by insurance claims for direct losses. For example, suppose an electronics merchant had $100,000 of electronic equipment stolen by burglars. Before the loss, the assets on the merchant's balance sheet included, "Inventory – $100,000." Immediately after the theft, the merchant's balance sheet would have to be adjusted to show, "Inventory – $0," but it would include a new asset, "Insurance claim receivable – $100,000." Amounts that other persons or organizations owe to the merchant are *assets* to the merchant, including any amount the merchant's insurance company owes the merchant for a claim (this example ignores any deductible or problems with limits). Once the claim is settled, the merchant's balance sheet would show, "Insurance claim receivable – $0," but "cash" would increase by $100,000. Exhibit 11-4 shows these transactions.

An insured loss to a building would be accounted for in a similar way. Ignoring any coverage problems or limitations, insurance claims convert other types of assets on the balance sheet into cash. Thus, typical insurance claims for direct

Exhibit 11-4
Loss Settlement for Theft of Merchandise

Loss Settlement for $100,000 Theft of Merchandise

Before Loss

Assets		Liabilities	
Cash	$ 50,000	Accounts payable	$ 75,000
Accounts receivable	50,000	Bank loan	50,000
Inventory	100,000	Mortgage	200,000
Building	500,000		
		Owners' Equity	$325,000

Immediately After Loss

Assets		Liabilities	
Cash	$ 50,000	Accounts payable	$ 75,000
Accounts receivable	50,000	Bank loan	50,000
Insurance claim receivable	100,000	Mortgage	200,000
Inventory	0		
Building	500,000		
		Owners' Equity	$325,000

After Settlement of Claim

Assets		Liabilities	
Cash	$ 150,000	Accounts payable	$ 75,000
Accounts receivable	50,000	Bank loan	50,000
Insurance claim receivable	0	Mortgage	200,000
Inventory	0		
Building	500,000		
		Owners' Equity	$325,000

physical losses affect only an organization's balance sheet. However, physical damage or destruction of property can affect an organization's income statement if it disrupts the organization sufficiently to cause a decrease in revenue, an increase in expenses, or both. An adjuster can evaluate business interruption losses only by examining the elements of an organization's income statement.

Effects of Property Losses on the Income Statement

Some property losses affect the income statement by causing reduced revenue, increased expenses, or both. Because net income is the difference between revenue and expenses, either lower revenue or increased expenses can reduce net income. For example, when revenue goes down, expenses do not automatically adjust downward in proportion, so net income is reduced. Likewise, after a property loss, a business might incur extraordinary expenses just to maintain its usual revenue. Ordinary revenue with *extraordinary* expenses results in lower net income.

Loss of net income would threaten any organization's survival. Insurance for business interruption responds to this exposure by covering an organization's loss of net income and continuing expenses during an interruption of operations. Adjusters evaluating business interruption claims must understand what happens to revenues and expenses after a loss.

Effect of a Loss on Revenue

A direct physical loss will reduce revenue if it disrupts sales. Many types of direct physical losses can reduce sales, including loss of inventory, destruction of the organization's manufacturing plant, and destruction of its operating premises. The duration of any disruption of sales depends on how long it takes to repair or rebuild the physical damage and the extent to which customers have transferred their loyalties elsewhere. An organization will continue to experience loss of income until (1) it has repaired any physical damage *and* (2) it has regained its old customers. Loss of sales that extends well beyond repair of the physical damage is generally not insured. Nevertheless, it is a very real loss.

Calculating loss of revenue is straightforward only when a business' sales are level and do not fluctuate. However, most businesses are dynamic. Product lines come and go, as do competitors. Some businesses have seasonal fluctuation, some have annual fluctuation, and some have monthly fluctuation. Most businesses show some overall trend in sales in addition to their regular fluctuations. In most cases, an adjuster must get expert accounting assistance to evaluate claims for loss of business income.

Effect of a Loss on Expenses

Direct physical losses can affect expenses in a variety of ways. Expenses might increase, decrease, nearly disappear, or remain the same. Some businesses must remain open and will incur extraordinary expenses to do so. For example, newspapers are a vital service to their readers and have contractual obligations to their advertisers. Many newspaper publishers feel a professional pride and obligation to publish without interruption. Banks and insurance companies must provide continuous service to their customers. Hospitals cannot expel their patients while a loss is repaired. Risk managers for such organizations plan to keep operations going after a loss or disaster, even at greatly increased expense.

Other businesses are unable or unwilling to remain in operation after a loss. However, a business that shuts down temporarily is unlikely to eliminate its expenses, especially if the shutdown is expected to be brief. A business that expects to reopen soon is unlikely to lay off its workforce since the cost of hiring and training new employees would exceed any savings from a layoff. Even a business that expects a prolonged shutdown will usually retain its key employees on its payroll and will incur some amount of other expenses such as utilities, professional fees, and insurance.

Some businesses might experience a combination of increased expenses (for example, to lease additional space or equipment) and decreased expenses (for example, layoffs caused by decreased sales). Adjusters evaluating such situations will usually need expert accounting assistance to identify how each item of expenses behaved.

In any case, expenses other than cost of goods sold do not change proportionately with changes in revenue. Expenses might increase significantly just to maintain usual sales, or, during a shutdown, sales might disappear while expenses are only cut in half. Alternatively, sales might decline significantly while expenses stay constant.

Cost of Goods Sold

Because of how cost of goods sold is determined, any reduction in sales will always be accompanied by a directly proportionate reduction in cost of goods sold. Whenever a direct loss causes a reduction of sales, the cost of goods sold decreases proportionately. In this respect, expenses for cost of goods sold are not a problem whenever a business has a shutdown. These expenses do not continue at disproportionately high levels when sales slump. This characteristic of cost of goods sold is important to business interruption insurance. In general, insurance covering business interruption need not and does not cover cost of goods sold.

The lack of coverage for cost of goods sold does not make it unimportant in business interruption losses. On the contrary, adjusters must calculate cost of goods sold accurately or net income will be wrong. Proper calculation of net income is crucial for determining business interruption losses. Net income is determined by subtracting all expenses, including cost of goods sold, from revenue.

Cost of goods sold during any period of time is determined as follows:

Beginning inventory

+ Additions to inventory
_____

= Amount that could have been sold during period

– End inventory (amount not sold)
_____

= Cost of goods sold

All of these amounts are stated in dollars. An error with respect to any of the first four numbers in this computation will cause an incorrect figure for cost of goods sold and, thus, for net income also. The most likely sources of error are the beginning and ending inventory figures. Valuing an inventory in which goods have been added and withdrawn at various times and at various prices is complex. Accounting rules recognize several valid methods for valuing inventories under these circumstances. These methods are beyond the scope of this text, but adjusters must be sure that the same method was used to evaluate the beginning inventory and the ending inventory.

Effect of a Loss on Net Income

Property losses that disrupt an organization's operations reduce net income in a variety of ways. Exhibits 11-5, 11-6, and 11-7 illustrate three different possibilities.

Exhibit 11-5 shows the effect on ABC of ceasing its normal operations during repairs of property damage. ABC earns no revenue, yet some of its expenses continue. (See Exhibit 11-2.) Although reduced, its expenses do not disappear. Its net income goes from $250,000 to –$350,000, a reduction of $600,000.

Exhibit 11-6 shows the effect on ABC of maintaining its normal sales, but incurring unusual expenses to do so. Although its sales are normal, its net income declines from $250,000 to –$125,000 because of the increased expenses.

Exhibit 11-7 shows the effect on ABC of maintaining some sales, but losing others. ABC also incurred extraordinary expenses to make its sales. Its net income is reduced by both the loss of sales and the increase of expenses. Net income declined from $250,000 to –$300,000, a reduction of $550,000.

Insurance for Loss of Business Income and Extra Expense

The Insurance Services Office's Business Income Coverage Form (and Extra Expense) (BIC) applies to a wide variety of organizations and time element losses these organizations might suffer. ISO also offers a BIC without extra expense coverage and a form that covers extra expense only. Thus, adjusters handling these losses must determine which coverage a policyholder has and must understand which losses are covered by each policy form.

Exhibit 11-5
Case One—No Revenue, Expenses Continue

ABC Inc.	
Income Statement During One-Year Interruption	
Revenue	
Sales	$ 0
Expenses	
Cost of goods sold	$ 0
Employee wages	100,000
Depreciation	100,000
Interest	100,000
Utilities	50,000
	$350,000
Net Income	–$350,000

Exhibit 11-6
Case Two—Revenue Unaffected, Expenses Increase

ABC Inc.	
Income Statement During One-Year Interruption	
Revenue	
Sales	$1,500,000
Expenses	
Cost of goods sold	$ 700,000
Employee wages	500,000
Equipment rental	150,000
Depreciation	100,000
Interest	100,000
Utilities	75,000
	$1,625,000
Net Income	–$ 125,000

Exhibit 11-7
Case Three—Revenue Decreases, Expenses Increase

ABC Inc. Income Statement During One-Year Interruption	
Revenue	
Sales	$ 750,000
Expenses	
Cost of goods sold	$ 350,000
Employee wages	400,000
Equipment rental	50,000
Depreciation	100,000
Interest	100,000
Utilities	50,000
	$1,050,000
Net Income	–$ 300,000

Coverages

The policy statements of coverage for business income and extra expense are brief and apparently simple, but they must be read carefully. These coverage clauses refer to accounting concepts not defined by the policy. Thus, adjusters handling losses under these coverages must understand accounting terminology.

Business Income

The essential coverage provision of the BIC policy makes the following statement:

> We will pay for the actual loss of Business Income you sustain due to the necessary suspension of your "operations" during the "period of restoration." The suspension must be caused by direct physical loss of or damage to property, including personal property in the open (or in a vehicle) within 100 feet, at the premises which are described in the Declarations and for which a Business Income Limit of Insurance is shown in the Declarations. The loss or damage must be caused by or result from a Covered Cause of Loss.

The BIC form defines **business income** as follows:

   a.   Net Income (Net Profit or Loss before income taxes) that would have been earned or incurred; and

   b.   Continuing normal operating expenses, including payroll, incurred.

The references to "operations," net income, and normal operating expenses make clear that this coverage is designed to protect policyholders from losses that result from interruption of its normal operations. Business income losses are determined by examining operating income and operating expenses. Receipts and expenditures that do not appear on an organization's income statement are not considered in the analysis of loss of business income.

Extra Expenses

The most important additional coverage in the BIC policy is for extra expense. The BIC provides the following:

> Extra Expense means necessary expenses you incur during the "period of restoration" that you would not have incurred if there had been no direct physical loss or damage to property caused by or resulting from a Covered Cause of Loss.

The coverage for extra expense is set forth in three subsections. The first extra expense coverage is for continuing operations:

   (1)   We will pay any Extra Expense to avoid or minimize the suspension of business and to continue "operations":

      (a)   At the described premises; or

      (b)   At replacement premises or at temporary locations including:

         (i)   Relocation expenses; and

         (ii)   Costs to equip and operate the replacement or temporary locations.

Subsection (1) above provides coverage if the insured tries to continue operations after a loss, but the expenses to do so are greater than those the insured would have incurred through normal business operations. Expenses covered under this section would include, for example, the cost to rent a temporary selling location in order to maintain sales levels.

The second extra expense coverage is for the cost to minimize the suspension of business operations:

   (2)   We will pay any Extra Expense to minimize the suspension of business if you cannot continue "operations."

Subsection (2) responds to situations in which the insured cannot continue operations but is incurring above-normal expenses to get back into business.

Typical expenses in this situation would be the cost to air freight a replacement part needed to repair a piece of production machinery without which the business cannot operate.

The third extra expense coverage provides the following:

> (3) We will pay any Extra Expense to:
>
> > (a) Repair or replace any property; or
> >
> > (b) Research, replace or restore the lost information or damaged valuable papers and records;
> >
> > to the extent it reduces the amount of loss that otherwise would have been payable under this Coverage Form.

Normally, the insured is limited to a reasonable value (either ACV or replacement cost, as applicable) for the repair or replacement of property. Subsection (3) allows the insured to incur "any Extra Expense" to repair or replace property to the extent that it reduces the amount of the BIC loss. Subsection (3) applies to items of property that are not insured under the property coverages and to the reconstruction of records, the expense of which might be limited under the property coverage.

Necessary Suspension of Operations

To recover a BIC loss, the insured must show that an "actual" loss has been sustained or incurred as a direct result of a "necessary" suspension of operations, either partial or total, caused by direct physical damage to insured property. The BIC defines "operations" as "Your business activities occurring at the described premises. . . ."

The manufacturing industry provides the best counter-example of a "necessary suspension of your operations." Manufacturing facilities typically have an annual "scheduled" shutdown of operations to perform maintenance on machinery and equipment. If an insured cause of loss resulted in damage to that machinery, the loss of use of the machinery during the shutdown would not be considered a "necessary" suspension of operations compensable by the BIC policy. In this case, because the insured had already scheduled a suspension of operations, the suspension was not made "necessary" by the physical damage.

The requirement that a suspension be "necessary" is consistent with the policyholder's typical duty under property insurance policies to minimize loss. Insurance should not reimburse an unnecessary suspension of operations.

Covered Causes of Loss

The policy provides the following regarding the causes of loss:

> See applicable Causes of Loss Form as shown in the Declarations.

The declarations page should show one of the Causes of Loss forms, Basic, Broad, or Special applicable to the business income coverage. These are the same Causes of Loss forms used with the BPP.

The BIC form represents stand-alone coverage for loss of business income, just as the commercial property form represents stand-alone physical damage insurance. Neither form describes what perils are insured. A separate causes of loss form is used to specify whether coverage is to be on a named peril or "all-risks" basis. This "modular" approach provides greater flexibility in designing coverages for a variety of risks. Although some type of property damage must occur for the loss of business income to be covered, the physical damage and loss of business income do not need to be covered for the same causes of loss. Although not common, different causes of loss forms can be used for physical damage and business income.

All of the Causes of Loss forms that might be attached to the BIC have special exclusions applicable to the BIC. These special exclusions are as follows:

- Loss caused by damaged or destroyed "finished stock." "Finished stock" is defined in the BIC as "stock you have manufactured." Thus, this exclusion only applies to manufacturers. For manufacturers, the stock itself should be covered as direct physical damage. If a manufacturer suffers loss to its inventory of finished goods but not to its productive capacity, it can work overtime to make up the lost inventory. This exclusion does not apply to extra expense.

- Loss caused by damage to radio or television antennas.

- Any *increase* of loss caused by interference of strikers at the location where repairs or rebuilding is occurring, or caused by loss of a contract, except to the extent the loss of contract affects loss of business income during the period of restoration.

- Extra expense caused by loss of a contract, beyond the period of restoration.

- Any other consequential loss.

Actual Loss

The term "actual loss sustained" is used to describe the extent of financial loss insured by the policy. The intent is to limit recovery to those losses that are real and direct, rather than speculative and remote. Losses must be real in the sense that not every property loss or interruption of operations results in loss of business income. For example, the owners of many small businesses are the chief salespersons. After a property loss, the owner might be occupied with the situation for a week or two, during which time no sales are made. Nevertheless, if the owner can make up all sales after he or she returns to selling, no business income might be lost.

Difficulties might arise in the adjustment of time element losses concerning the degree of "directness" of the financial loss incurred by the insured. The last listed exclusion from the Causes of Loss form is for "Any other consequential loss." This wording can create confusion because all time element losses are "consequential" in the true sense of the word, that is, the business interruption loss sustained by the insured is always a consequence of a physical damage loss.

In order to resolve this issue, various approaches have been used to distinguish a direct loss from a remote one. One common approach is based on the "intent to insure" concept, which is based on the question, "Was this risk of loss contemplated by the parties at the time the policy was issued?" This approach is similar to the "meeting of the minds" requirement in contract law. In order to have a binding contract, the parties to the contract must agree as to the contract's essential terms. However, in insurance contracts, the two parties whose minds must meet, the insured and the insurer, have often never discussed terms. The insurer offers a form contract covering commercial losses and is anticipating losses of a general type usual to commercial enterprises. The insured is a unique business with a specific commercial purpose that requires an analysis of its unique risks of financial loss.

The Causes of Loss forms include an exclusion for a specific type of indirect loss, loss of contract. Direct physical damage can sometimes cause a policyholder to lose certain contracts. For example, an owner of a shopping mall might lose its tenant leases if the shopping mall is damaged by fire. After the shopping mall is repaired, the owner will continue to suffer loss because the leases terminated, allowing the tenants to depart. At this point, the losses are caused by the loss of contract, not by the physical damage. The Causes of Loss forms exclude both loss of business income and extra expense that occur after the period of restoration because of loss of contract.

Determining Loss of Business Income and Extra Expense

The policy definitions of business income and extra expense *cannot* be used as formulas to calculate losses. Adjusters must be guided by the principle that insureds should be made whole, consistent with the coverages selected by those insureds. Adjusters must distinguish between business income losses and extra expenses for those policyholders with one type of coverage but not the other.

In all cases, the adjuster or an expert accountant working for the adjuster must determine the revenue, expenses, and net income that the insured *would have experienced* had no physical damage occurred. This determination might not be easy if the insured is in a dynamic business environment of growth, decline, new products, or new competitors. Nevertheless, it is an essential first step to determining loss of business income or extra expense. Only after the revenue, expenses, and net income that would have occurred have been determined can the adjuster specifically consider loss of business income or extra expense.

Loss of Business Income

The BIC form makes the following statement regarding loss determination:

    a. The amount of Business Income loss will be determined based on:

        (1) The Net Income of the business before the direct physical loss or damage occurred;

        (2) The likely Net Income of the business if no loss or damage occurred, but not including any Net Income that would have been earned as a result of an increase in the volume of business due to favorable business conditions caused by the impact of the Covered Cause of Loss on customers or on other businesses;

        (3) The operating expenses, including payroll expenses, necessary to resume "operations" with the same quality of service that existed just before the direct physical loss or damage; and

        (4) Other relevant sources of information, including:

            (a) Your financial records and accounting procedures;

            (b) Bills, invoices and other vouchers; and

            (c) Deeds, liens or contracts.

The above loss determination clause makes clear that many factors can be considered in determining business income loss. The second listed item is included to avoid compensating policyholders for loss of windfall business that only would have existed because of the covered loss. For example, an insured building supply company would expect windfall business following a hurricane. However, the intent of the BIC is to place the insured in the same position it would have been in had no loss occurred.

Normal operating expenses should be included in any determination of business income. The definition of business income clarifies that it intends to cover the insured's expected net income plus *normal* operating expenses that continue. In contrast, only extra expense insurance covers operating expenses above normal.

Extra Expense Loss

Condition 4 on loss determination in the BIC makes the following provision for extra expense:

b. The amount of Extra Expense will be determined based on:

(1) All expenses that exceed the normal operating expenses that would have been incurred by "operations" during the "period of restoration" if no direct physical loss or damage had occurred. We will deduct from the total of such expenses:

(a) The salvage value that remains of any property bought for temporary use during the "period of restoration", once "operations" are resumed; and

(b) Any Extra Expense that is paid for by other insurance, except for insurance that is written subject to the same plan terms, conditions and provisions as this insurance; and

(2) All necessary expenses that reduce the Business Income loss that otherwise would have been incurred.

The evaluation of how much extra expense incurred by the insured is compensable by the BIC policy is a two-step process. First, the adjuster can determine that the expense is "extra" if it "exceeds the normal operating expenses" that would have been incurred had no loss occurred.

The second step, set forth in paragraph (2) above, is to determine whether the expense reduced the BIC loss that would have been incurred had the additional money not been spent. For example, the use of air freight might expedite the repair of damaged machinery, thereby reducing the loss of productive capacity from that machine, as shown below:

	Anticipated	Actual	Difference
Freight in :	$1,000	$1,500	$500
Income value of production per day			$500
Days saved by air freight			3
Income value saved			$1,500
Difference between income saved and additional air freight			$1,000

By spending $500 more on freight, the insured was able to reduce the BIC loss by $1,500.

Extra expense need only "avoid or minimize" the suspension of business under Subsection (1) or "minimize" the suspension under Subsection (2), but it is payable under Subsection (3) only to the extent that it "reduces the amount of loss that otherwise would have been payable under this Coverage Form." Only when dealing with the repair or replacement of physical property or restoration of records must the insured actually reduce the BIC loss to at least the extent of the extra expense payment. Expenses that lessen the effect of the business income loss will be fully compensable under Subsections (1) and (2), even if the expenses exceed the reduction of business income loss.

Case One—No Revenue, Expenses Continue

In the classic example of business interruption loss, the insured shuts down completely during the period of restoration. Such an insured has no sales and no revenue but continues to experience expenses. Operating expenses, other than cost of goods sold, might be reduced, but not necessarily. Expenses for cost of goods sold disappears when sales disappear.

A policyholder in this situation only needs business income coverage. Indeed, a policyholder that had only extra expense coverage would not collect anything for this loss.

Determining loss in this situation comes closest to the definition of business income. The adjuster should add (1) the net income that would have been earned had no shutdown occurred and (2) the normal operating expenses incurred. The policy definition of business income makes clear that continuing expense can include payroll. Thus, an insured is not required to lay off its workforce during a shutdown.

Case Two—Revenue Unaffected, Expenses Up

Some insureds will incur any expense to stay in operation. Such insureds might succeed in maintaining their revenue, but they will experience increased expenses. Although these insureds experience reduced net income, or even negative net income, their situations are purely extra expense claims. The definition of business income is clearly limited to normal operating expenses. A loss of net income caused solely by increased expenses is covered by extra expense insurance, not by business income insurance. A policyholder that has only business income insurance would be better off not incurring expenses to maintain its revenue.

The loss determination clause for extra expense explains that it covers "All expenses that exceed the normal operating expenses that would have been incurred by 'operations' during the 'period of restoration' if no direct physical loss or damage had occurred." An adjuster should subtract from the expenses that *were* incurred for operations the expenses that *would* have occurred had there been no loss.

A loss settlement based on this difference will restore to the insured the net income it expected to enjoy had no loss occurred. For example, assume that, in the absence of loss, the insured would have had revenue of $100,000, expenses of $85,000, and net income of $15,000. After a loss, this insured maintained revenue of $100,000, but incurred expenses of $105,000. The loss settlement for this insured is calculated as expenses incurred, $105,000, minus expenses it expected, $85,000, or $20,000. This $20,000 difference also makes up the difference between the expected net income of $15,000 and the actual net income of –$5,000.

An insured entitled to recover extra expense might incur and recover extra expenses that are not items on the income statement. For example, an insured might buy equipment, other than what is covered for direct physical loss, if such equipment enables the insured to reduce the loss that otherwise would occur. This is the third type of expense specified in the definition of extra expense, but it is not the sort of expense that appears on an income statement. Nevertheless, such expenses are covered and must be added to the calculation of extra expense determined above.

Case Three—Revenue Down, Expenses Up

Some insureds have a partial shutdown and loss of revenue but incur extraordinary expenses to maintain even a reduced level of sales. Adjusters should get expert accounting assistance to analyze these situations. Nevertheless, with certain qualifications, loss settlement in these cases can be determined as follows:

$$\begin{array}{l} \text{Net income that would have been earned} \\ \underline{- \text{ Net income that was earned}} \\ = \text{Loss settlement} \end{array}$$

This formula works because net income reflects both revenue and expenses. "Net income that would have been earned" reflects both the revenue and expenses that would have been earned had no loss occurred. "Net income that was earned" reflects both the lower revenue and increased expenses that were actually experienced.

The first qualification to this formula is that it only applies to insureds with both business income and extra expense coverage. For a policyholder with only business income coverage, an adjuster would have to deduct from the loss settlement computed above any operating expenses in excess of normal. The second qualification is that for insureds with extra expense coverage, some covered extra expenses might not be part of net income. This situation was explained in Case Two.

Determining the Period of Restoration

Recovery for loss of business income and extra expense is limited to the "period of restoration." Determining this period can present some complex adjusting issues. This section sets forth the policy definition of this period and explains the insured's typical duty to mitigate loss. The actual time period in which repairs to the insured property *are* made is not necessarily the time period in which such repairs *should* be made. Loss adjustments can be based on either time period, each of which presents advantages and disadvantages. This section also presents the special limitations on the time periods for recovery following loss to electronic media and records and for delays caused by strikers.

Definition

The BIC policy covers losses of business income and extra expense that occur during the **period of restoration**. This period is defined in the policy as follows:

> "Period of Restoration" means the period of time that:
>
> a. Begins:
>
> > (1) 72 hours after the time of direct physical loss or damage for Business Income coverage; or
> >
> > (2) Immediately after the time of direct physical loss or damage for Extra Expense coverage; caused by or resulting from any Covered Cause of Loss at the described premises; and
>
> b. Ends on the earlier of:
>
> > (1) The date when the property at the described premises *should* be repaired, rebuilt or replaced with *reasonable speed* and similar quality; or
> >
> > (2) The date when business is resumed at a new permanent location.

[Emphasis added.]

The beginning date for the period of restoration creates a three-day deductible for loss of business income. However, extra expense is covered beginning immediately after a loss. In most cases, for the sake of determining the period of restoration, the date of loss is not at issue. However, the parties to the adjustment process might have to make a considerable effort to determine when the restoration period should have ended.

Due Diligence Requirement

The BIC policy definition of the period of restoration requires the insured to use "reasonable speed" to repair or replace the property with that of "similar quality." The use of the word "reasonable" reinforces the traditional view that the efforts of the insured should be judged according to the insured's abilities, both physical and financial, to get back to the same position as before the loss. In addition, under the insured's duties in the event of loss, the insured is required to "resume all or part of your 'operations' as quickly as possible" if the insured intends to continue in business.

The BIC form further includes the following loss conditions :

4.c.   Resumption Of Operations

We will reduce the amount of your:

a.   Business Income loss, other than Extra Expense, to the extent you can resume your "operations"; in whole or in part, by using damaged or undamaged property (including merchandise or stock) at the described premises or elsewhere.

b.   Extra Expense loss to the extent you can return "operations" to normal and discontinue such Extra Expense.

d. If you do not resume "operations," or do not resume "operations" as quickly as possible, we will pay based on the length of time it would have taken to resume "operations" as quickly as possible.

The "reasonableness" standard, which applies to all BIC evaluations, is important. For example, if a manufacturer could reduce the amount of his BIC loss by using a competitor's facilities, but would as a result reveal to a competitor a trade secret manufacturing process, the insurer would not be entitled to require such action because it would be unreasonable for the insurer to require the insured to give up a trade secret. Likewise, even if a retailer could arrange for delivery of merchandise to a nearby competitor's location because its premises were damaged, requiring the insured to direct customers to the competitor in order to continue to sell merchandise would be unreasonable. An insurer cannot ask the insured to sacrifice customers to reduce a BIC loss. Nevertheless, an insured cannot remain idle and allow BIC losses to accumulate. The insured's duty to mitigate the loss is inherent in all first-party insurance contracts and is especially important in a BIC loss. Although an insurer can assist an insured in the repair or replacement of physically damaged property, the insurer cannot step in and run the insured's business.

Time Needed To Repair or Replace

Since the time element portion of an insured loss is measured by the time necessary to repair or replace the damaged property, the first step in determining the extent of a BIC loss is to determine the extent of the physical damage loss. To make an accurate determination, the adjuster must speak early in the adjustment process with the people involved in assessing and/or restoring the damage. Discussions with the insured and his or her representatives, including architects, engineers, contractors, and other consultants, are required as soon as possible in order to gain an early understanding of the probable duration of the financial loss.

The methods used to repair the damaged property will always have a direct effect on the extent of the financial loss. For example, overtime labor can shorten the reconstruction period, as can other forms of "fast-track" construction techniques. The BIC form anticipates this possibility in its treatment of expediting expenses as covered extra expense.

Obviously, not every possible type of loss and method of repair can be anticipated. Circumstances of the reconstruction, such as delays in the adjustment process itself, weather conditions, availability of materials, labor, alternative sites, and governmental restrictions, all affect the actual time needed for repairs.

Time in Which Repairs Should Be Complete

Because of the circumstances that affect actual repair time, a reasonably expected time for repairs, rather than an actual one, is often preferred in determining the extent of a BIC loss. A reasonably expected time period is the time in which restoration *should* be completed, as opposed to the time in which it is completed. The use of a reasonably expected time period allows loss adjustments to be made prospectively, that is, before the period of restoration is complete. If the insured and adjuster can agree on when restoration *should* be completed, they can settle the business income loss immediately.

Depending on the circumstances of a given loss, all parties might benefit from the use of a reasonably expected time standard. In interpreting similar language that describes the period of restoration in previous business interruption policies, the courts have found that the intent of the policy is to use a reasonably expected time standard rather than the actual time required to repair the damaged property. Courts have applied this standard based on two premises: (1) the physical damage is sometimes never repaired, or it is repaired in such a fashion that it bears no relationship to the extent of originally damaged property; and (2) certain extraneous circumstances not contemplated by the parties might affect the restoration period.

The fact that the insured, for whatever reason it feels appropriate, chooses not to repair or replace the insured property does not prevent it from recovering a BIC loss. In such a case, the parties must agree on what time should have reasonably been necessary to accomplish whatever repairs were insured by the property damage coverage. Experts can establish that time frame, depending on the degree of difficulty of the repair work.

Using a reasonably expected time element has some advantages. First, factors affecting the actual time to repair can be eliminated from consideration, such as extraordinary delay in obtaining permits or materials. Second, because neither the insured nor the adjuster must wait for the suspension period to end and the insured to resume normal operations before establishing the extent of the loss, the BIC loss can be agreed to prospectively, when the scope of the property damage loss is established. As a result, both parties have greater freedom during the adjustment period—the adjuster to expedite the settlement, and the insured to use settlement proceeds to the advantage of the business as he or she sees fit.

Prospective settlement has some disadvantages as well. The insurer might feel that the extent of the loss cannot be projected with enough certainty to prevent it from paying for a period beyond which repairs would be complete. On the other hand, the insured might fear that its actual loss will be greater than anticipated by any projection and that it will therefore be underpaid. A reasonably expected time element estimate might turn out to be longer than the actual time needed to repair the physical damage, which would be a disadvantage for the insurer. Unforeseen events can also arise, such as a delay in the replacement of an essential component, which would lengthen the suspension period beyond the projection, creating a disadvantage for the insured. Any lengthening of the actual time period would be uncompensated, but the insured would still have received a certain sum well before property damage repairs were completed and, as mentioned, freedom to use the BIC loss proceeds as he or she sees fit. In each claim, the insurer and insured must carefully weigh the advantages and disadvantages of a prospective approach to the adjustment process.

Limitation—Electronic Media and Data

The BIC form states the following:

> We will not pay for any loss of Business Income caused by direct physical loss of or damage to Electronic Media and Records after the longer of:
>
> a. 60 consecutive days from the date of direct physical loss or damage; or
>
> b. The period, beginning with the date of direct physical loss or damage, necessary to repair, rebuild or replace, with reasonable speed and similar quality, other property at the described premises due to loss or damage caused by the same occurrence.

The intent of this section of the BIC policy is to limit the time during which coverage is provided for loss of business income caused by damage to electronic media. Business income losses resulting from physical loss to electronic media and records could extend for a very long time, even beyond the time needed to restore other property damaged by the same cause of loss. This section of the policy provides up to sixty days of coverage regardless of how quickly the other property is restored. After sixty days, the coverage would end, unless the time estimated to repair other property is longer than sixty days. If an insured has a large exposure in this area, it should purchase specific electronic data processing (EDP) coverage, which does not have time limitations.

Electronic media and records losses are occurring more often with the increased use of computers in all areas of business. For example, if a retail store maintains its inventory by computer and the software is damaged by an insured peril, the store might be unable to sell undamaged stock because the insured cannot properly document the sale. The policy would insure this type of BIC loss, subject to the sixty-day time limitation.

Delays Caused by Strikers

All of the Causes of Loss forms that might be attached to the BIC include a Special Exclusion that states the following:

> We will not pay for:
>
> . . .
>
> (3) Any increase of loss caused by or resulting from:
>
> (a) Delay in rebuilding, repairing or replacing the property or resuming "operations," due to interference at the location of the rebuilding, repair or replacement by strikers or other persons. . . .

This limitation applies only to striker interference at the insured premises. It does not apply to strike activities elsewhere. The last three words quoted above could be construed to mean that any delay caused by any person is not covered. However, the sense of this entire clause is to exclude delays caused by strike activities, not every delay. The broad wording of the last three words is necessary because identifying perpetrators during strike activities is not always possible.

Additional, Optional, and Extended Coverages Under the BIC

The BIC provides valuable additional, optional, and extended coverage for interruptions caused by civil authorities, alterations and new buildings, business income losses that extend beyond the period of restoration, and newly acquired locations.

Civil Authority

The BIC provides the following additional coverage:

> We will pay for the actual loss of Business Income you sustain and necessary Extra Expense caused by action of civil authority that prohibits access to the described premises due to direct physical loss of or damage to property, other than at the described premises, caused by or resulting from any Covered Cause of loss. This coverage for Business Income will begin 72 hours after the time of that action and will apply for a period of up to three consecutive weeks from the date of that action.
>
> The coverage for Extra Expense will begin immediately after the time of that action and will end:
>
> (1) 3 consecutive weeks after the time of that action; or
>
> (2) When your Business Income coverage ends;
>
> whichever is later.

This coverage applies in the event of damage to property away from the described premises. The intent is to insure the loss of income that results from, for example, cordoning off an entire city block by civil authorities. Thus, this additional coverage is also limited to three weeks.

Alterations and New Buildings

Another additional coverage provided by the BIC is for alterations and new buildings. The policy provides the following:

> We will pay for the actual loss of Business Income you sustain due to direct physical loss or damage at the described premises caused by or resulting from any Covered Cause of Loss to:
>
> (1) New buildings or structures, whether complete or under construction;
>
> (2) Alterations or additions to existing buildings or structures; and
>
> (3) Machinery, equipment, supplies or building materials located on or within 100 feet of the described premises and:
>
> > (a) Used in the construction, alterations or additions; or
> >
> > (b) Incidental to the occupancy of new buildings.
>
> If such direct physical loss or damage delays the start of "operations," the "period of restorations" will begin on the date "operations" would have begun if the direct physical loss or damage had not occurred.

The Alterations and New Buildings coverage parallels the extension of property damage coverage under the BPP policy for the same items. If the adjuster determines that the damaged property is covered, the resulting loss of use of that property is insured as well. The BIC policy anticipates that property insured under this section might not yet be income-producing at the time of the loss. In that case, the time element is measured from when the property was to begin generating income to when the property actually does generate income after being repaired or replaced.

Extended Business Income

The additional coverage for extended business income (other than rental value) provides the following:

> We will pay for the actual loss of Business Income you incur during the period that:
>
> (a) Begins on the date property (except "finished stock") is actually repaired, rebuilt or replaced and "operations" are resumed; and
>
> (b) Ends on the earlier of:
>
>> (i) The date you could restore your "operations" with reasonable speed, to the level which would generate the business income amount that would have existed if no direct physical loss or damage occurred; or
>>
>> (ii) 30 consecutive days after the date determined in (1)(a) above.
>
> However, Extended Business Income does not apply to loss of Business Income incurred as a result of unfavorable business conditions caused by the impact of the Covered Cause of Loss in the area where the described premises are located.
>
> Loss of Business Income must be caused by direct physical loss or damage at the described premises caused by or resulting from any Covered Cause of Loss.

This feature of the BIC policy provides up to an additional thirty days after the restoration of the property within which the insured can regain whatever business was lost because of the interruption. For example, a retail store whose business is interrupted by a covered cause of loss often continues to lose sales income even after the shelves are restocked and the store has reopened. Once consumers discover alternative stores to shop in, insured store owners cannot easily recapture their business. To that end, an insured might offer a "grand reopening sale," which would be unnecessary if no loss had occurred. The extent to which the sale negatively affects the income that would have been anticipated for the additional thirty-day period had no loss occurred would be insured under this extension of coverage. Nevertheless, Extended Business Income does not include loss of income caused by unfavorable business conditions caused by the Covered Cause of Loss. For example, after a catastrophe such as a hurricane, the economy in an entire area might be depressed. Losses caused by such a general business depression are not covered.

Optional Coverage—Extended Period of Indemnity

This coverage allows an insured to extend the period of indemnity beyond the automatic thirty days granted under the BIC form. This extension usually applies to businesses with a marked seasonal selling period. For example, a retailer selling Christmas ornaments might have a peak season of approximately sixty days before Christmas. If the normal "period of restoration" and the normal thirty-day extended period ended shortly before the insured's peak season, an additional amount of time would be required for the insured to regain its share of the seasonal market.

Limits of Insurance Apply to Additional Coverages

The Limits of Insurance section of the BIC form provides the following:

> The most we will pay for loss in any one occurrence is the applicable Limit of Insurance shown in the Declarations.

This clause also *restricts* recovery to the stated limit for the following additional coverages: (1) Alterations and New Buildings, (2) Civil Authority, (3) Extra Expense, and (4) Extended Business Income.

Coverage Extension

The BIC provides extended coverage, beyond the stated limits, as follows:

> If a Coinsurance percentage of 50% or more is shown in the Declarations, you may extend the insurance provided by this Coverage Part as follows:
>
> Newly Acquired Locations
>
> a. You may extend your Business Income Coverage to apply to property at any locations you acquire other than fairs or exhibitions.
>
> b. The most we will pay for loss under this Extension is $100,000 at each location.
>
> c. Insurance under this Extension for each newly acquired location will end when any of the following first occurs:
>
> (1) The policy expires;
>
> (2) 30 days expire after you acquire or begin to construct the property; or
>
> (3) You report values to us.
>
> We will charge you additional premium for values reported from the date you acquire the property.
>
> This Extension is additional insurance. The Additional Condition, Coinsurance, does not apply to this Extension.

The intent of this language is to parallel the property coverages for locations acquired during the term of the policy. This coverage is limited in dollar amount and in duration, but it is additional to the Limits of Insurance. If an insured acquires a new location, it should report its value to the agent as soon as possible to obtain appropriate coverage.

Coinsurance

Like most property insurance policies, the BIC has a coinsurance requirement. However, determining coinsurance compliance under the BIC can be complex. This section explains the figure against which coinsurance compliance is measured and over what period of time this figure is determined. The section goes on to present several optional coverages that substitute for coinsurance and explains why coinsurance is not a problem under the businessowners policy (BOP).

Policy Requirement

The BIC sets forth the coinsurance requirement as an additional condition:

> If a Coinsurance percentage is shown in the Declarations, the following condition applies in addition to the Common Policy Conditions and the Commercial Property Conditions.
>
> We will not pay the full amount of any loss if the Limit of Insurance for Business Income is less than:
>
> a.   The Coinsurance percentage shown for Business Income in the Declarations; times
>
> b.   The sum of:
>
> > (1)   The Net Income (Net Profit or Loss before income taxes), and
> >
> > (2)   Operating expenses, including payroll expenses,
> >
> > that would have been earned or incurred (had no loss occurred) by your "operations" at the described premises for the 12 months following the inception, or last previous anniversary date, of this policy (whichever is later).

The policy lists a variety of expenses that are deducted from all operating expenses for purposes of determining coinsurance compliance. The effect of deducting these expenses is to reduce the limit of insurance required for coinsurance compliance. If the limit of insurance is less than it should be, losses are settled as follows:

$$\frac{\text{Actual limit}}{\text{Required limit}} \times \text{Loss} = \text{Loss settlement (subject to actual limit)}$$

The "required" limit is only required if the policyholder wishes to have losses paid in full, but policyholders can justifiably carry inadequate limits. The BIC policy itself includes illustrations of both underinsurance and adequate insurance.

Values Against Which Compliance Is Measured

Coinsurance compliance is measured against the sum of net income plus *all* operating expenses. Operating expenses do not include cost of goods sold. Thus, coinsurance compliance is measured against a business' total gross profit, or gross margin.

The BIC Income Report/Worksheet, shown in Exhibit 11-8, is designed to help policyholders determine the coverage limits they must have in order to comply with coinsurance requirements. Line A is gross sales. Line F, net sales, is determined by adjusting line A. Total revenue, line H, is determined by adding other sources of revenue to line F. Line I is the cost of goods sold calculation. Line J, determined by subtracting line I from line H, is the basis for coinsurance compliance.

Line J of the BIC Income Report/Worksheet is the policyholder's gross margin for an entire year. This amount might seem excessive to businesses that cannot foresee a business interruption lasting that long. Indeed, policyholders are not necessarily required to carry limits equal to line J. The coinsurance percentage on the declarations page can range from 50 percent to 125 percent, thus requiring from six months (line J x 50 percent) to fifteen months (line J x 125 percent) of coverage. Even six months of coverage might be too much for some policyholders, but that is the minimum allowed by the BIC without a coinsurance penalty. For other policyholders, fifteen months of coverage might be inadequate. Policyholders with fifteen months of coverage would never suffer a coinsurance penalty, but they might not have sufficient limits for some losses.

Values Projected From Policy Inception

The values for coinsurance purposes are determined at the inception or anniversary date of the policy. If the insured accurately completes the BIC Report/Worksheet, a coinsurance penalty should not be assessed. However, since the values are predicated on a projection of the experience made at the beginning of the policy term, the question arises as to whether using hindsight to determine the accuracy of those projections is fair.

For example, assume an insured conscientiously projects a business income value of $1,000,000 for the succeeding twelve-month period using all of the

Exhibit 11-8
Business Income Report/Worksheet

POLICY NUMBER: COMMERCIAL PROPERTY

BUSINESS INCOME REPORT/WORK SHEET

Your Name _____ Date _____

Location _____

_____

This work sheet must be completed on an accrual basis in conformity with generally accepted accounting principles.

Indicate the inventory valuation method used by your company:

_____ Specific Identification Method	_____ Last-In, First-Out (LIFO) Method	
_____ Average-Cost Method	_____ Other (specify):	
_____ First-In, First-Out (FIFO) Method	_____	

_____

APPLICABLE WHEN THE AGREED VALUE COVERAGE OPTION APPLIES:

I certify that this is a true and correct report of values as required under this policy for the periods indicated and that the Agreed Value for the period of coverage is $ _____ , based on a Co-insurance percentage of _____%.

Signature _____

Official Title _____

_____

APPLICABLE WHEN THE PREMIUM ADJUSTMENT FORM APPLIES:

I certify that this is a true and correct report of values as required under this policy for the 12 months ended _____

Signature _____

Official Title _____

Agent or Broker _____

Mailing Address _____

Continued on next page

BUSINESS INCOME REPORT/WORK SHEET
FINANCIAL ANALYSIS
(000 omitted)

Income and Expenses	12 Month Period Ending 12/31/94		Estimated for 12 Month Period Beginning 4/1/95	
	Manufacturing	Non-Manufacturing	Manufacturing	Non-Manufacturing
A. Gross Sales	$ 10,050	$ ___	$ 10,350	$ ___
B. DEDUCT: Finished Stock Inventory (at sales value) at Beginning	- 500 9,550		- 550 9,800	
C. ADD: Finished Stock Inventory (at sales value) at End	+ 533		+ 480	
D. Gross Sales Value of Production	$ 10,083		$ 10,280	
E. DEDUCT: Prepaid Freight	0			
Returns & Allowances	+ 20			
Discounts	+ 30			
Bad Debts	+ 25			
Collection Expenses	+ 0			
Total	- 75		- 80	
F. Net Sales Net Sales Value of Production	$ 10,008	$ ___	$ 10,200	- $ ___
G. ADD: Other Earnings from your business operations (not investment income or rents from other properties): Commissions or Rents	0			
Cash Discounts Received	+ 0			
Other	+ 10			
Total Other Earnings	+ 10		+ 15	
H. Total Revenues	$ 10,018	+ $ ___	$ 10,215	+ $ ___

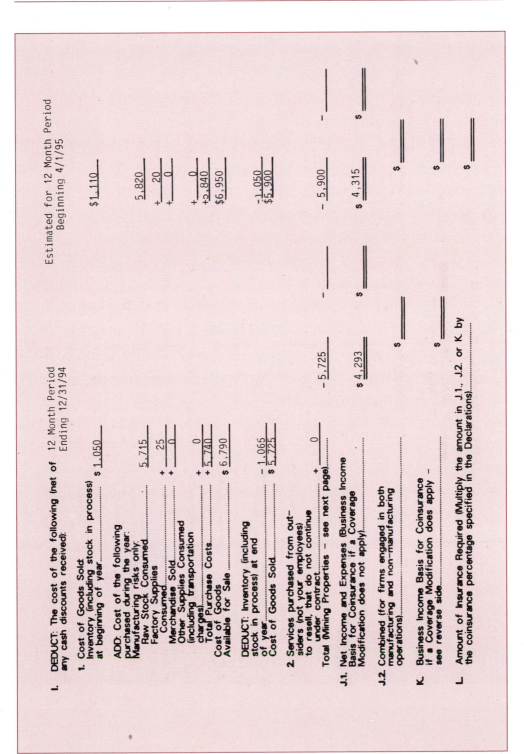

	12 Month Period Ending 12/31/94	Estimated for 12 Month Period Beginning 4/1/95
I. DEDUCT: The cost of the following (net of any cash discounts received):		
1. Cost of Goods Sold:		
Inventory (including stock in process) at beginning of year	$ 1,050	$ 1,110
ADD: Cost of the following purchased during the year:		
Manufacturing risks only:		
Raw Stock Consumed	5,715	5,820
Factory Supplies Consumed	+ 25	+ 20
Merchandise Sold	+ 0	+ 0
Other Supplies Consumed (including transportation charges)	+ 0	+ 0
Total Purchase Costs	+ 5,740	+ 5,840
Cost of Goods Available for Sale	$ 6,790	$ 6,950
DEDUCT: Inventory (including stock in process) at end of year	– 1,065	– 1,050
Cost of Goods Sold	$ 5,725	$ 5,900
2. Services purchased from outsiders (not your employees) to resell, that do not continue under contract	+ 0	—
Total (Mining Properties – see next page)	– 5,725	– 5,900
J.1. Net Income and Expenses (Business Income Basis for Coinsurance if a Coverage Modification does not apply).	$ 4,293	$ 4,315
J.2. Combined (for firms engaged in both manufacturing and non-manufacturing operations).	$	$
K. Business Income Basis for Coinsurance if a Coverage Modification does apply – see reverse side.	$	$
L. Amount of Insurance Required (Multiply the amount in J.1, J.2, or K by the coinsurance percentage specified in the Declarations).	$	$

Continued on next page

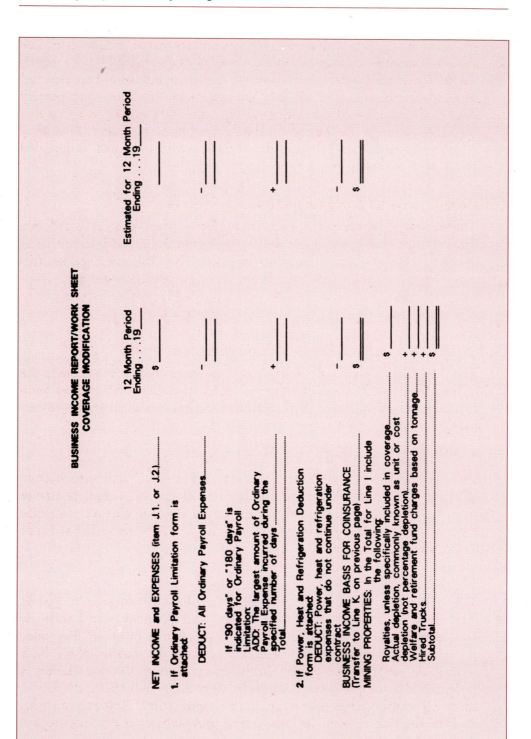

BUSINESS INCOME REPORT/WORK SHEET COVERAGE MODIFICATION

	12 Month Period Ending . . .19____	Estimated for 12 Month Period Ending . . .19____
NET INCOME and EXPENSES (item J.1. or J.2.)	$_____	$_____
1. If Ordinary Payroll Limitation form is attached:		
DEDUCT: All Ordinary Payroll Expenses	−_____	−_____
If "90 days" or "180 days" is indicated for Ordinary Payroll Limitation: ADD: The largest amount of Ordinary Payroll Expense incurred during the specified number of days		
Total	+_____	+_____
2. If Power, Heat and Refrigeration Deduction form is attached: DEDUCT: Power, heat and refrigeration expenses that do not continue under contract	−_____	−_____
BUSINESS INCOME BASIS FOR COINSURANCE (Transfer to Line K on previous page)	$_____	$_____
MINING PROPERTIES: In the Total for Line I include the following:		
Royalties, unless specifically included in coverage	$_____	
Actual depletion, commonly known as unit or cost depletion (not percentage depletion)	+_____	
Welfare and retirement fund charges based on tonnage	+_____	
Hired Trucks	+_____	
Subtotal	$_____	

information available at that time, but actually receives $1 million in income value ten months into the policy period and has an insured loss in month eleven. Could the insurer reasonably say that the insured should have reported a twelve-month value of $1,200,000? The application of a coinsurance penalty in this situation would *not* withstand the "reasonableness" test applied to insurance coverage. As long as the insured used its best efforts to determine what would have been earned had no loss occurred and based its reported values on those efforts, no penalty should be applied.

Extra Expense and Coinsurance Calculations

The amount of extra expenses needed to reduce a given business income loss cannot be reasonably forecast and therefore cannot be included in the insurable values upon which coinsurance is based. The BIC policy follows this reasoning by excluding amounts insured under extra expense from the coinsurance condition: "This condition does not apply to the Extra Expense Additional Coverage."

Optional Coverages Instead of Coinsurance

The BIC policy contains three "optional" coverages that are available to the insured when certain conditions are met regarding either additional premium or reporting requirements. Each allows the coinsurance clause to be suspended.

Maximum Period of Indemnity

This optional coverage allows the insured to limit the period of restoration to 120 days. When that is done, the requirements of the coinsurance section of the policy are suspended, thus allowing the insured to purchase less insurance than would otherwise be required. This option is useful for insureds that do not expect an interruption to last long.

Monthly Period of Indemnity

This optional coverage allows the insured to limit coverage to a specific fraction of the total limit for each thirty-consecutive-day period after the beginning of the period of restoration. The example given in the policy illustrates how the dollar limit is calculated when one-quarter of the limit is available per thirty-day period. In the example given, the policyholder is not required to use one-quarter of its limit every thirty days; that is the most it can use. It could use less—for example, one-tenth of its limit for ten months. As with the first option, the coinsurance provisions of the policy are suspended.

Business Income Agreed Value

This option suspends the operation of the coinsurance provisions of the policy when the insured reports BIC values before the policy's inception date. However, the Agreed Value coverage operates like a new coinsurance requirement. The insured can preselect the amount of coverage it must maintain, but Section d. of the Agreed Value coverage applies a factor to any loss settlement determined by the proportion of the actual limit to the values agreed at the inception of the policy. In the example given in the policy, recovery is reduced by 50 percent since the business income limit of insurance is half of the agreed value reported at the policy inception date. Therefore, for the insured to recover it must purchase 100 percent of any insured BIC loss, it must purchase 100 percent of the agreed value as the business income limit of insurance.

Limits Under Businessowners Policies

The ISO businessowners policy (BOP) provides package property coverages including coverage for loss of business income and extra expense. This coverage is substantially identical to the BIC coverage, except that the BOP has *no* limit of insurance or coinsurance clause. Instead, the BOP limits both the loss of business income and extra expense to twelve consecutive months after the date of loss.

Homeowners Loss of Use

When their homes are damaged or destroyed, homeowners can suffer losses beyond the direct cost to repair or replace the property. Although property losses typically do not affect their incomes, homeowners suffer increased expenses when their homes are uninhabitable. Coverage for loss of use of the insured premises is included in homeowners policies. The coverages are simple, but adjusters must analyze expenses against several criteria to determine loss settlements.

Coverages

The HO-3 is typical of ISO's homeowners policies with respect to loss of use. Coverage D—Loss of Use provides three types of coverage for such losses. The main coverage is for additional living expense. Alternatively, a homeowner can recover fair rental value for damage to premises held for rental. The third possibility is coverage for loss of use caused by civil authorities.

Additional Living Expense

The coverage for additional living expense is straightforward:

> If a loss covered under this Section makes that part of the "residence premises" where you reside not fit to live in, we cover the Additional Living Expense, meaning any necessary increase in living expenses incurred by you so that your household can maintain its normal standard of living.

This coverage only applies when a loss otherwise covered by the policy has occurred. For example, the HO-3 does not cover flood damage, so loss of use caused by a flood would not be covered under Coverage D.

An important phrase in this provision is "not fit to live in." The determination that the insured premises are "not fit to live in" is obviously subjective. Making this determination requires an assessment of both the insured's lifestyle and the physical damage. For example, substantial damage to an insured's kitchen or only bathroom would probably make the premises "unfit"; damage to an attached garage would probably not. Certainly, the inability to use utilities, such as water or electricity, would render the premises uninhabitable. However, even relatively minor smoke damage loss can render the premises uninhabitable for a day or so because of the odor. The problem of determining whether a home is fit to live in is common in the adjustment of claims for loss of use. Its resolution requires common sense on the part of the adjuster.

Property Held for Rental

Some homeowner policyholders rent part of their homes to others. If the part held for rental is damaged, the homeowner might lose rental income or be unable to rent the premises. The second coverage under Coverage D applies to such a situation:

> If a loss covered under this Section makes that part of the "residence premises" rented to others or held for rental by you not fit to live in, we cover the:
>
> > Fair Rental Value, meaning the fair rental value of that part of the "residence premises" rented to others or held for rental by you less any expenses that do not continue while the premises is not fit to live in.

The premises do not have to be rented at the time of the loss for the insured to be compensated. They can be "held for rental" as long as they are not occupied by the insured.

This coverage does not apply to every rental property that a policyholder owns, but only to rentals of the "residence premises." "Residence premises" is defined to mean the place where the policyholder resides. Thus, this coverage typically applies to a room held for rental to boarders or to one floor of a residence in which the policyholder occupies the rest of the property. Coverage D of the homeowners policies is not intended to substitute for business income coverage for commercial landlords.

Applicable to all the Coverage D provisions, but especially to the coverage for Fair Rental Value, is the limitation, "We do not cover loss or expense due to cancellation of a lease or agreement." After damage to rental premises, an existing lease might terminate, either by its own provisions or by operation of law. The policyholder might not be able to find a new tenant until well after the premises are repaired and would lose rental income while the premises are vacant. Nevertheless, the policyholder can only recover for losses occurring while the premises are not fit to live in.

Civil Authorities

Sometimes a policyholder cannot use his or her home even though it has not suffered damage. In case of damage to a neighboring property, the HO-3 also makes the following provision:

> If a civil authority prohibits you from use of the residence premises as a result of direct damage to neighboring premises by a Peril Insured Against in this policy, we cover the Additional Living Expense or Fair Rental Value loss as provided under 1 and 2 above for no more than two weeks.

This clause is similar to clauses found in commercial property policies and limits coverage to two weeks for loss of use resulting from a declaration by civil authorities (police, fire, or civil defense) that the insured may not occupy the residence premises. The only part of the coverage that differs from commercial coverages is that the two weeks do not have to be *consecutive*. This difference allows some flexibility in the adjustment since civil orders related to a single event are often issued and rescinded several times.

Determining Settlement for Loss of Use

Adjusters should determine loss settlements for additional living expenses differently from settlements for fair rental value. Settlements for additional living expenses require analysis of many specific items of expense. Settlements for fair rental value require analysis of market rental prices.

Under either approach, the time period for loss payment is limited to "the shortest time required to repair or replace" the damage in question. The "shortest time" standard might seem to call for an ideal recovery from loss, but common sense should tell an adjuster to consider such factors as weather, the severity of the loss, and the difficulty in adjusting the loss. For additional living expense, if the insured chooses to relocate permanently, the period of recovery is additionally limited to the shortest time required to settle elsewhere. Under either approach to loss settlement, recovery is not limited by the expiration of the policy. Thus, if a major fire occurs on the last day of a policy and the time needed for repairs lasts many months, the insured can recover all of his or her loss of use.

Additional Living Expense Losses

Although the coverage for additional living expense is simply stated, expenses must meet several criteria to be paid. Such expenses must be (1) necessary, (2) increases above normal, (3) incurred, and (4) to maintain the insured's normal standard of living.

Necessary Expenses

The requirement that expenses be necessary reinforces the insured's duty to minimize loss. For example, an insured should not rent an apartment as temporary living quarters under a year-long lease when satisfactory month-to-month rentals are available. Likewise, an insured who faces a longer commute to work from a new temporary location cannot rent a car just to save mileage on his or her own car. Such an insured should be fairly compensated for the additional use of his or her own car, but rental of a substitute is unnecessary.

Expenses must also be necessary in the sense of being caused by the damage to the insured premises. For example, while his or her home is being repaired, an insured might coincidentally decide to join a health club. The expense of the health club might be worthwhile, even necessary for the insured's health, but it is not related to the damage to the insured's home.

Increases Only

Following damage to his or her home, an insured remains responsible for his or her normal amount of living expenses, since this amount would have been incurred without a loss. Any normal expense, such as a regular mortgage payment, is not covered. Coverage D only applies to increases in living expenses. Determining what expenses increase when an insured must live elsewhere and while the insured premises are being repaired is usually simple. The best example of this is the cost of food. If an insured normally spends $150 a week for food, but after the loss spends $250 because the insured has no kitchen to use, this expense was necessarily increased by $100 per week.

Like operating expenses for commercial risks, certain living expenses for homeowners automatically discontinue to some extent if the premises are vacated. Electricity, fuel oil, and natural gas, billed on an as-used basis for residential purposes, normally stop while the premises are repaired. However, they do not *always* stop. If the loss occurs during the winter and in a partially exposed building and the heat must be maintained to prevent weather-related damage to undamaged areas, heating costs could increase during the repair period and be compensable under Coverage D. Common sense and good judgment should be used to determine the extent to which living expenses discontinue.

Adjusters should also be aware of certain types of expenses that *might or might not* be affected by the loss. If the insured hires a lawn-care service, depending on the terms of the agreement, the insured might be obligated to continue to pay for the service even though the insured is not present. Septic or sewage treatment costs are similar.

Incurred Expenses

The insured's increased expenses must actually be *incurred* in order to be payable under Coverage D. Unlike business interruption insurance in which a reasonably expected time period should be used to determine loss, under Coverage D a comparison must be made between what an insured has spent in a similar period before the loss and what the insured actually spent during the loss of use period. The adjuster must advise the insured immediately after a loss to retain all receipts that document expenditures during the repair time, including receipts for all normal expenses. These receipts must be tallied against previous similar bills in order to determine which expenses have increased. The adjuster must also decide whether the loss or some other situation caused the increase.

The requirement that expenses be incurred does not mean that adjusters cannot make advance payments for additional living expenses. Indeed, making such payments is among the most valuable and important services that adjusters perform. People who have lost their homes are in desperate circumstances. The insurance industry never looks better than when an adjuster appears, literally before the ashes are cold, and hands the insured a check for living expenses. An adjuster making advance payments must explain, though, that such payments will be deducted from any final settlement and that the final settlement will be based on expenses actually incurred.

Normal Standard of Living

Additional living expense coverage extends only to expenses necessary to maintain the insured's normal standard of living. Although the calculation for increased expenses appears to be straightforward, interpreting an insured's "normal standard of living" can be difficult. The adjuster should be careful not to insult the insured by insisting or assuming that all the meals consumed during the repair period should be bought at a fast-food restaurant. At the same time, the adjuster should ascertain whether dining at a five-star restaurant every night is above the insured's "normal standard of living."

Some expenses will be common for one insured but extraordinary for another. An insured who normally entertains at home would bear the additional expense of entertaining out. This is a compensable increased expense under Coverage D for an insured whose lifestyle includes formal entertaining. In some cases this type of entertainment expense is actually business-related and is therefore not insured under a homeowners policy. However, if entertainment is clearly part of the insured's personal lifestyle, even this expense is insured because Coverage D contains no language to the contrary.

Other factors important in determining the lifestyle of the insured can include any of the following: number of family members; employment of the family members; location of the insured premises; social and professional memberships; and health considerations. Each of these factors must be considered singly and in combination with one another in order to determine what is recoverable under loss of use coverage.

Fair Rental Value

Loss settlements based on fair rental value do not require detailed review of numerous items. Indeed, such settlements do not even require showing that the insured actually suffered loss. The insured is deemed to have suffered a loss when property held for rental is uninhabitable, even if it was uninhabited before the loss.

A good source for determining fair rental value is a local real estate broker who normally handles residential rental property. A knowledgeable broker should be able to provide the adjuster with the rental values of comparable properties. The adjuster must then determine which properties are similar enough to the insured's premises to establish the "fair rental value."

After the rental value has been determined, the next step is to subtract from that value the expenses that do not continue during the restoration period. Similar to the additional living expense requirement of incurred expense, this section of Coverage D indicates that only those expenses that *actually discontinue* are to be deducted from the rental value. Although this language suggests that the loss cannot be adjusted until the restoration is complete, it can still be handled like a BIC loss—by prospectively establishing a reasonably expected time period and projecting discontinued expenses.

Summary

Time element losses can affect both homeowners and organizations. Damage to or destruction of property can result in loss of income, increased expenses, or both. Insurance settlements for such losses are measured over the time necessary to repair or replace the damaged or destroyed property, so such claims are called time element losses.

Claim adjusters cannot understand insurance or claims for time element losses for organizations unless they first understand basic accounting for organizations. The two principal accounting statements for organizations are the balance sheet and the income statement. The balance sheet lists an organization's assets and its liabilities. The difference between assets and liabilities is the organization's net worth. An organization's income statement lists the revenue and expenses for the organization for a given period of time. The difference between revenue and expenses is net income. Damage or destruction of property appears on an organization's balance sheet. However, if such damage or destruction results in loss of income or increased expenses, those effects appear on the income statement. Loss of revenue, increased expenses, or both together result in reduced net income.

The Business Income Coverage Form (and Extra Expense), BIC, covers an organization's loss of net income, its continuing expenses, and its extraordinary expenses that result from a suspension of its operations. Claim adjusters must be careful when determining losses under other coverage forms. Some other forms apply only to loss of "business income" and some apply only to extra expenses. In all cases, claim adjusters must be able to evaluate the separate effects and coverage for reduced revenue and increased expenses. The BIC covers losses occurring during the "period of restoration," defined to end when repairs should be completed. This definition allows adjusters and policyholders to settle claims prospectively, before restoration is completed.

Homeowners are insured for loss of use of their homes under Coverage D of the homeowners policies. Such losses generally consist of additional living expense, but homeowners policies can also cover fair rental value for damage to property held for rental. Although the coverage provision for additional living expense is very simple, claim adjusters must analyze all of a policyholder's items of expense against several criteria to determine loss settlements. The expenses must be necessary increases that are incurred to maintain the policyholder's normal standard of living.

Chapter 12

Specialty Losses

This chapter discusses several essentially unrelated topics that are called "specialty losses" because they are less common than most property losses or because they require some specialized knowledge to analyze and adjust. This chapter covers (1) inland marine losses, (2) losses under the National Flood Insurance Program (3) condominium losses (4) builders risk losses and (5) differences in conditions policies. Adjusters should be familiar with these topics first because they account for losses themselves and second because they often arise in the handling of more "typical" losses. Chapter 13 will continue this discussion with several additional specialty losses.

Inland Marine Losses

Inland marine insurance includes a variety of insurance coverages. These coverages are grouped together as inland marine as much because of their history as because of any logical relationship. Nevertheless, inland marine coverages share certain characteristics that adjusters must recognize and understand. This section reviews the inland marine market and three major categories of inland marine losses: transportation losses, bailee losses, and contractors equipment losses. Builders' risk losses and computer losses are two other types of inland marine losses treated elsewhere in this chapter and the next chapter.

The Inland Marine Market

In the late nineteenth and early twentieth centuries, the property-liability insurance industry was divided among fire, marine, and casualty lines of business, each of which was regulated differently and authorized to conduct only certain types of business. For example, fire insurance companies provided coverage to property at fixed locations, and casualty insurers provided theft coverage.

As the economy grew, shippers needed to insure goods in transit without buying multiple policies. Ocean marine underwriters were the least regulated types of insurers, and they already had experience in evaluating risks to goods in transit and in providing all-risks coverage. Ocean marine underwriters were able to address a need that traditional fire insurers could not handle, so the inland marine business was born. **Inland marine insurance** is not "marine" insurance in the sense that it usually has nothing to do with the oceans or navigable waterways. Instead, this line of insurance usually relates to property in transit or not at fixed locations.

Soon after the inland marine business began, it attracted a variety of risks that had little in common except the need for broader or more flexible coverage than traditional fire insurers offered. Since fire insurers were more tightly regulated, they were at a competitive disadvantage. Naturally, they resented the encroachment of inland marine insurers. In 1933, the **Nation-Wide Marine Definition,** summarized in Exhibit 12-1, was created to delineate the scope of inland marine underwriting. Although modern property-liability insurers have full legal power to write all types of property insurance, the Nation-Wide Marine Definition remains important because inland marine business is less regulated and less standardized. This definition specifies which business is part of inland marine insurance.

Common Characteristics of Inland Marine Losses

Although the property and situations subject to inland marine coverage are diverse, certain circumstances are common.

"All-Risks" or Specialized Coverage

Many inland marine policies are written on a specified perils basis, but "all-risks" coverage is the norm. However, an adjuster cannot assume that "all-risks" coverage is equivalent to the perils of the BPP causes of loss—special form or to any other familiar standard. Because inland marine policies were developed to meet specialized needs, the coverages are often distinctive. The "all-risks" coverage of an inland marine policy might be broader than typical "all-risks." For example, it might extend to earthquake or flood. On the other hand, it might be narrower because of exclusions unique to certain types of property.

Exhibit 12-1
Summary of The Nation-Wide Marine Definition

☐ *Transportation*, covering the shipper or owner's goods, or the interests of the common carrier

☐ *Bridges, Tunnels, Instrumentalities of Transportation or Communication*

  Piers, dry docks

  Pipelines

  Telephone and telegraph property, including transmission lines and generating equipment

  Radio and television communication equipment, including towers and antennas and electrical apparatus

  Cranes and equipment to load and unload

☐ *Bailee—Bailor*

  Garment contractors' floater

  Bailee customer

  Warehousemen's legal liability

  Furrier's customer

☐ *Floater policies (personal)*

  Personal effects

  Furs

  Jewelry

  Silverware

  Fine arts

  Stamp and coin

  Musical instrument

☐ *Floater policies (commercial)*

  Physicians' and surgeons' instruments

  Patterns and dies

  Theatrical

  Live animals

  Salesmens' samples

  Exhibitions

☐ *Installment sales, covering the vendor or purchaser of property*

☐ *Contractors' equipment*

☐ *Builders' risk*

☐ *Dealers' policies (floor plan)*

☐ *Miscellaneous policies*

  Jewelers' block

  Valuable papers

  Accounts receivable

  Fine arts

  Differences in conditions

  Electronic data processing

The additional coverages of inland marine policies are often more generous than conventional property insurance policies. For example, loss of use coverage is included in many policies. Other inland policies have attractive extra features, such as coverage for additional expenses and broadened coverage for property of others.

Adjusters must be aware of the nonstandard nature of many inland marine policies. Policy clauses or conditions that an adjuster might take for granted might not even exist, or they might be substantially different. Thus, adjusters must read the policy in question with every loss.

Multiple Parties

Inland marine scenarios often include transportation, custody, or use of property by someone who is not the owner. Losses often involve more than one party, even when is only one named insured is on a given policy. The presence of more than one party can result in multiple insurance policies applicable to a given loss. These policies might only cover the respective interests of the various parties in the property, or they might cover the same interest. An adjuster must be alert to these possibilities and must resolve overlapping coverage and loss-sharing problems when they arise.

Need To Consult Contracts and Documents

Because several parties can be involved in inland marine losses, adjusters must often consult contracts or documents to determine interests or property values. These contracts and documents include bills of lading, consignment contracts, warehouse receipts, equipment leases, construction contracts, and sales invoices. These documents might specify or determine who has an interest in property and who must insure the property. Adjusters must also become familiar with the business practices and jargon of various industries.

Transportation Losses

Transportation coverages were the historic origin of the inland marine business and still account for a significant amount of the business. Transportation losses require adjusters to determine legal interests and responsibilities for the damaged property.

Parties in Transportation Losses

Transportation losses sometimes involve one party, if the property is being transported by its owner on the owner's trucks to the owner's locations. Usually, though, transportation losses involve three parties.

The **shipper** is the party with whom transportation of property begins. The shipper of property is usually a seller sending property to a buyer. In any case, the shipper is usually in some business other than carrying goods and will usually hire a carrier to transport goods.

Carriers transport goods. They can operate by truck, railroad, aircraft, barge, or ship. The following discussion concerns truck transportation. Rail, air, and ship carriers are subject to different laws of liability than truck carriers, often dictated by federal statute. Even truck carriers face different liabilities depending on whether they are contract carriers or common carriers, as explained below.

The **consignee** is the party to whom goods are to be delivered. The consignee is usually a buyer and, depending on the terms of sale, might also own the goods during their journey.

Responsibility for Loss

Responsibility for loss to goods in transit depends on the answers to several questions. Who owns the goods? Who agreed to insure them? Is the carrier liable? Did any party limit its liability?

Who owns goods depends on the terms of sale. The seller and buyer can agree to any one of a number of sales terms, as shown in Exhibit 12-2. Ownership might transfer to the buyer at any point from the seller's warehouse to the buyer's receiving dock. Thus, an adjuster must check the terms of sale to see who owns goods at the time of a loss.

Exhibit 12-2
Terms of Sale

FOB (free on board) point of origin—Ownership passes from the seller to the buyer as soon as the carrier picks up the goods from the seller's premises. The point of origin might be specified by name.

FOB destination—Ownership passes from the seller to the buyer when the carrier delivers the goods to the buyer's premises. The destination might be named.

FAS (free along side) vessel at a named port—Ownership passes from the seller to the buyer once the seller delivers the goods alongside a vessel for loading onto that vessel.

C.I.F. (cost, insurance, and freight)—The seller is obligated to pay for the insurance and freight charges for delivery to the buyer. However, ownership passes once the seller has delivered the goods to the carrier. The insurance and freight charges become part of the insured value of the goods.

C.F. or C.&F.—The same as C.I.F., except the seller is not obligated to provide insurance coverage.

No agreed terms—If the agreement requires or authorizes the seller to ship by carrier, the risk of loss is like FOB point of origin. If the agreement is silent about shipping terms, the seller bears the risk of loss until the goods are delivered to the buyer.

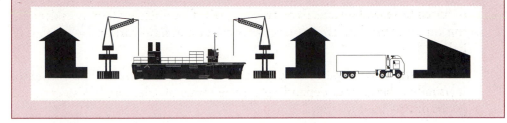

Normally, the owner of goods would have the greatest incentive to insure them, but when goods are being transported, the parties involved can agree on any arrangement. The adjuster must check the sales invoice and the bill of lading to see who has agreed to insure the goods. A **bill of lading** is both a contract of carriage between the carrier and the shipper and a receipt for the goods. Although an agreement to insure property does not automatically create insurance coverage, an adjuster who sees an agreement by a party other than the policyholder to insure the goods should investigate that party's coverage.

A carrier is usually legally liable for loss or damage to goods in its custody. A common carrier offers its services to the general public and is liable in all cases, except for losses caused by acts of God, acts of a public enemy, exercise of public authority, shipper's neglect, or inherent vice of the goods. A contract carrier operates under contract with a shipper. Its liability depends on the terms of contract. Its liability might be as strict as a common carrier's or less strict. For example, a contract carrier might only be responsible for losses caused by its negligence.

Carriers often limit their liability by the terms of a bill of lading. In particular, they often limit their liability to a specified dollar amount. Adjusters should not conclude that a carrier will cover a loss without first checking for such a limitation. The buyer and seller might also limit their liability for loss, although liability between these parties usually depends entirely on ownership. The owner of goods at the time of loss bears the loss.

Adjusting Considerations

Shippers and consignees can insure goods in transit with **transit insurance**. Coverage under transit insurance does not depend on ownership. It certainly covers owned property, but it might also cover property for which the policyholder is liable or has agreed to insure, or for which the policyholder is the consignee. Transit insurance applies only while goods are "in transit," which usually includes transit on a vehicle owned by the policyholder or while on a loading dock in the custody of a carrier.

Coverage for carriers is called **motor truck cargo insurance**. It generally applies only for losses for which the carrier is legally liable. Thus, shippers need their own coverage, even when their carriers are insured, for losses not covered by the motor truck cargo insurance.

Theft is a significant risk for goods in transit. Transit policies exclude theft by the policyholder or its employees and usually exclude voluntary parting with the goods because of trick, pretense, fraud, or swindling. Some policies require evidence of forcible entry into a locked truck for theft to be covered.

Adjusters must read the valuation clause carefully. Valuation is usually at invoice value, but it can be at actual cash value point of origin or point of destination or according to whatever terms to which the buyer and seller have agreed. The insurer might cover prepaid freight charges and the cost of new packaging materials.

Adjusters who expect to handle a volume of transportation losses should arrange nationwide salvage services. Losses can occur in remote places or require immediate action, such as when a cargo is spilled along a highway in an ice storm.

Bailee Losses

A **bailment** is the transfer of possession of property from one person to another for a specified purpose. Title to the property remains with the owner, the **bailor,** and the property is expected to be returned to the bailor once the specific purpose has ended. The person entrusted with the property is the **bailee** and is responsible for the property while it is in his or her control.

A bailment differs from both a lease and agency. In a lease, the tenant-lessee has full rights during the lease to use the property *in any way*, even to the exclusion of the owner. In a bailment, use of the property by the bailee is limited to a specific purpose. If an agent or employee holds property, the law considers that condition as equivalent to possession by the principal/owner.

Liability in Bailment Situations

There are three types of bailment situations. First is a **bailment for the benefit of the bailor** only, such as when one neighbor agrees to take care of a vacationing neighbor's plants. The owner of the property enjoys the sole benefit. In such a bailment, the bailee owes only a slight duty of care and would probably be liable to the owner only for intentional wrongdoing and gross recklessness.

The second type is a **bailment for the benefit of the bailee** only, such as when one neighbor borrows another's lawn mower. In this situation, the bailee owes a high duty of care and is presumably liable for any damage.

The third type is a **bailment for the mutual benefit of bailee and bailor.** For example, a dry cleaner/bailee receives payment for the service of laundering, and the customer/bailor receives clean clothing in return for his or her payment. This situation is also known as a **commercial bailment.** The bailee owes a duty of ordinary care for the property in his or her possession.

Bailee Coverages

Just as the types of bailment situations differ, so do the types of bailment coverages. Bailment coverages are as varied as the businesses involved in bailment contracts. They range from warehouse legal liability policies to tailored coverages for specific risks such as repair shops, jewelry stores, or consignees of property on consignment.

Coverage purchased by bailees typically falls into two broad categories, the bailee liability policy and the bailee's customers policy. The **bailee liability policy** covers the insured for sums he or she becomes legally obligated to pay as a result of loss caused by a covered peril. As the name implies, this is a liability coverage, and the insured would have to be legally liable for the loss for the policy to respond. Under the **bailee's customers policy,** coverage is provided for property in the bailee's custody with no need to prove liability or negligence on the part of the insured. The coverage is often invoked when bailees want to maintain customer goodwill by replacing the customer's damaged property, even when the bailee has not been at fault. Bailee's customers policies always involve dual interests: both the bailee and the customer have interests in the property and in the claim settlement proceeds.

Bailor Coverages

Bailors do not necessarily rely on the bailee's coverage. Often when a bailment is created, either the bailee provides no coverage or the bailee's coverage will not respond, such as when the bailee is found not to be legally liable for the loss. Sometimes bailors insure an exposure despite coverage available from the bailee. Perhaps the property involved is of particularly high value or is hard to replace, or perhaps its loss would interfere with the bailor's regular business.

Most bailors seeking coverage for their property when it is off-premises first check the built-in extensions contained in their own homeowners or commercial property forms. The homeowners policy covers personal property "while it is anywhere in the world." The building and personal property form provides tightly limited off-premises coverage. Coinsurance requirements must apply, and the loss must occur at a place the insured does not own, lease, or operate. In addition, the covered property cannot be in or on a vehicle; in the care, custody, or control of a salesperson; or at a fair or an exhibition. The limit for this extension is $5,000.

Because the built-in off-premises coverages are limited and might not be adequate for losses, several types of bailors policies are available. In personal lines coverages, various inland marine floaters cover specific property such as jewelry, cameras, and fine arts. These floaters cover more than just a bailment situation, but they do apply to losses occurring to property in the hands of a bailee. Commercial bailors can use numerous inland marine floaters and endorsements, such as a processing floater, which businesses that send their goods to other businesses for processing use.

Adjustment of Bailment Losses

Because of the many coverage possibilities, as well as the possibility of overlapping or joint coverage, a bailment loss requires special handling. Adjusters must determine all parties to the bailment and the nature and extent of their specific interest in the property damaged. Adjusters must also examine all documents related to the bailment to determine the contractual rights of the parties and whether either party has waived any rights before the loss. For example, the contract might contain a hold harmless agreement or might require a specific party to insure the property.

Adjusters must also be familiar with industry practices concerning specific types of property. For example, in the jewelry business, retailers typically hold property of others on a consignment basis. While the property is in the hands of the retailer, he or she must usually provide insurance.

Adjusters should also be aware of differences in valuation clauses between policies. For example, under a bailee liability policy, the insurer would be liable to cover property on an actual cash value basis; under a homeowners form, the coverage could be written either on an actual cash value or a replacement cost basis.

Each bailment requires the adjuster to develop all the facts of the bailment contract and the property loss and determine how the applicable coverages address those facts. In dealing with the garment industry, general warehousing, or any of the other industry covered by bailee or bailor policies, adjusters must be aware of the traditions and practices unique to that trade. Adjusters must know how the business operates and be familiar with the financial aspects of the industry.

If a bailee's customer policy insures a laundry or dry cleaner and the loss involves virtually all of the bailor's property in the store, the adjuster can set up a claims operation on the premises. The policy usually covers the actual cash value of the customer's property. The adjuster might be dealing with 300 or more customers, so a standard procedure would be necessary. The adjuster might require each claimant to complete a claim form, then negotiate the claim and issue a check on the spot. The adjuster would handle claims involving a few shirts or a pair of slacks in this manner, but if a large value is involved, the adjuster might go to the claimant's home to settle the loss. Alternatively, the adjuster might simply have the insured distribute claims forms to its customers to be completed and then sent to the adjuster's office, after which negotiations are handled by phone.

In some cases, insurers allow of the businessowners to settle losses up to a certain dollar amount with their customers, for example, up to $100 or $250.

The insurer might believe that the insured knows the customer and the garments and is therefore better able to negotiate a reasonable actual cash value. This method, of course, has its drawbacks. The insured might be only interested in keeping its customers happy and might not subject their claims to much scrutiny. Another method of settlement is to settle directly with the insured with a **policy release,** which allows the insured to handle the customers' claims.

Contractor's Equipment Losses

Contractor's equipment represents one of the largest markets for inland marine insurance. Contractor's equipment policies can insure road-building equipment, asphalt plants, farm machinery, mining equipment, and many other related items. Bulldozers, harvesters, concrete mixers, portable equipment such as compressors and chain saws, and hundreds of other pieces of equipment used by many different types of contracting firms might be covered. The policy might provide named perils or "all-risks" coverage and applies while the equipment is on the job site or stored.

Coverage

A contractor's equipment policy usually describes the equipment and has a dollar limit of liability per piece of equipment. Nonscheduled property such as tools valued at less than $1,000 and an aggregate coverage limit might be included. Many policies are written at actual cash value, but replacement cost coverage is available. Policies can cover the insureds' equipment or equipment that is leased.

Coverage can be "all-risks" or specified perils. Specified perils coverage usually includes unusual perils peculiar to contractors equipment, such as "blowout" on drilling rigs. Fire is a common cause of loss on job sites. In addition, unsafe practices by employees and poorly trained operators contribute to the frequency of loss. Vandalism is common because most machinery is left on the job site overnight, usually without a guard. Wear and tear and mechanical or electrical breakdown are typically excluded, even under "all-risks" policies.

Coverage can include rental reimbursement to enable the contractor to hire substitute equipment. Alternatively, the contractor might have full business income and extra expense coverage, especially for equipment essential to the contractor's operations.

Appraisal

Contractor's equipment losses are usually adjusted by heavy equipment appraisers. Specialized knowledge of the equipment is necessary. The appraiser must be able to confirm what parts are necessary to repair the equipment, the prevailing labor rates, the value of equipment for coinsurance purposes, and how to depreciate the repair. Depreciation is often computed by the number of hours that the equipment has been in service. Value on a total loss can be determined by the market value of a comparable piece of equipment. An expert appraiser can be invaluable in controlling down-time and rental expense.

Catastrophes can severely disrupt an affected area. As a result, the daily claims activity of an insurance company would be also disrupted. With a catastrophe-preparedness plan, the insurance company can maintain its normal daily activities while handling claims for insureds in the damaged areas expeditiously.

Losses Under the National Flood Insurance Program

Although hundreds of standard property insurance forms cover many perils, coverage for flood is excluded from virtually all of them. Floods can result from melting snows, rising rivers and lakes, hurricanes, or heavy rains.

The market for flood insurance among private insurers is characterized by adverse selection. **Adverse selection** occurs when only those with a high probability of experiencing loss are interested in purchasing insurance. For example, only people living in a flood-prone area need flood insurance. Some of these areas have seasonal flooding, but other areas flood much less often. In some areas, premiums for flood insurance in the private market would be prohibitive, so only those who face a high probability of flood would pay these premiums. Adverse selection makes underwriting these risks over a great number of diverse insureds extremely difficult. Since insurance cannot provide indemnification against nearly certain loss, private insurers have avoided writing this catastrophic coverage.

History of the National Flood Insurance Program

Because of the problems associated with flood insurance in the private market, the government has made flood insurance widely available through the National Flood Insurance Program (NFIP). The National Flood Act of 1968 made flood insurance available to certain communities. It subsidized rates for insurance and created an office to administer the insurance. The act also required eligible communities to implement plans to reduce future flood problems. In 1969, the act was amended to provide an emergency program and to expand the definition of "flood" to include mudslides and mudflows. In 1973, the Flood Disaster Protection Act restricted federal disaster relief funding for flood-prone areas where flood insurance was available but not purchased. It also expanded the definition of "flood" to include flood-related erosion.

The National Flood Insurance Act was originally a joint venture between the government and private insurers. In 1978, that partnership ended. Since then, the Federal Insurance Administration (FIA), of the Federal Emergency Management Agency (FEMA), has underwritten all flood coverage. In 1983, FIA invited private insurers to participate in a **Write Your Own** (WYO) program to increase the base and geographic distribution of flood insurance and to improve service and claims handling. A WYO company sells flood policies under its own name, collects premiums, services the policyholders, adjusts the claims, and pays the losses. FEMA reinsures 100 percent of these losses. FEMA pays commissions on premiums and reimburses expenses and costs. If the insurer loses money on the program, FEMA makes up the difference. Any profits are returned to the government.

NFIP Coverage

The NFIP has three policy forms. A **dwelling form** (DF) insures a one- to four-family residential dwelling or condominium unit and residential contents. A **general property form** (GPF) insures other residential and nonresidential buildings and contents. Another form insurers condominium associations.

Definition of Flood

The NFIP policies cover the described property from direct loss by flood. **Flood** is defined in both policies as a *general* and *temporary* condition of partial or complete inundation by water of what is normally dry land caused by any of the following:

1. The overflow of inland or tidal waters
2. The rapid and unusual accumulation of runoff or surface waters from any source
3. Mudslides proximately caused by flood, as defined in subparagraph 2
4. Collapse or subsidence of land along a lake shore or other body of water caused by erosion, waves, or currents of water exceeding normal cycles that cause a flood, as defined in subparagraph 1

Removal Coverage

Although the purpose of the flood policy is to cover direct damage from flood, it also has a provision to pay in the event of *impending* loss. The cost of removing covered property to protect and preserve it against flood is covered. This includes all reasonable expenses incurred, including the value of labor of the policyholder and members of the policyholder's household at minimum wage. Removal coverage applies for forty-five days while property is secured above ground level or outside the flood area and is protected from the elements. Failure to protect property could lead to a denial of coverage.

Exclusions

Consequential or indirect loss is not covered. Loss of use, additional living expenses, and business interruption are indirect losses resulting from flood and are thus not covered. Increased costs of construction resulting from ordinance or law are not covered. A loss already in progress at the inception of the policy term is not covered.

The following perils are excluded from both flood policies:

- Theft
- Fire
- Wind or windstorm
- Explosion
- Earthquake
- Landslide, movement of land from subsurface water, or gradual erosion, except to the extent covered as mudslide
- Rain, snow, sleet, hail, and waterspray
- Freezing, thawing, and pressure or weight of ice or water
- Sewer backup, seepage of water, or land subsidence unless caused by a flood and occurring within seventy-two hours after the flood has receded

Several exclusions explain that a flood must be a general, not an individual, condition. Flood policies exclude water, moisture or mudflow confined to the insured property, or any damage resulting from conditions within the policy-holders' control. This exclusion applies to any design, structural or mechanical defects, or any failures, stoppages, or breakages of water or sewer lines, drains, pumps, fixtures, or equipment. Any modification by the insured of the property or premises that increases the hazard of flooding can exclude subsequent losses from coverage. Any intentional act by the policyholder is also excluded. A flood confined to the insured premises is not covered unless the flood covers more than two acres of the premises.

Property Covered—Dwelling Form

Building coverage under the dwelling form is written similar to that under other property forms. Extensions and additions to the buildings are covered, as are building materials and supplies, and certain specifically described fixtures. Automatic coverage applies for a separate garage or carport for up to 10 percent of the overall building coverage limit. If the value of the detached building exceeds 10 percent, a separate policy should be obtained on that building. The 10 percent extension is not an additional amount of insurance, so using this coverage reduces the limit otherwise available for the dwelling.

Contents coverage applies to personal property usual and incidental to a dwelling owned by the insured or by household family members. Property must be contained in a fully enclosed building on the residence premises or secured against floating out of a partially enclosed building.

Debris removal coverage pays for incurred expenses and the policyholder's labor (at federal minimum wage rates) to remove debris caused directly by flood. This is not an additional amount of insurance. This coverage extends to property and debris from other properties that float onto the insured location and to debris of insured property that has floated onto other locations.

Replacement cost coverage is provided only for single-family principal residences. It is not available for condominiums, appurtenant building structures, or personal property. Outdoor antennas, equipment, and awnings in addition to carpeting and appliances are excluded from replacement cost coverage. These items are insured for actual cash value. To qualify for replacement cost coverage, the building must be insured for at least 80 percent of its replacement cost or for the maximum amount of coverage available under the NFIP. Failure to meet these conditions reduces the insurer's liability to actual cash value or to that portion of the full cost of repair or replacement that the total amount of insurance on the building bears to 80 percent of the full replacement cost. Exhibit 12-3 is a statement, required by the NFIP, that enables adjusters to apply the replacement cost provision to a given loss. Replacement cost is not due until replacement or repairs are completed, but repairs are not required for total losses.

Property Covered—General Property Form

Building coverage under this form includes the described building, attached additions and extensions, permanent fixtures, and building service equipment while within an enclosed building on the premises or adjacent to the premises. Appurtenant structures are not included and must be insured under a different policy.

Contents are covered as either household contents or personal property other than household contents. If the coverage is written to cover personal property other than household contents, the covered property includes merchandise and stock, furniture, fixtures, machinery and equipment owned by the insured, and improvements and betterments if the insured does not own the building. All contents must be within the described building to be covered under this form.

Exhibit 12-3

National Flood Insurance Program Replacement Cost Determination

O.M.B. NO. 3067-0021
Expires May 31, 1996

NATIONAL FLOOD INSURANCE PROGRAM

**Statement as to full cost of repair or replacement
under the replacement cost coverage, subject
to the terms and conditions of this policy***

(See reverse side for Privacy Act Statement and Paperwork Burden Disclosure Notice)

Policy No. FL ....

Agency at .... Agent ....

Insured ....

....

Location ....

....

Type of property involved in claim ....

Date of loss ....

1. **Full Amount of Insurance** applicable to the property
   for which claim is presented was. . . . . $ ....

2. **Full Replacement Cost** of the said property at the time
   of the loss was. . . . . : . . . . $ ....

3. **The Full Cost of Repair or Replacement** is. . . . . $ ....

4. Applicable Depreciation is. . . . . $ ....

5. Actual Cash Value loss is. . . . . $ ....
   (Line 3 minus Line 4)

6. Less deductibles and/or participation by the insured. . . . . $ ....

7. **Actual Cash Value Claim** is . . . . $ ....
   (Line 5 minus Line 6)

8. **Supplemental Claim,** to be filed in accordance with the
   terms and conditions of the Replacement Cost Coverage
   within............days from date of loss as shown above,
   will not exceed. . . . . $ ....
   (This figure will be that portion of the amounts shown on Lines 4 and 6
   which is recoverable)

   *The Standard Flood Insurance Policy is subject to the National Flood Insurance Act of 1968 and any Acts Amendatory thereof, and Regulations
   issued by the Federal Insurance Administration pursuant to such statute(s).

.... Insured

.... Adjuster

FEMA Form 81-44, MAY 93   REPLACES EDITION OF APR. 90, WHICH IS OBSOLETE.   593-113B (5/93)

Additional living expenses, loss of use, and business interruption are not covered. Debris removal is covered similar to the dwelling form. It is not an additional amount of coverage.

Property Not Covered

The dwelling form excludes personal property in the open and animals, livestock, birds, and fish. Both the dwelling form and general property form exclude the following types of property:

- Accounts, bills, currency, deeds, evidences of debt, money, coins, medals, postage stamps, securities, bullion, manuscripts, and other valuable papers or records.

- A building and its contents located entirely in, on, or over water or seaward of mean high tide if the building was newly constructed or substantially improved on or after October 1, 1982.

- Structures other than buildings, such as fences, retaining walls, seawalls, swimming pools, bulkheads, wharves, piers, bridges, docks; other open structures located on or over water, including boathouses or other similar structures or buildings into which boats are floated; and personal property in the open.

- Other real property, including land values, lawn, trees, shrubs or plants, growing crops, underground structures and equipment including wells, septic tanks or septic systems; and those portions of walks, walkways, driveways, patios, and other surfaces, of any kind of construction, located outside the perimeter, exterior walls of the insured building.

- Other personal property, including aircraft, any self-propelled vehicle or machine and motor vehicles, trailers on wheels, and other recreational vehicles, whether affixed to a permanent foundation or on wheels; and watercraft, including their furnishings and equipment.

- Basements and personal property in basements.

- Property below ground, meaning a building and its contents, including machinery and equipment, which are part of the building, when more than 49 percent of the actual cash value of such buildings is below ground.

- A manufactured (that is, mobile) home located or placed within a FEMA-designated Special Flood Hazard Area that is not anchored to a permanent foundation to resist flotation, collapse, or lateral movement.

- Units that are primarily containers, rather than buildings (such as gas and liquid tanks, chemical or reactor container tanks or enclosures, brick kilns, and similar units) and their contents. (Silos and grain storage buildings, including their contents, can be insured even though they are of container-type construction.)

- A building and its contents ineligible for flood insurance under the Coastal Barrier Resources System established by the Coastal Barrier Resources Act.

Adjustment Procedures

The adjustment of flood losses involves numerous special procedures, most of which are dictated by NFIP requirements.

NFIP Authorization

All independent adjusters must have NFIP authorization to handle losses, or they will not be paid for their work. NFIP sets standards for adjusters in three categories: residential, commercial, and mobile homes. These standards are set forth in Exhibit 12-4. Applications for authorization must be sent to NFIP for approval.

Exhibit 12-4
NFIP Adjuster Qualifications

Residential—Adjusters who handle residential claims must:
(1) have three years of flood or general property adjusting experience;
(2) be able to write their own estimates up to $15,000;
(3) have spent the past three years actually adjusting claims (claims management work does not count).

Commercial—Adjusters who handle commercial claims must:
(1) have three years of flood or five years of general property adjusting experience;
(2) be able to write their own estimates up to $50,000;
(3) have spent the past three years actually adjusting claims.

Manufactured Homes (mobile homes)—Adjusters who handle manufactured home claims must:
(1) have three years of general property adjusting or familiarity with mobilehome claims;
(2) be able to write their own estimates up to $15,000;
(3) have spent the past three years actually adjusting claims.

Adjusters with WYO insurers must meet whatever criteria are set by the insurer employing the adjuster. The NFIP standards are generally followed, but the WYO insurer can modify them. In catastrophic situations, adjusters should check licensing requirements in the state or jurisdiction where the disaster occurred.

Wind Versus Water Damage

The NFIP's **Single Adjuster Program** was formed to assign a single property adjuster to handle combined wind and flood claims during catastrophes such as hurricanes. The participating wind insurers and the NFIP agree on qualified adjusters. In adjusting the wind and water damage claims, adjusters assess which portion of the total claim is to be paid under which policy.

FICO

If a catastrophe produces a large enough volume of claims to warrant the opening of a Flood Insurance Claims Office (FICO), FICO personnel assign all adjusters at the FICO site. FICO does not make claim assignments for WYO participants.

NFIP Adjusting Requirements

The NFIP also sets standards for how certain aspects of a claim are to be adjusted.

Depreciation

Depreciation is determined on an item-by-item basis. No lump sum depreciation is accepted. The actual cash value is determined in the policy as the replacement cost of the item of property at the time of loss, less depreciation.

Overhead and Profit

Overhead and profit are applied to the depreciated total and are reflected in the actual cash value of the loss. Overhead and profit should not be applied to carpeting, to the insured's own labor, or when the insured does its own repairs. An allowance can be made for an insured's time and expense in purchasing materials. Overhead and profit are not applied to service charges for plumbers, electricians, or appliance service calls.

Proofs of Loss

Proofs of loss are required on all advance payments and claim settlements. This requirement can be waived for losses under $7,500. Exhibit 12-5 is a sample of the required proof-of-loss form. The insured must sign the NFIP final report form if the proof of loss is waived.

Denials and Rejections

Only NFIP personnel can deny claims or reject proofs of loss, based on the adjuster's recommendations.

Exhibit 12-5

National Flood Insurance Program Proof of Loss

POLICY NO. FL_____

FEDERAL EMERGENCY MANAGEMENT AGENCY

NATIONAL FLOOD INSURANCE PROGRAM

O.M.B. NO. 3067-0021
Expires May 31, 1996

POLICY TERM

AGENT _____

PROOF OF LOSS

AMT OF BLDG COV AT TIME OF LOSS

AGENCY AT _____

(See reverse side for Privacy Act Statement and Paperwork Burden Disclosure Notice)

AMT OF CNTS COV AT TIME OF LOSS

TO THE NATIONAL FLOOD INSURANCE PROGRAM:

At time of loss, by the above indicated policy of insurance, you insured the interest of

_____

_____

against loss by flood to the property described according to the terms and conditions of said policy and of all forms, endorsements, transfers and assignments attached thereto.

TIME AND ORIGIN

A_____ loss occurred about the hour of _____ o'clock _____ M., on the _____ day of _____ 19____, the cause of the said loss was:_____

OCCUPANCY

The premises described, or containing the property described, was occupied at the time of the loss as follows, and for no other purpose whatever:_____

INTEREST

No other person or persons had any interest therein or incumbrance thereon, except:_____

CHANGES

Since the said policy was issued, there has been no change in the property described, except_____

1. FULL AMOUNT OF INSURANCE applicable to the property for which claim is presented is......................... $_____
2. ACTUAL CASH VALUE of building structures .... $_____
3. ADD ACTUAL CASH VALUE OF CONTENTS or personal property insured .... $_____
4. ACTUAL CASH VALUE OF ALL PROPERTY .... $_____
5. FULL COST OF REPAIR OR REPLACEMENT (Building and Contents) .... $_____
6. LESS APPLICABLE DEPRECIATION .... $_____
7. ACTUAL CASH VALUE LOSS is .... $_____
8. LESS DEDUCTIBLES .... $_____
9. NET AMOUNT CLAIMED under above numbered policy is .... $_____

The said loss did not originate by any act, design or procurement on the part of your insured, nothing has been done by or with the privity or consent of your insured to violate the conditions of the policy, or render it void; no articles are mentioned herein or in annexed schedules but such as were destroyed or damaged at the time of said loss no property saved has in any manner been concealed, and no attempt to deceive the said insurer as to the extent of said loss, has in any manner been made. Any other information that may be required will be furnished and considered a part of this proof.

Subrogation - To the extent of the payment made or advanced under this policy; the insured hereby assigns, transfers and sets over to the insurer all rights, claims or interest that he has against any person, firm or corporation liable for the loss or damage to the property for which payment is made or advanced. He also hereby authorizes the insurer to sue any such third party in his name.

The insured hereby warrants that no release has been given or will be given or settlement or compromise made or agreed upon with any third party who may be liable in damages to the insured with respect to the claim being made herein.

The furnishing of this blank or the preparation of proofs by a representative of the above insurer is not a waiver of any of its rights.

State of_____   _____

County of_____   _____

Insured

Subscribed and sworn to before me this _____ day of _____   , 19____

_____
Notary Public

FEMA Form 81-42, MAY 93   REPLACES EDITION OF APR. 90, WHICH IS OBSOLETE.   593-111B (5/93)   *U.S.GPO.1993-0-721-134/60138

Subrogation

Adjusters identify subrogation possibilities and report them in the preliminary report. Once the possibility of subrogation has been identified and reported to NFIP, the NFIP is responsible for further investigation and directing the possibility for subrogation.

Reports

The NFIP sets the reporting requirements for independent adjusters. WYO adjusters follow their own insurers' reporting procedures. However, all adjusters are required to complete the NFIP preliminary and final reports on all flood losses. Samples of these forms are shown in Exhibits 12-6 and 12-7. Each portion of these reports must be completed and submitted to the NFIP when the claim is settled. Packets of these forms can be obtained from the NFIP. WYO companies can reproduce the forms on their own letterhead. These forms provide not only the facts on the claim, but also the basis on which fees are paid.

Condominium Losses

Condominiums are a special form of property ownership that present several unique legal, coverage, and adjusting issues. A **condominium** is one of the units in a multiple-unit structure, each of which is separately owned. These units can be dwelling or business-type units. Each unit owner receives a deed of record independent of any other unit owner. A single unit often consists of nothing more than a cubicle, or "box of air," of one or more levels of space within the unfinished surfaces of walls, floors, or ceilings of the structure. Once a developer has sold a certain percentage of the units, it relinquishes authority to the condominium association.

Common Elements

A **condominium association** manages the condominium complex and is responsible for the **common elements**. The common elements, or areas, are jointly owned by all unit owners and include the land on which the building is located as well as other real property, consisting of foundations, roofs, main support walls, halls, stairways, entrances and exits, lobbies, yards, gardens, parking areas, power, light, gas, plumbing, heating and air conditioning systems, elevators, pumps, duct work, storage areas or basements, and pools, playgrounds, and any other recreation facilities on the grounds.

Exhibit 12-6
National Flood Insurance Program Preliminary Report

O.M.B. NO. 3067-0021
Expires May 31, 1996

FEDERAL EMERGENCY MANAGEMENT AGENCY

THE NFIP REQUIRES THAT A PRELIMINARY REPORT BE RECEIVED WITHIN 15 DAYS OF ASSIGNMENT,
AND AN INTERIM OR FINAL REPORT NOT LATER THAN EVERY 30 DAYS THEREAFTER.

NATIONAL FLOOD INSURANCE PROGRAM PRELIMINARY REPORT

(See reverse side for Privacy Act Statement and Paperwork Burden Disclosure Notice)

INSURED _____   POLICY NUMBER _____

PROPERTY ADDRESS _____   DATE OF LOSS _____

MAILING ADDRESS _____   CATASTROPHE NO. _____

INSURED TELEPHONE NUMBER: HOME _____ WORK _____   ADJ. FILE NO. _____

ADJUSTING COMPANY _____   TAX ID NO. _____

ADJUSTER ADDRESS _____   ADJ. PHONE NO. _____

DATE LOSS ASSIGNED _____ DATE INSURED CONTACTED _____ DATE LOSS INSPECTED _____

ENCLOSURES

☐ Building worksheets ( )   ☐ Photographs ( )   ☐ Proof of Loss   ☐ Other _____
☐ Contents worksheets ( )   ☐ Narrative (pp)   ☐ R/C Proof   ☐ Other _____

INSURANCE

Coverage verified from: ☐ NFIP   ☐ Agent's Daily   ☐ Insured's Policy   Program: ☐ Emergency ☐ Regular

Term _____ to _____   Edition: ☐ 79 ☐ 82 ☐ 83   Form: ☐ Dwelling ☐ General Property

	Coverage	Deductible	Reserve
RESERVES: Building	$ _____	$ _____	$ _____
Contents	$ _____	$ _____	$ _____

ADVANCE PAYMENT REQUESTED?   ☐ No   ☐ Yes: Building $ _____   Contents $ _____

If yes, Proof of Loss for amount of payment and supporting documentation must be submitted with this report.

RISK

Type of Building: ☐ Single Family   ☐ 2-4 Family   ☐ Condo Assn   ☐ Condo Unit   ☐ Other Residential   ☐ Non-residential
☐ Mobile Home: Make _____   Model _____   Serial No. _____

Occupancy: ☐ Owner   ☐ Tenant   ☐ State government owned   ☐ Unoccupied   Residency: ☐ Principal ☐ Seasonal

Title verified?   ☐ Yes   ☐ No   Source of verification: _____

Number of floors in building including basement: ☐ 1   ☐ 2   ☐ 3 or more   Is building a split level?   ☐ Yes   ☐ No

In case of multiple occupancy, indicate floor(s) occupied by insured: ☐ Basement   ☐ First   ☐ Second and/or above

Type of basement: ☐ None   ☐ Unfinished   ☐ Finished   Is basement floodproofed?   ☐ Yes   ☐ No

Building elevated?   ☐ No   ☐ Yes: Foundation area enclosure: ☐ None   ☐ Breakaway walls   ☐ Unfinished   ☐ Finished

Is risk under construction?   ☐ No   ☐ New building   ☐ Improvement in progress

Prior condition of
Building: ☐ Poor   ☐ Fair   ☐ Good   ☐ Very Good
Contents: ☐ Poor   ☐ Fair   ☐ Good   ☐ Very Good

Foundation structure:

Piles: ⑪ Concrete   ⑫ Wood   ⑬ Steel   Piers: ㉑ Reinf. concrete   ㉒ Reinf. block   ㉓ Unreinf. block   ㉔ Brick   ㉕ Other

㉚ Wood posts   Walls: ㊶ Reinf. concrete   ㊷ Block   ㊸ Reinf. concrete shear   ㊹ Treated plywood   ㊺ Brick   ㊻ Other

㊿ Concrete slab   ⑥⓪ Other _____

Exterior wall structure:
① Reinf. concrete   ④ Steel and glass
② Concrete block   ⑤ Brick or stone
③ Wood stud   ⑥ Other _____

Exterior wall surface treatment:
① Unfinished   ③ Stucco   ⑤ Metal sheathing/siding
② Stone/brick veneer   ④ Wood siding   ⑥ Vinyl sheathing/siding
⑦ Other _____

Contents are   ☐ household   ☐ other than household

Contents located in   ☐ basement   ☐ basement and first floor   ☐ first floor   ☐ first floor and above   ☐ second floor and above

Nearest body of water: _____   Distance from risk: _____

ORIGIN

Was there a general and temporary condition of flooding;   ☐ No: Explain fully under Remarks.   ☐ Yes: Indicate cause of loss —

Cause of Loss: ① Tidal water overflow   ② Stream, river, or lake overflow
③ Alluvial fan overflow   ④ Accumulation of rainfall or snowmelt

Flood Characteristics: ① Velocity flow   ② Low velocity flow or ponding
③ Wave action   ④ Mudflow   ⑤ Erosion

Was flood associated with failure of a dam, storm drain system, pump(s), other flood control measure, etc.?   ☐ Yes   ☐ No
Did other than natural cause contribute to flooding?   ☐ Yes   ☐ No

If "yes" to either question, complete "Cause of Loss and Subrogation Report"

Water Height or Wave Action:	Exterior	Interior
Main Building/Condo Assn.:	_____	_____
Appt. Building/Condo Unit:	_____	_____

Date/time water entered building _____
Date/time water receded from building _____
Length of time water remained in building _____

Date of Report _____   Adjuster's Signature _____   Adjuster's SSN _____

FEMA Form 81-57, MAY 93   REPLACES EDITION OF APR. 90, WHICH IS OBSOLETE.   593-101B (5/93)

Exhibit 12-7
National Flood Insurance Program Final Report

FEDERAL EMERGENCY MANAGEMENT AGENCY

O.M.B. NO. 3067-0021
Expires May 31, 1996

THE NFIP REQUIRES THAT A PRELIMINARY REPORT BE RECEIVED WITHIN <u>15</u> DAYS OF ASSIGNMENT, AND AN INTERIM OR FINAL REPORT NOT LATER THAN EVERY <u>30</u> DAYS THEREAFTER.

NATIONAL FLOOD INSURANCE PROGRAM FINAL REPORT

(See reverse side for Privacy Act Statement and Paperwork Burden Disclosure Notice)

INSURED _____   POLICY NUMBER _____

PROPERTY ADDRESS _____   DATE OF LOSS _____

ADJUSTING COMPANY _____   ADJ. FILE NO. _____

PREMISES HISTORY

Date risk was originally constructed: _____   Insured at premises since: _____

Date of Alteration	Brief Description of Alteration	Market Value	Cost of Alteration	Type of Alteration	*Substantial improvement?
_____	_____	_____	_____	☐ Repair ☐ Recon ☐ Improve	☐ Yes ☐ No
_____	_____	_____	_____	☐ Repair ☐ Recon ☐ Improve	☐ Yes ☐ No
_____	_____	_____	_____	☐ Repair ☐ Recon ☐ Improve	☐ Yes ☐ No

*Defined as any repair, reconstruction, or improvement the cost of which equals or exceeds 50% of the market value of the structure before the damage occurred or the reconstruction or improvement was begun.

Prior losses (approximate dates and amounts of loss):

_____ Repairs completed? ☐ Yes ☐ No   Insured? ☐ Yes ☐ No   ☐ Insured but no claim made
_____ Repairs completed? ☐ Yes ☐ No   Insured? ☐ Yes ☐ No   ☐ Insured but no claim made
_____ Repairs completed? ☐ Yes ☐ No   Insured? ☐ Yes ☐ No   ☐ Insured but no claim made

(Continue under Remarks if additional space is needed for alterations or prior losses.)

INTERESTS

Mortgagee(s): _____

Loss Payee(s): _____

Other Insurance: _____   ☐ Yes ☐ No

(Company)   (Type)   (Policy Number)   (Coverage bldg/cts)   (Covers flood?)

CLAIM SUMMARY

Duration building will not be habitable: ☐1 0-2 days   ☐2 3-7 days   ☐3 2-4 weeks   ☐4 1-2 months   ☐5 more than 2 months

CLAIM RECAPITULATION (See worksheets for details)

	Building		Contents		Totals
	Main*/Assn	Appurtenant/Unit	Main*/Assn	Appurtenant/Unit	
Property Value (ACV)					
Covered Damage (ACV)					
Removal/Protection					
Total Loss (ACV)					
Less Salvage					
Less Deductible					
Excess Over Limit					
Claim Payable (ACV)					
Damage From Other Cause					
Identify Cause:					

Main building RCV: $ _____   Insured qualifies for R/C coverage? ☐ Yes ☐ No ☐ Not Applicable

If yes, R/C claim: $ _____   Total building claim: $ _____

*Includes mobile home.

EXCLUDED DAMAGES

	Approximate value of property excluded:	Approximate damage to property excluded:

Excluded building damages:
☐1 Less than 1,000   ☐4 5,000 - 10,000   ☐1 Less than 1,000   ☐4 5,000 - 10,000
☐2 1,000 - 2,000   ☐5 10,000 - 20,000   ☐2 1,000 - 2,000   ☐5 10,000 - 20,000
☐3 2,000 - 5,000   ☐6 More than 20,000   ☐3 2,000 - 5,000   ☐6 More than 20,000

Excluded contents damages:
☐1 Less than 1,000   ☐4 5,000 - 10,000   ☐1 Less than 1,000   ☐4 5,000 - 10,000
☐2 1,000 - 2,000   ☐5 10,000 - 20,000   ☐2 1,000 - 2,000   ☐5 10,000 - 20,000
☐3 2,000 - 5,000   ☐6 More than 20,000   ☐3 2,000 - 5,000   ☐6 More than 20,000

ENCLOSURES

☐ Building worksheets ( )   ☐ Photographs ( )   ☐ Proof of Loss   ☐ Other _____
☐ Contents worksheets ( )   ☐ Narrative (pp)   ☐ R/C Proof   ☐ Other _____

CERTIFICATION

The above statements are true and correct to the best of my knowledge. I understand that any false statements may be punishable by fine or imprisonment under 18 U.S. Code Sec. 1001.

County of _____   Insured _____

State of _____   Insured _____

Signed this _____ day of _____ , 19 ____   Witness _____

Date of Report _____   Adjuster's Signature _____   Adjuster's SSN _____

FEMA Form 81-58, MAY 93   REPLACES EDITION OF APR. 90, WHICH IS OBSOLETE.   593-102B (5/93)

State Law

Because of the complexity of the relationship between unit owners and the association, condominiums are created and defined by legislation in most jurisdictions. These statutes also address insurance requirements. Most states require the association to provide insurance to cover loss or damage to the common elements. A unit owner must insure the contents and his or her interest in his or her unit. Some statutes state that improvements and betterments are to be covered under the unit owner's insurance because the improvements increase the value of the unit itself. Other statutes require improvements and betterments, whether to the individual units or to common areas, to be insured under the association's policy.

Master Deed and Bylaws

To determine who is responsible for specific property, adjusters must check not only the statutes of the state, but also the **master deed** and the unit deeds of the condominium. The master deed might also be called the "declarations of the condominium association" or the "condominium association agreement." The developer or builder of the condominium usually draws up the deed or declarations.

Either the master deed or separate bylaws describe the relationship between the unit owners, the duties of the association, maintenance fees, how assessments are to be made, and insurance requirements. The deed or bylaws also describe the transference of properties, how the association is to be governed, and requirements for any modifications or amendments to the bylaws.

Nature of the Unit Owner's Interest

After reviewing a copy of the master deed and bylaws, adjusters can determine insurable interests and which policy is to provide coverage for damaged items. Condominium deeds set out the insurable interests in two possible ways: the barewalls concept and the all-encompassing concept.

The Barewalls Concept

Under the **barewalls concept**, a unit owner's property consists only of what is within the bare walls, including paint, wallpaper, carpet or flooring, appliances, fixtures (electrical or plumbing), and interior walls. An adjustment of a claim under an association's policy would not consider these items. Conversely, the unit owner's policy would not provide coverage for damage to drywall that forms an exterior, or load-bearing, wall, floor decking, joists, studs, rafters, foundations, or roofing in the event of a loss.

For a loss adjustment based on the barewalls concept, the adjuster for the association and the adjuster for the unit owner must decide which policy provides coverage for which items. This issue should be decided before repairs are made so that no misunderstanding occurs during the final settlement or payment of the claim. When the structural damage is serious, a unit owner's insurer often allows the condominium association insurer to cover all repairs and reimburses it for the portion of the damages covered by the unit owner's policy.

The All-Encompassing Concept

Under the **all-encompassing concept**, the condominium association owns and is responsible for all exterior and interior items within the unit at the time of its original purchase by the unit owner. When the unit is sold with appliances, flooring, and fixtures already installed, the association is responsible for insuring these items. The purchase contract describes these items.

For a loss adjustment based on the all-encompassing concept, the condominium association insurer repairs or replaces all original installations. The unit owner's insurer covers damage to improvements and betterments and any personal property involved in the loss and installed by the unit owner.

Coverage Forms

The Insurance Services Office (ISO) provides a separate, simplified commercial property insurance program for condominium associations. Unit owners are protected by a special type of homeowners form or a commercial unit owners form.

Condominium Association Coverage Form

The condominium association coverage form is used in conjunction with the common declarations, common and commercial property conditions, causes of loss forms, and other assorted forms. The condominium association form is similar to the building and personal property form and contains the same coverages, additional coverages, extension of coverage, optional coverages, and property not covered. The condominium association coverage form provides coverage for the building. It also covers certain types of property within a unit, such as fixtures, improvements, and appliances, if the condominium master deed or bylaws require the association to insure it. This coverage applies whether or not the unit owner owns these items. Under the unit owner's insurance provision, the insurance for the association is primary. It is not contributory with any insurance carried by the unit owner covering the same property.

Business personal property is covered if it is owned by the association or indivisibly by all unit owners. It is not covered if owned solely by a unit owner. Property under this coverage could include clubroom furnishings, deck or lawn chairs, lobby or hall decorations, and recreational equipment. The coverage does not address tenant improvements and betterments because it provides coverage for building owners only. The condominium association form, like the building and personal property form, provides coverage for personal property of others if shown in the declarations. This coverage includes property of unit owners.

Associations commonly appoint a trustee to act on behalf of the unit owners. The condominium association coverage form has added a provision under loss payment to state that the insurer may adjust the loss with the association but pay the insurance to a trustee. Any payment made to the trustee satisfies the claims of all unit owners.

The association is made up of individual unit owners. Accordingly, the right of subrogation by the insurer against individual unit owners has been waived in the **waiver of rights of recovery provision.**

Unit Owner's Coverage Form

Two types of unit owner's coverage are available—one for commercial unit owners and one for residential unit owners.

Commercial Unit Owners

The popularity of ownership, as opposed to leasing, has given rise to the growth of commercial or business condominiums. The condominium commercial unit owner's coverage complements the association policy and has many of the same provisions of the other commercial property coverages. It includes no building coverage because the building is insured under the association policy.

It does include coverage for building fixtures, improvements, and alterations owned by the unit owner and not insured by the association. Any settlement on these items is subject to the coinsurance provision of the policy. If the same property is covered under both the unit owner's policy and the association policy, the unit owner's coverage is excess over the association coverage. The condominium commercial unit owner's coverage has two optional coverages: loss assessment coverage and miscellaneous real property coverage.

A loss assessment is a charge by the condominium association against the unit owners. The association has the right to make such charges, under certain circumstances, as described in the master deed or bylaws. Loss assessment coverage is limited to liability for assessments resulting from direct physical loss or damage by a covered peril to common property in which all unit owners have an interest. The unit owner purchases loss assessment coverage for protection in case the association's insurance is not sufficient to cover a loss. Loss assessment coverage can be purchased for multiples of $1,000, with a $250 deductible. If the assessment is made to cover a large deductible in the association's coverage, the limit of liability is $1,000 regardless of the amount purchased by the unit owner.

Miscellaneous real property coverage is provided under a separate limit of insurance. This class of real property includes property owned by the condominium unit insured only or required by the association agreement to be insured by the unit owner. An example is a storage structure located in the common areas and used solely by a unit owner.

Residential Unit Owners

Residential unit owners' coverage is provided by a homeowner's unit owner's form (HO-6). The policy insures against all broad form perils, including fire; lightning; windstorm; hail; explosion; riot; civil commotion; aircraft; vehicles; smoke; vandalism; malicious mischief; theft; breakage of glass; falling objects; weight of ice, snow, or sleet; accidental discharge of water or steam; tearing, cracking, burning, or bulging of a steam or hot water system; freezing; artificially generated electrical current; and volcanic eruption.

Coverage against these named perils is important for the insured's personal property, but it also applies to building improvements and betterments and other building items owned by the unit owner and not insured under the association agreement. It also applies to other structures owned solely by the unit owner (other than the residence premises) and located on the residence premises. In the event of a loss, insurance provided under this form is excess to the association's policy covering the same property.

Loss assessment coverage is an additional coverage under the unit owner's form. When an assessment is made as a result of direct loss to property owned collectively by all unit members and caused by a peril insured against, the insurer will pay up to $1,000.

Builders' Risk Losses

Buildings under construction have special loss exposures. **Builders' risk coverage** responds to these exposures. This coverage is different from standard commercial property insurance. Loss adjustment of builders' risk claims can be accomplished in a number of ways.

Builders' Risk Exposures

When a contractor or builder is prepared to begin construction of a new building, it faces the difficult situation of insuring a structure whose value is constantly changing. Initially, machinery, equipment, tools and supplies, building materials, scaffolding, fencing, temporary buildings, and sheds might be on the site. If the contractor were to secure ordinary commercial property insurance to cover the completed value of the structure, it would pay excessive premiums while the building was under construction. Because of increased costs, the contractor might also be underinsured as the structure is nearing completion.

The contractor might be required to protect not only its own interests in the building, but also the interests of the owners, the mortgagees, and the subcontractors that work on the structure. The contractor might even be required to protect the interests of its suppliers. The contractor's obligation to protect these other interests comes from the construction contracts. Although the contractor might not bear each of the preceding obligations, rarely is a contractor only obligated to protect its own interest.

The building also faces special hazards while the building is under construction. Building materials are difficult to protect while on a construction site. They are subject to theft and severe damage by windstorms and by fire. While under construction, the building itself is also exposed to these types of losses and to vandalism or collapse. Protecting the building from loss is difficult because it lacks safeguards such as sprinkler systems or even adequate access to water.

Coverage Forms

The builder's risk form was devised to address the special problem of changing values and the unique exposures to loss of a building under construction. The policy is written for one year but normally terminates when the building has been completed or occupied. A builder's risk policy can be written for basic, broad, or "all-risks" coverage.

Types of Builders' Risk Policies

The policy can be written under a commercial property form as a manuscript policy or as an inland marine form.

Commercial Property

A common builders' risk form is attached to a commercial property policy and becomes subject to the common declarations and conditions, as well as the commercial property declarations and conditions and basic, broad, or special causes of loss forms that make up the basic policy.

Commercial property builder's risk forms do not cover collapse during construction unless it is added back by an endorsement that covers collapse caused by faulty design, plans, or workmanship. Nor do they cover theft of building materials not attached to a building under any cause of loss form. Even the cause of loss special form eliminates theft coverage for building materials and supplies and any coverage for machinery, tools, and equipment owned by, or in the care, custody, or control of the insured.

Manuscript Forms

The policy can be written in a manuscript form to cover uncertain or uncommon exposures. The builder might be building over many years an unusually large complex and might require more coverage than provided by the standard commercial form.

Inland Marine Policies

Builders' risk coverage is also provided as an inland marine coverage under a builders' risk policy or an installation floater, usually on an "all-risks" basis. Inland marine builders' risk policies usually have broader coverage than commercial property policies because they can cover property in transit and at other job sites, they cover collapse and theft, and they can be endorsed to cover earthquake and flood. Most important, inland marine policies cover increased **"soft" costs**, such as interest, real-estate tax, advertising, architects' and engineers' fees, legal and accounting fees, and insurance. Adjusters need professional assistance to identify and evaluate increased "soft" costs.

Property Covered

Builders' risk provides coverage for buildings or structures in the course of construction on the described premises, including foundations and materials used for construction. It extends coverage to fixtures, machinery, and equipment that service the building. Inland marine forms cover building materials and supplies owned by the insured, building materials and supplies of others in the insured's care, custody, or control, and temporary structures including scaffolding, cribbing, and construction forms.

As in most coverage forms, there is no coverage for land, water, or certain outdoor property such as lawns, trees, shrubs, plants, radio or television antennas or towers, and detached signs. Builders' risk coverage forms might also exclude the preexisting part of a building to which alterations, additions, repairs, or renovations are being made.

Handling Changing Values

The builders' risk policy is written on a completed value approach or a reporting form. Insurance is usually written for the completed value of the building or structure. The premium charged is reduced because the value of the policy exceeds the value at risk to the insurer until the building is completed.

The completed value form includes a condition called "need for adequate insurance" that is effectively a 100 percent coinsurance clause. The policy limit must equal the expected completed value, or a penalty is imposed.

The reporting form requires the insured to make monthly reports of value. The initial premium is generally determined by computing the actual cash value of the property brought onto the insured premises at the start of construction. As the monthly reports are filed, the limits of liability are increased accordingly, and additional premium is computed. If the reports are late or undervalued, the insured can face severe penalties in the event of a covered loss. Because the coinsurance clause in a full reporting form is 100 percent, failure to report will limit the insurer's liability to the actual cash value at the inception of the policy. Failure to report on time can limit the insurer's liability to the last reported value.

Subrogation

Because of the various interests covered by the policy and the relationship between these parties, adjusters should check both the policy and the contracts between the parties to determine whether subrogation is possible. Determining who is an insured, the extent of the interest insured, and whether subrogation has been waived in writing by agreement before an actual loss is important.

The older commercial property builders' risk form required an insured to obtain the insurer's written permission to waive any rights to recovery. This provision read as follows:

> You may not waive your rights to recover damages from an architect, engineer or building trades contractor or subcontractor with respect to the described premises except as agreed to in writing by us. This provision supersedes any provisions to the contrary in the TRANSFER OF RIGHTS OF RECOVERY AGAINST OTHERS TO US Commercial Property Condition.

The inland marine form limits this provision to architects or engineers, thus permitting waiver of subrogation against other contractors or subcontractors. These provisions are especially important because many form contracts in the construction business, such as those provided by the American Institute of Architects, require waiver of actions by the parties. Such waivers might threaten a contractor's insurance coverage unless the insurer approves them.

Termination of Coverage

The coverage of the builders' risk form ends when *any* one of the five following conditions is met:

1. The policy is canceled, the policy expires, or ninety days have passed since the completion of the project.

2. The owner or purchaser accepts the property. This acceptance, of course, should mean that other specific insurance on the completed building is in place.

3. The insured no longer has any interest in the property; therefore, the insured cannot suffer a loss if the property is damaged.

4. The construction is abandoned, and the insured has no intention of completing the building and has given up his or her right or interest in the building.

5. Sixty days after the building has been wholly or partially occupied or put to its intended use, or leased to others.

Loss Adjustment

The investigation and adjustment of builder's risk losses require a careful examination of who is insured, what his or her interest is, what is insured, and how the coverage is written. Adjusters should check reporting forms for accuracy and timeliness and must determine values properly. The settlement of these losses follows the same course as any other structural loss except that the insured's status as a contractor often expands the adjustment options. Since the insured is often the contractor that built the building, losses can be adjusted in various ways.

As with any loss to a structure, adjusters can write an estimate of damages showing the actual scope of repairs to be made. Alternatively, insureds can submit a detailed claim based on actual time and materials costs necessary to make the repairs. Finally, the loss can be calculated by using the insured's books and records to assess the costs or value of the damaged property before the loss. Even though the policy might be written at actual cash value, this value would ordinarily be the same as the replacement cost on newly constructed property.

Differences in Conditions Policies

Differences in conditions (DIC) insurance is written to supplement commercial property policies. The DIC reduces the chance of an uninsured loss by covering additional perils and by filling gaps in the coverage provided by the ordinary property forms. DIC policies are generally written on an "all-risks" basis, but most policies exclude damage caused by fire and the perils of the extended coverages, as well as certain other perils.

The intent of "all-risks" coverage is to address those exposures not covered in the basic property forms. For example, earthquake and flood are excluded in the basic property forms but are the most important exposures covered by the DIC policy. They are covered either because of the "all-risks" nature of the coverage or because flood and earthquake are named as perils under a non-standard form or manuscript form. DIC coverage is primarily used by risk managers as flood and earthquake coverage.

Standardized DIC forms do not meet the needs of most insureds and insurers. As a result, insurers provide their own nonstandard DIC forms. If the non-standard forms provided by insurers do not meet the requirements of a large insured corporation, the corporation's risk manager might produce a policy or form to cover that business' unique exposures. These forms are called "manu-script policies." Adjusters handling DIC losses cannot assume they understand the coverage until they carefully read the policy in question.

Exclusions

Although they provide very broad coverage, DIC policies include important exclusions of certain types of property and certain perils.

Because of the diversity of coverage and the use of nonstandard or manuscript forms, adjusters must examine each DIC policy for all clauses and conditions. Some policies cover all property, but others only cover buildings. Some policies are written on an actual cash value basis, but others are written for replacement cost. Even though DIC forms provide "all-risks" coverage, they contain exclusions for certain property similar to those in the BPP. DIC policies generally exclude currency, money, deeds, evidences of debt, notes, securities, jewelry, gems or precious stones, furs, fine arts, crops, watercraft, aircraft, motorized vehicles licensed for highway use, and animals and birds.

Some DIC policies contain the exclusions found in most "all-risks" forms. These exclusions include, but might not be limited to, wear and tear, deterio-ration, dampness of atmosphere, smog, shrinkage, evaporation, and wet and dry rot. Employee infidelity is also not covered because this coverage is generally available under a fidelity form. Mysterious disappearance and unex-plained loss or shortage are also excluded.

Summary

Specialty losses differ from typical property loss in that they are rare or require special knowledge or expertise in the adjustment process.

Inland marine insurance covers a wide variety of exposures. Losses can arise in numerous circumstances, but especially to property in transit, bailed property, and contractor's equipment. Adjusters must recognize that inland marine coverage is usually specialized and "all-risks." Losses often involve two or more parties. Adjusters must understand the business relationships and contracts among these parties.

Flood is a peril that the private insurance market does not cover. The federal government has filled the need for coverage with the National Flood Insurance Program. The NFIP issues its own policies and has its own standards for loss adjusting. Through the Write Your Own Program, many adjusters have the opportunity to handle flood losses.

Condominium losses almost always involve both the condominium association and the unit owners. Adjusters must carefully review the deeds, bylaws, and respective insurance policies to determine liability and coverage for any specific damage.

In adjusting builders' risk losses, adjusters must study the construction contracts and insurance policies to determine liability and coverage for a loss. Several parties are likely to have an interest in a given item of damaged property and in the applicable insurance coverage. In builders' risk policies, because the insured is usually a builder, several additional options might be available for loss settlement.

Differences in conditions policies are designed to fill in coverage gaps left by other primary insurance to handle perils such as earthquake or flood. Although the coverage is very broad, certain perils and types of property are excluded.

Chapter 13

Specialty Losses, Continued

Like Chapter 12, this chapter examines less common property loss adjustment situations. It addresses crime losses, boiler and machinery coverage, computer losses, and contamination claims.

Crime Losses

Crime losses are among the most challenging an adjuster can face. An adjuster must verify coverage thoroughly and must understand the coverage applicable to a given loss. Crime coverage varies considerably from personal lines to commercial lines and from one commercial insured to another. Investigation of crime losses is difficult and sensitive. In cases of actual crime, the perpetrator would have tried to prevent discovery. In other cases, a policyholder might have staged a loss, or an insider might be involved.

Common law and modern criminal statutes define various crimes. **Theft** is the broadest category of illegally taking property with the intent to deprive the owner of it. **Burglary** is entry into a building with the intent to commit a crime, usually theft. **Robbery** is the act of taking property from a person, or taking it in the presence of that person, by threatening the person with violence. Burglary and robbery are forms of theft. Insurance policy definitions might not be identical to common law or crime statute definitions. For example, insurance policies usually define burglary as having "marks of forcible entry or exit," a characteristic that might be absent from crime codes.

Thefts of property often occur in office, residential, retail, or warehouse-type occupancies where a quick, secretive act can go unnoticed. Personal property often disappears under a coat, in a shopping bag, or in the toolbox of an employee. Property can be easily disposed of in a pawn shop or kept for the use of the thief.

Burglaries account for the largest dollar loss amounts among all thefts. The secrecy with which burglary is accomplished affords a perpetrator ample time to carry off large quantities of merchandise without detection. Notwithstanding burglar alarms, watchdogs, security guards, and other security measures, burglaries are common events and are easier for criminals to commit than robbery.

Robberies often occur in establishments that hold cash and have only one or two attendants, such as convenience stores, dry cleaners, and gas stations. Couriers for banks or high-volume retail stores are particularly susceptible to attack. Trucking companies are likely targets for robbery or theft of merchandise, because the driver is usually alone. Criminals target stock high in value and easily disposed of, such as liquor, cigarettes, and appliances.

Crime Coverages

Insurance coverage evolved as exposures to perils changed and grew. As crime became more prevalent, insurers saw an opportunity to offer marketable coverage at a price that would cover expected losses. Insurers first acted on this opportunity in the commercial lines. Under the commercial robbery and burglary coverages, they insured businesses against loss from outsiders, and under fidelity bonding coverages, they insured against losses from within by employees.

In the early twentieth century, the first ventures into personal lines theft and robbery coverage involved marine coverages, specifically under the personal property floater policy and the personal articles floater forms. These coverages were very broad and included protection for robbery, burglary, and theft. Personal theft coverage became more available in the late 1940s. Insurers saw a market for theft and robbery coverage for the average homeowner, and a policy was developed. Its price was low, and it sold well because no such coverage had been provided with the fire and extended coverage forms then in use. The only coverage previously available for theft of personal goods was through the relatively expensive marine coverages noted above.

In the early 1950s, the insurance regulatory climate relaxed, insurers were authorized to expand their writings, and the first homeowners policy was introduced. That policy included five coverages that had been sold separately, one of which was personal theft coverage. Sold as part of the homeowners package policy, personal theft coverage was not optional. Few losses were expected, and little or no premium was allocated to the coverage. Underwriters referred to this crime coverage as "an accommodation coverage." It could be broadened by endorsement or schedule, but it could not be eliminated. Very few homeowners today would feel secure without some protection against crime. Since the advent of the homeowners package policy, property values have risen many times, and the number of losses has doubled and redoubled.

Along with a resulting increase of personal crime coverage, the commercial lines coverage has been broadened and made more accessible. All commercial package policies include crime coverage directly or make it available by endorsement. Coverages available for commercial lines can be loosely grouped into two classes: (1) coverage against crime from outside and (2) coverage against crime from within. Crime from outside is usually a burglary, a theft, a fraud, or a robbery. Crime from within is often subtle and even petty, but it can grow to major proportions if it goes undetected for a long time. Most theft policies exclude coverage for loss committed by an employee. That risk is underwritten with fidelity bonds.

Personal Lines

Crime coverage is a standard part of all homeowners policies and is essential to a well-constructed personal insurance package. One need only read a newspaper to understand why most homeowners consider such coverage necessary.

Crime against a private citizen can take many forms and can cause loss to both personal and real property. When copper was extremely expensive, many homes were stripped of copper gutters and downspouts, which were then sold for scrap. Stained glass windows are also tempting targets. Even woodwork, trim, or plumbing fixtures can be targets for thieves. Building materials awaiting installation are favorite and easy targets.

Standard homeowners policies cover the real and personal property of an insured against theft losses, but the policies limit classes of property that have an extremely high loss potential, such as firearms, gems, gold, jewelry, furs, and other expensive articles. (Chapter 3 discussed the HO-3's special limits of liability in detail.) However, these articles can be scheduled on an endorsement to the policy for an agreed value and for an additional premium. When these articles are listed on the policy, they are said to be **scheduled articles**. They are covered against a broader range of perils and for a wider geographical scope.

Crime coverage limited to the home would not apply to the insured's entire exposure. At times, all insureds leave their residence and travel, often with substantial valuables on them or in their baggage. For many reasons, the exposure to loss increases substantially when the owner leaves home. Articles are lost or misplaced and believed to have been stolen. Luggage is lost and believed stolen. Articles are left unattended. Travelers often innocently stray into high-risk areas. Insurers recognize this off-premises exposure and provide coverage for the insured's protection. In most policies, coverage extends to losses to personal property "anywhere in the world." Coverage is for the named insured and other members of the household.

Theft of personal property at other locations owned by, rented to, or occupied by an insured is covered only while the insured is temporarily living there. Thus, theft from a summer home while an insured is living there would be covered. The status of a student insured is slightly different. The student only needs to establish that he or she was at the temporary residence where theft occurred within forty-five days before the theft. The student's property is thus protected over long holiday periods, but not for a full summer. Theft coverage away from the residence premises does not apply to watercraft, their furnishings or equipment, outboard motors, or trailers or campers.

Homeowners policies usually have an Additional Coverage for losses caused by unauthorized use of a credit card, check forgery, or loss by receipt of counterfeit money. No deductible applies to any loss under this coverage. This coverage does not apply to losses arising out of business use or out of an insured's dishonesty. In the Additional Coverage, the insurer also agrees to settle or defend actions against an insured arising out of fraudulent fund transfer or credit card use. The insurer bears the cost of such a defense, which is not deducted from the available loss coverage. Defense costs are in addition to the policy coverage limit.

The BPP

Unlike the homeowners policy, which is a package, the commercial lines of coverage are offered separately. Insureds choose the coverages they want. Exposures vary so widely by business that a package approach would not be an efficient way of meeting business insurance needs. A policy is built by selecting various forms that meet a customer's needs.

Nevertheless, the building and personal property coverage form (BPP) provides certain limited crime coverages. They are so limited or restricted that a business with any significant crime exposure must consider the ISO crime program, explained below. Particularly important to the insured in purchasing crime coverage, however, is the exclusion of "accounts, currency, deeds, evidences of debt, money, notes and securities" from any coverage by any causes of loss form.

The causes of loss—basic form or broad form include crime coverage only for "vandalism" and looting accompanying a riot. Breakage of glass by vandals when the glass is part of a building is excluded, but damage to other property resulting from broken glass is covered. This is the extent of the crime coverage provided under the basic and broad forms.

The causes of loss—special form is written to cover all losses that it does not specifically exclude or limit. This form includes crime coverage except to the extent that it is excluded or limited. This form specifically excludes losses caused by a dishonest act of the policyholder or employees or by voluntary parting of property caused by a fraudulent scheme, trick, device, or false pretense. The following limitations also apply to theft claims:

> We will not pay for loss of or damage to:. . .

> d. Building materials and supplies not attached as part of the building or structure. . .caused by or resulting from theft. . . .

> e. Property that is missing, where the only evidence of the loss or damage is a shortage disclosed on taking inventory, or other instances where there is no physical evidence. . . .

The following sublimits apply to covered theft losses:

> For loss or damage by theft, the following types of property are covered only up to the limits shown:

> a. $2,500 for furs, fur garments and garments trimmed with fur.

> b. $2,500 for jewelry, watches, watch movements, jewels, pearls, precious and semiprecious stones, bullion, gold, silver, platinum, and other precious alloys or metals. This limit does not apply to jewelry and watches worth $100 or less per item.

> c. $2,500 for patterns, dies, molds, and forms.

> d. $250 for stamps, tickets, and letters of credit.

Coverage is extended to owned property in transit on the insured's owned or leased vehicle to a limit of $1,000, but coverage for theft is restricted to "theft of an entire bale, case or package by forced entry into a securely locked body or compartment of the vehicle. There must be visible marks of the forced entry."

The ISO Crime Program

The crime coverage provided by the BPP and the standard cause of loss forms are inadequate for many businesses. To meet the need for expanded crime coverage, ISO has developed a commercial crime coverage program. The following is the ISO menu of coverages:

- Form A—Employee Dishonesty
- Form B—Forgery or Alteration
- Form C—Theft, Disappearance, and Destruction
- Form D—Robbery and Safe Burglary (property other than money and securities)
- Form E—Premises Burglary
- Form F—Computer Fraud
- Form G—Extortion
- Form H—Premises Theft and Robbery Outside the Premises
- Form I—Lessees of Safe Deposit Boxes
- Form J—Securities Deposited with Others
- Form K—Liability for Guests' Property—Safe Deposit Box
- Form L—Liability for Guests' Property—Premises
- Form M—Safe Depository Liability
- Form N—Safe Depository Direct Loss
- Form O—Public Employee Dishonesty (per loss)
- Form P—Public Employee Dishonesty (per employee)
- Form Q—Robbery and Safe Burglary (money and securities)

Exhibit 13-1 summarizes these forms. The most significant forms, A, C, D, Q, E, and H, are further explained later.

One or more of these forms can be used to create a monoline coverage policy. The forms can also be included as a coverage part on a multiline policy. Combining these forms into a cohesive and appropriate unit is the responsibility of an agent or underwriter and goes beyond the scope of this discussion. However, adjusters should be aware of the variety of coverages represented by these coverage parts.

The commercial crime program has so many endorsements that they cannot be extensively discussed in this text. The various crime forms often include endorsements enabling the underwriter to meet the insured's needs without requiring coverage that is not useful to that customer. Endorsements can add coverage to or delete coverage from the form to which they are attached. An adjuster must never assume that because he or she recently encountered a similar policy, the policy in force on a new loss is the same. A careful examination of the policy as written should guide the adjustment. Failure to detect and

Exhibit 13-1
ISO Crime Program

Coverage Form	Type of Property	Cause of Loss	Place
A—Employee Dishonesty	Any	Employee Dishonesty—either on a blanket or scheduled basis	U.S. and Canada
B—Forgery or Alteration	Checks and similar instruments drawn on the insured	Forgery or alteration	Worldwide
C—Theft, Disappearance, and Destruction	Money and securities	Theft, disappearance, or destruction	Inside the premises or outside while in the care of a messenger
D—Robbery and Safe Burglary	Any property other than money or securities	Robbery or safe burglary (actual or attempted)	Inside (robbery or burglary) or outside in the custody of a messenger (robbery)
E—Premises Burglary	Any property other than money or securities	Actual or attempted burglary—robbery of a watchperson	Inside the premises
F—Computer Fraud	Any	Theft by use of any computer	U.S. and Canada
G—Extortion	Any	Threat of bodily harm to a captive	U.S. and Canada
H—Premises Theft and Robbery Outside Premises	Any property other than money or securities	Actual or attempted theft—actual or attempted robbery	Inside (theft) or outside in the custody of a messenger (robbery)
I—Lessees of Safe-Deposit Boxes	Securities or property other than money or securities	Theft, disappearance, or destruction of securities— Burglary or robbery of other property	Inside depository premises

Exhibit 13-1
ISO Crime Program, Continued

Coverage Form	Type of Property	Cause of Loss	Place
J—Securities Deposited With Others	Securities	Theft, disappearance, or destruction	Custodian or depository premises
K—Liability for Guests' Property— Safe-Deposit Box	Property belonging to the insured's guests	Any legal liability for covered property	Safe-deposit box inside the premises
L—Liability for Guests' Property— Premises	Property belonging to the insured's guests, not excluded	Any legal liability for covered property	Inside the premises, or in insured's possession
M—Safe Depository Liability	Customer's property on deposit	Any legal liability for covered property	Inside the premises
N—Safe Depository Direct Loss	Customer's property on deposit, other than money or securities	Robbery, burglary, destruction, or damage	Inside the depository premises
O—Public Employee Dishonesty	Any (pe-loss limit of coverage)	Employee dishonesty	U.S. and Canada
P—Public Employee Dishonesty	Any (per-employee limit of coverage)	Employee dishonesty	U.S. and Canada
Q—Robbery and Safe Burglary	Money and securities	Robbery or safe burglary (actual or attempted)	Inside (robbery or safe burglary) or outside in the custody of a messenger (robbery)

consider any narrowing or broadening of coverage produces an adjusted claim that is inequitable to the insured or the insurer.

Crime General Provisions Form

As in all multicoverage part policies, a policy for crime coverage is built on a foundation form. The **crime general provisions form** contains a section of general exclusions followed by a section of general conditions for the ISO crime program. The general conditions section deals with such items as discovery period for loss, insureds' duties after loss, valuation for settlement, and distribution of recoveries.

The most significant exclusions are those for indirect loss (which includes loss of profit or business income), legal expense, government action, and acts committed by the policyholder or a partner. Acts committed by employees are specifically excluded in all the individual forms, except those designed for employee losses (Form A, Form O, and Form P).

The crime policies are essentially occurrence policies. The general provisions form includes the following statement: "We will pay only for loss that you sustain through acts committed or events occurring during the Policy Period." However, many of the losses covered by the crime coverages are neither readily discoverable nor reported until years after coverage has expired. The general provisions limit the duration of coverage under an existing policy as follows: "We will pay only for covered loss discovered no later than one year from the end of the policy period." The general provisions also extend coverage to losses that an earlier policy would have covered if the losses had been discovered in time. This extended coverage applies only if the current policy became effective upon termination of the previous policy and would have also covered the loss had it occurred while the current policy was in effect.

The insured's duties in the event of loss are standard provisions and are applicable upon discovery of a loss or "a situation that may result in loss. . . ." Thus, the insured should inform the insurer when anything suspicious arises to avoid the risk of failing to comply with the requirement of prompt notice. Apart from the complying with Crime General Provisions, within almost every specific form, the insured should notify police of any loss.

For purposes of valuation for settlement, money is valued at face value. Losses of foreign currency can be paid in that currency or in U.S. dollars. Securities are valued at their market value on the day the loss is discovered, but they can also be replaced in kind. Other property is valued at no more than its actual cash value, the cost to repair, or the cost to replace.

After a loss is settled, property might be recovered. The Crime General Provisions are clear about the order in which recovered property is distributed:

1. Any expenses of recovery
2. To the insured for any loss in excess of the policy limits plus the deductible
3. To the insurer to the extent of the loss settlement
4. To the insured for the deductible

Coverage Form A—Employee Dishonesty

This coverage part protects an insured from dishonest acts committed by its own employees. It is the only form in the crime program that protects private employers against acts of employees. Coverage extends to loss of money, securities, and any other type of property directly caused by employee dishonesty. Coverage also extends to damage to these covered items if the damage is created by an employee's dishonest act.

A problem arises when the insurer learns that an employee has committed dishonest acts before the one causing the loss. The prior incidents should have warned the employer of the deviant nature of this employee. In such a situation, the policy does not cover the current loss. Coverage is voided for an employee who has already demonstrated unreliability.

Coverage can be purchased in either of two forms: blanket or scheduled. **Blanket coverage** protects the owner from dishonest acts of any employee. **Scheduled coverage** limits coverage to named employees, to employees in titled positions, or to groups of employees. In scheduled coverage, a limit of liability is specified for each person, position, or group, together with a deductible. In blanket coverage, the insured must only establish that a loss resulted from employee dishonesty and does not have to identify the guilty employee. Under the scheduled form, the insured must show that a dishonest act was committed by a particular employee or member of a group or in a particular job. The insurer must identify the offending employee.

An insured often purchases scheduled coverage only for key employees. The employer often retains the exposure from the rank and file of workers and tolerates a certain amount of internal loss. This practice, however, becomes a problem for an adjuster trying to verify a theft, a burglary, or even a robbery loss from an employer's books and records. An internal loss often appears as part of the "shortage" indicated by the records. Sometimes, when several losses coexist, separating them or even recognizing that more than one loss is demonstrated is difficult. As a result, Form A excludes losses for which proof of their existence or amount depends on an inventory calculation or profit and loss calculation.

Coverage under either the blanket or scheduled employee dishonesty forms can be modified by adding any of a number of endorsements. These endorsements limit, expand, or modify coverage for certain types of property or certain circumstances.

Coverage Form C—Theft, Disappearance, and Destruction Coverage

This form has two sections. The first section extends coverage to money and securities *inside* the insured premises. Coverage is for *theft, disappearance, or destruction*. The second section covers outside loss from these same perils but only while the money or securities are in the care and custody of a messenger. Under both sections, coverage extends to *money* or *securities* owned or held by the named insured or for which the named insured is legally liable.

Theft is defined as "any act of stealing" and includes coverage for robbery and burglary. Disappearance and destruction are not defined but are broadly interpreted. Employee dishonesty is excluded in this coverage, as are acts of trustees, directors, and representatives. Form C also excludes losses caused by accounting and arithmetic errors, an exchange or purchase of property, fire damage to the premises, and voluntary parting of the property.

Coverage Forms D and Q—Robbery and Safe Burglary

Form D covers robbery and safe burglary of property other than money and securities. Form Q covers money and securities only. Section 1 of these coverage parts offers coverage *inside the premises* for two risks: (1) robbery or attempt of robbery of a custodian and (2) attempted or actual safe burglary. These two coverages can be purchased separately or together. Both robbery and safe burglary are defined terms. Section 2 of this form covers loss from actual or attempted *robbery of a messenger outside the insured premises*. Exclusions include acts of employees, fire damage, transfer or surrender of property, and vandalism. There is a $5,000 per-occurrence limit for loss of precious metals, precious or semiprecious stones, pearls, furs, or any article with most of its value consisting of these materials, and for manuscripts, drawings, and records, or the cost to reproduce them. These coverage parts can be modified by the use of one or more of the numerous endorsements.

Coverage Form E—Premises Burglary

The coverage provided by Form E supplements the coverage provided by Forms D and Q. Coverage in this part extends to actual or attempted burglary of the premises or actual or attempted robbery of a watchman. No coverage applies outside the covered premises. Coverage is limited to "property other than money and securities," but motor vehicles and trailers are excluded. **Burglary** is defined in this form as "the taking of property from inside the premises by a person unlawfully entering or leaving the premises, as evidenced by marks of forcible entry or exit." **Robbery** is the taking of property from another through bodily harm or threat of such harm or an obviously unlawful taking witnessed by another. Coverage extends to damage to a building if an insured owns it or when the insured is legally liable for its repair. Exclusions include acts of employees, changes in conditions, fire, and vandalism.

Coverage Form H—Premises Theft and Outside Robbery

This form provides *theft* coverage, except for money and securities, inside the insured premises. **Theft** is defined as "any act of stealing," which includes robbery and burglary, but extends to other crimes as well. Coverage is also provided for robbery of messengers outside the insured premises. This form can be used in place of forms D and E. Coverage extends to repairs to the real property if the insured is the owner or is legally liable for repairs.

The following are excluded from this coverage part:

1. Acts of employees, directors, trustees or representatives
2. Changes in conditions if the change increases the risk of loss
3. Exchanges or purchases—losses in business transactions are not covered
4. Fire and theft during a fire, although the latter can be endorsed back onto the policy for a fee
5. Inventory shortages—coverage does not apply to losses that require an inventory calculation to be established or measured
6. Transfer or surrender of property as might occur through computer fraud or extortion
7. Vandalism not covered as theft, but the form can be endorsed to provide coverage for vandalism committed along with a theft
8. Voluntary parting of title to or possession of property (through trick or device)

Coverage in this form is written on an "occurrence" basis, which is defined to include a series of related events as a single loss. Coverage is suspended after a loss until the premises are restored to the pre-loss condition or until a full-time guard is stationed on premises whenever the insured is not open for business.

Investigation of Crime Losses

As in most investigations, the adjuster should tour the insured premises, survey the physical conditions of the property to see where the premises were entered and where the property was located, and get a general overview of the circumstances related to the loss. The adjuster should then investigate with the insured or whoever knows the most about the circumstances of the loss and the property itself. For commercial losses, the adjuster should obtain tape-recorded or written statements regarding the type of business; how it operates; how long it has been at the location; its loss history; its financial data, including inventory records, cost of goods, and markups; its customer relationships; and other details of the loss. For homeowners losses, the adjuster should obtain documentation concerning purchase dates, invoices, and the condition of the property. The adjuster must know as much as possible about the property, the insured, and the circumstances of the loss.

Verification of the Event

Under any of the crime coverages, the adjuster's primary goal, after determining that coverage applies for the type of loss and property involved, is to establish that a loss has actually occurred. Staged crime losses are among the easiest types of frauds to accomplish. Unlike other perils, which show evidence of having occurred, a theft might leave no overt sign at all. Even if a fire might be an arson, the adjuster would know that a fire occurred. But with a staged burglary or other theft, the insured could move or sell the property to create the appearance that a crime has occurred.

Since suspicion is a natural response to crime losses, adjusters need to be highly trained to interview insureds and others without offending them and creating an impression of bad faith. Interviews with employees, neighbors, or police might also be appropriate. Neighbors often inform adjusters that they witnessed the insured carrying large amounts of property from the premises shortly before the alleged loss.

The insured might try to prove a loss by indicating the absence of three pallets or two shelves of merchandise. The decision to accept that a loss has occurred rests partly on the adjuster's assessment of the insured's integrity and partly on proof. For instance, an adjuster would have little reason to doubt the integrity of three teachers who attest to the theft loss of gym equipment from a high school since they would not have a personal interest at stake. In that case, the word of the teachers would probably be enough proof. Still, each case must be weighed on its merits, and the degree of proof required should be assessed accordingly. Significant dollar losses, of course, call for significant investigation. Many crime claims, especially under homeowners policies, are small and can be handled by telephone or inside adjusters. Though ostensibly cost-effective, such investigations are often not as thorough as an on-the-scene investigation and might be confined to securing a police report.

Indicators of Fraud

Although many losses are undoubtedly totally fraudulent, fraud usually occurs when a legitimate loss occurs and the insured uses the opportunity of filing a claim to exploit the loss, claiming many times the amount actually stolen. The National Insurance Crime Bureau checklist in Exhibit 5-7 identified the indicators of a fraudulent or exaggerated claim. Any of these indicators might also be present on legitimate claims, so the adjuster must interpret them carefully.

Insured's Statement

In some circumstances, adjusters are required to take a signed or recorded statement from the insured or other individuals. When a theft, burglary, or robbery occurs, a statement is almost mandatory except when the value of the claim is small. The statement should record facts that are fresh in the insured's or witness's mind. It should also serve as an inventory of what was taken. If the adjuster asks questions logically and chronologically, a statement can evoke other thoughts and facts that might have been overlooked. Taking a statement puts the adjustment process into a more formal atmosphere and might deter an insured from some intended dishonest act. Statements might also be used to identify property or to recall facts years later during litigation.

The examination under oath, permitted by the policy under "Duties in the Event of Loss or Damage," is a more serious and formal statement. Insurers often use this approach when they have doubts about the validity of a claim. Coverage, the cause, or the extent of loss might be in doubt. The statement is usually taken by the insurance company's attorney with the insured's attorney in attendance.

Employee Involvement

In a commercial setting, after determining that a commercial covered crime loss has actually occurred and that the insured is not involved, the adjuster must then ascertain whether an employee is involved. All policies exclude losses caused by employees, except those specifically written for employee dishonesty or fidelity losses. Unless such coverage is purchased, the exclusions under all other crime coverages will bar recovery for theft by an employee. Employees, by definition, must be employed when the loss occurs. Independent contractors and other like associates are not considered employees.

Determining the involvement of an employee is often difficult, and the evidence is often circumstantial. If the only way a loss could conceivably have occurred is through the participation of a specific employee, such evidence should be enough to deny a claim. Whether the employee dishonesty coverage (which is often purchased separately from a different insurer) or the crime coverage should pay the loss is often a question. Certainly the insured should not suffer as the two insurers try to discover which is responsible. Complete payment to the insured should be made under an agreement between the insurers to arbitrate their differences. The insurers should agree that any payments made to the insured would not prejudice the rights of the insurers at arbitration.

Amount of Loss

After being satisfied that a covered loss has occurred and that neither the insured nor an employee is involved, the adjuster must measure the loss. For many commercial crime losses, salvors and accountants can assist the adjuster in this effort. First to be determined is the type and amount of property that was at the insured's premises just before the loss. Salvors might be needed to count what remains after a loss. An accountant can work backward with records of purchases and sales and with previous physical inventory to prove what existed just before the loss. Properly kept books and records are thus helpful. An insured with poor records causes much inaccuracy in this procedure. In fact, the adjuster might encounter a wide variety of accounting records—anything from a shoebox full of receipts to the formal journals of a CPA. Nevertheless, the adjuster must deal with whatever records are available. The policy requires that the insured divulge all records, regardless of their nature and quality.

Recovery of Property

Both the commercial and homeowners forms explain what must be done with property recovered after a theft. The policy might state that such property could be exchanged for the amount paid by the insurance company to the insured or that the insured would have the option to keep the payment, in which case the company would dispose of the property as salvage. Recovery expenses might be separately reimbursable on the commercial form, subject to the limit of insurance.

Experience shows that most property is recovered within a reasonably short time after a loss or it is not recovered at all. The adjuster must check with law enforcement authorities to determine the likelihood of recovery. This is important because the amount the insurer will likely realize from salvage after a recovery is usually minimal compared to the actual value of the property. If recovery is imminent or has been made, the insured might be asked to consider a delay in the settlement. Authorities sometimes hold recovered property as evidence, and it can be in their possession for a considerable time awaiting the thief's trial date. Various insurers solve this dilemma differently. Some contend that when the authorities have the property, it is no longer "stolen property" and is no longer subject to a claim. Others might pay the loss if the insured is actually unable to take possession of the property. Stolen property discovered by police in pawnshops or held by others might be recovered. The authorities are less likely to recover property or to identify a thief in a simple theft or cash robbery than they are in a burglary in which a large stock of merchandise can be trailed. The recovery of stolen property is, however, relatively rare.

Boiler and Machinery Coverage

Boiler and machinery coverage is different from other property coverages. Only a small group of adjusters who commonly handle boiler and machinery claims understand the coverage. The following brief review explains how it functions and fits into the overall insurance market.

Need for Boiler and Machinery Coverage

A business might need coverages other than those provided by the BPP because that form excludes causes of loss and types of property that are very real exposures for an insured. Boiler and machinery coverage responds to an important category of these causes and property.

Limitations Under the BPP

The causes of loss—broad form includes "explosion" as a covered peril but includes the following limitations within the definition of the peril:

3. Explosion, including the explosion of gases or fuel within the furnace of any fired vessel or within the flues or passages through which the gases of combustion pass. This cause of loss does not include loss or damage by:

    a. Rupture, bursting or operation of pressure relief devices; or

    b. Rupture or bursting due to expansion or swelling of the contents of any building or structure, caused by or resulting from water.

Coverage is excepted for loss by rupture, bursting, or operation of pressure relief devices.

The broad form contains exclusions that read as follows:

2. We will not pay for loss or damage caused by or resulting from:

    a. Artificially generated electrical current, including electric arcing, that disturbs electrical devices, appliances or wires. But if loss or damage by fire results, we will pay for that resulting loss or damage.

    b. Explosion of steam boilers, steam pipes, steam engines or steam turbines owned or leased by you, or operated under your control.

        But if loss or damage by fire or combustion explosion results, we will pay for that resulting loss or damage.

    c. Mechanical breakdown, including rupture or bursting caused by centrifugal force.

        But if loss or damage by a Covered Cause of Loss results, we will pay for that resulting loss or damage.

As these provisions indicate, an "ignition of gases" explosion is covered, but not an explosion of a pressure vessel. The causes of loss—special form has similar exclusions. Additionally, the special form has exclusions for loss by electric arcing; bursting of pipes; breaking or cracking of a steam pipe; explosion of steam boilers, engines, or turbines; or mechanical breakdown or centrifugal disintegration. Any one of these excluded items can and often does represent a high value exposure to loss for its owner.

The Boiler and Machinery Market

Recognizing the limitations in standard commercial property insurance, some insurers have developed the expertise to insure **boiler and machinery (B&M) exposures** using special forms and rates. These companies also have a staff of engineers who are highly skilled in the inspection and evaluation of hazards associated with these exposures and who regularly visit the insureds to examine the materials and machines or devices that contribute to the exposure. These inspection engineers perform a valuable service to the insured and the insurer. Indeed, the inspection service feature of B&M insurance might be the primary feature of interest for as many as half the purchasers of such coverage.

Boiler and machinery policies provide coverage against perils that standard property insurance avoids. Businessowners cannot operate without a power source (steam boiler or electric motor), heavy and very specialized power transfer devices and switches, and air conditioning systems. The failure of a pressure boiler, a critical transformer, or a rotating flywheel would represent failure *within* the item itself. Ordinary insurance treats such an event as the result of an inherent defect in the item and deems it to have served a useful life and to be of no further value. Because the article is of no value the instant it fails, the insurer does not need to indemnify the owner.

That position is generally a valid reflection of coverage principles. However, the businessowner must replace the machine. The costs are often enormous, as for a large gas-fired boiler. Further, a delay usually follows the loss, during which the repairs must be made before the business can be restarted.

This coverage protects against losses to classes of equipment that the standard commercial property policy cannot cover. Coverage includes internal failure, breakage, or explosion of the covered objects. However, if a fire starts as a result of an accident to an object, both the B&M coverage and the commercial property coverage would be activated. The current ISO B&M coverage has language that makes it excess coverage when two or more insurers share a common area of loss. However, some insurers do not use an ISO form, and their policies might provide primary coverage.

B&M coverages usually do not overlap with building and contents coverage. Instead, these coverages normally complement each other. One exception is when the cause of a fire cannot be established as internal or external to an object. An adjuster discovering that power machinery was involved in the cause of the loss should inquire about the existence of B&M coverage. A

B&M policy might provide coverage for damage also covered by the fire policy. If there is any mutually covered loss, the adjuster should be guided by respective policy provisions on "other insurance."

Boiler and Machinery Coverage

This section presents the important features of the ISO boiler and machinery policy.

Declarations Page

The declarations page records the basic facts related to the insured. At the top of the declarations is the information found in most policy declarations. This is followed by the schedule of insured objects, along with the location of each and the coverage limit applying to each. This declaration page must be completed carefully. The policy text refers to it often, and this information is needed to activate coverage.

The Essential Coverage Provision

The essential coverage provision states: "We will pay for direct damages to Covered Property caused by a Covered Cause of Loss." This is the entire insuring agreement. All that follows is by way of definition, exclusion, or explanation.

Coverage extends to property owned by an insured; property in the care, custody, or control of the insured; and property for which the insured is legally liable. Should any disagreement arise over payment for property held by an insured, the insurer would defend the insured and pay what is legally owed to the owner. All of the policyholder's property is protected from the covered cause of loss, not just the insured object.

The coverage peril for this policy is "accident" to an "object," identified in the declarations. The policy text further states that an object must be in use or connected and ready for use at the insured location at the time of the accident.

Throughout all forms of B&M coverage, the definition of "object" and "accident" are the most important.

Object

The **object** is the equipment shown in the declarations. It might be one article, a group of similar articles, or a group of related articles. It might be very specifically scheduled, down to its serial number, or it might be listed on the policy in a general fashion. In the section titled "General Conditions," an explanation of the object group reads as follows:

> All "objects" in use or connected ready for use and included in an "Object" Group Definition will be considered as individually described in the Declarations.

This provision reaffirms coverage for all component parts of any one object group—coverage of an object group covers every part thereof and is not limited to important machinery. Examples of what the provisions consider include cables and wiring of a machine or piping, valving, and controls of a refrigeration system.

A complete description of specific object categories is found in one or more of the following in the object definitions endorsement(s) that might be attached to the coverage:

- Object Definition No. 1—Pressure and Refrigeration Objects
- Object Definition No. 2—Mechanical Objects
- Object Definition No. 3—Electrical Objects
- Object Definition No. 4—Turbine Objects
- Object Definition No. 5—Comprehensive Coverage (Excluding Production Machines)
- Object Definition No. 6—Comprehensive Coverage (Including Production Machines)

The need for this variety of forms becomes obvious as they are compared. Each class of object is defined and circumscribed by its individual form.

Historically, B&M coverage excluded from the definition of "object" all production machinery or systems. Processing or manufacturing systems were not eligible for this coverage, nor were objects that were disconnected, were in disuse, or that did not in some way relate to the generation or distribution of power. The concept of "power" applied to steam boilers, transformers, shafting (line shafts), transformers and electric switching and distribution systems, motors and generators, and all related equipment. Over time, this group was expanded to include refrigeration systems (because of their pressure lines), turbines, much broader electrical coverage, various mechanical objects such as pumps and compressors, gear sets, and many other types of machinery.

In 1988, ISO added Object Definitions No. 5 and No. 6, which provide comprehensive coverage for objects. In addition, the ISO B&M essential coverage form no longer excluded production machinery as a defined group. Rather, this limitation of coverage must appear in the applicable object definition. For example, Object Definition No. 5 states:

Object does not mean any:

. . .

Production or process machine or apparatus that processes, forms, cuts, shapes, grinds, or conveys raw materials, materials in process, or finished products. . . .

By contrast, Object Definition No. 6 does not exclude production machinery as a group. If a production component can qualify as an object in every other respect, it is not barred from coverage solely because it is a production component.

Accident

Accident means "a sudden and accidental breakdown of the 'object' or a part of the 'object.' At the time the breakdown occurs, it must manifest itself by physical damage to the 'object' that necessitates repair or replacement." This definition goes on to list seven types of damage that are *not* accidents. These include: (1) deterioration, depletion, corrosion or erosion; (2) wear and tear; (3) valve or seal leakage; (4) vacuum tube, gas tube, or brush breakage; (5) breakdown of any electronic computer; (6) breakdown of any foundation supporting the object; and (7) the functioning of any safety valve or protective device. Turbine units might have separate definitions of "accident," cited in the Turbine Object Definitions endorsement. "Accident" extends to cover damage resulting from an accident caused by a strike, by sabotage, by civil commotion, or by vandalism.

Conditions

Boiler and machinery loss conditions address duties of an insured in the event of loss or damage, insurance under two or more coverages, and legal action against the carrier. They contain a loss payable clause as well as an "other insurance" provision, a transfer of "right to recovery against others" to the insurer, and a lengthy section on valuation. Valuation is essentially based on the cost to repair or replace damaged property with property of like kind, capacity, size, and quality. The valuation clause also addresses special circumstances: when a part of an object is more expensive than the object; when property is obsolete or is replaced with better property; and when repair or replacement is not made.

Defense

If a suit is brought against an insured to recover for damage to property of others on the insured's property or in the insured's care, custody, and control, the insurer will defend the insured and has the right to settle as it deems appropriate. Costs of defense include all expenses, such as those for certain bonds, investigation, lost wages, any taxes or suits, and pre-judgment and post-judgment interest.

Historically, B&M policies provided liability coverage for injury to the public (excluding employees of an insured) payable from any funds left after payment of the property loss. This coverage was conditioned on the legal liability of the insured. Such coverage is no longer found in the basic B&M policy but is available by endorsement. The commercial general liability coverages now generally cover the risk of injury to the public.

Boiler and Machinery Business Interruption

Business interruption coverage for B & M losses can be written as a monoline or as a multiline coverage. Deductibles are available in time (number of days) or in money.

Why is there a separate B&M coverage for business interruption? The answer lies in the cause of the loss. The standard commercial property policy and the B&M policy require a covered loss on the primary coverage before the business interruption coverage is triggered. For example, if an electrical fault causes a loss, the commercial property coverage and its business interruption would not respond. However, the B&M coverage would be activated (if electrical cables were an insured object), and the business interruption coverage on the B&M form would apply.

Small Business Boiler and Machinery Coverage

ISO has developed this coverage form for small businesses. Provisions are essentially the same as for the standard policy, but there is less opportunity to adjust or alter the form. Unlike the standard form, the small business form is self-contained and does not require object definition forms. All definitions, including "object," appear in the form. The "object" definition is limited to (1) boiler and pressure vessels and (2) air conditioning units. The policy includes a list of items that are defined as "*not* objects."

This coverage is available as a monoline policy or as part of a multiline package. Also available is a small business broad form that covers a broader range of objects, including electrical and refrigeration items.

Computer Losses

Handling computer losses is one of the fastest changing areas in loss adjusting. Most people are generally acquainted with various computer types and sizes, but the field is broadening daily. The present electronic data processing field includes, in addition to computers, machine control systems, building mechanical control systems, communications relay systems, medical diagnostic tools, and technical test equipment. Telephone and intercom systems are often computer-driven. Almost all of these systems can be insured. Claims for repair or replacement are surfacing with greater frequency.

The following is a review of some terms used in insurance policies and in the computer trade.

- **Data** include any information used in or with a computer. It is recorded in a magnetic code that is usable by a computer. Data includes programs (software), raw information that has been placed in the system, calculations, and memory system content.

- **Hardware** includes the physical machine and all of its component parts as well as connecting cables.

- **Media** are any computer-readable devices that can hold information. They include punch cards, magnetic tapes, and magnetic disks (hard or floppy) and their carriers. Media are tangible and serve only as the vehicle to carry or store information. Some insurance policies define media to include data and programs.

- **Programs** (or software) are a series of logically connected steps that are loaded into the computer, allowing it to perform any given function when directed by an operator. They are carried on a disk or tape. Programs can be proprietary (fully owned and protected by copyright) or in the public domain. Some are general purpose and sold widely in the market, but others are so specialized that they have no value outside a particular application.

Causes of Loss

Following are several causes of loss that can do the most damage to computers:

- Heat damage (with or without fire)
- Water damage/humidity
- Smoke
- Contamination
- Head crash
- Impact or crushing

- Voltage variation
- Magnetic field intrusion

Heat

A computer is built with many heat-sensitive materials. Plastics distort or degrade at relatively low temperatures. Solder melts, and wire insulation softens or breaks down at 465 degrees Tolerances change as materials expand. Heat damage might be produced internally because of cooling system failure, or externally, such as when a room heats up unexpectedly. Damage occurs at connections and joints. Panels warp, and insulation breaks down. Space tolerances deteriorate. Conductivity of systems changes, and some cosmetic discoloration is likely to occur in the system or at the console. Heat caused by fire raises additional concerns about contamination.

Water/Humidity

Water falling into a computer or rising around it is extremely destructive. Excessive humidity can have the same effect. Water cross-conducts between pin connectors and also deposits chemicals whose corrosive action erodes and destroys connectors and circuit boards.

Repairing a water-damaged computer is best left to an expert. The *machine should be shut down* until it has been cleaned and decontaminated. Any effort to turn it on to "see whether it will work" might do new and irreparable damage. If restoration personnel are not available for several hours or days, the cabinet should be opened and warm air from a hair dryer should be blown gently across the wet areas, concentrated particularly on cable plugs and connectors. A dehumidifier should be used to reduce the humidity in the area where the computer is located.

Smoke

Smoke is made up of carbon and other chemicals that can be destructive to a computer. When smoke invades a computer and settles onto its connections and circuit boards, the result can be disastrous. As with water infiltration, the system should be turned off and protected against further invasion of smoke. It can be wrapped in plastic. Professionals should be called to dismantle and clean it. The smoke residue must be tested to identify the chemicals it carries and to enable the restorer to select a detergent that will remove those chemicals. Acids in the smoke can etch metal and even cut the trace lines on a circuit board. After twenty-four hours, rapid degradation of the affected areas or systems is likely.

Smoke particles are measured in microns (one millionth of a meter) but are large enough to cause a crash in the read/write head in a mainframe. Other losses include internal and external discoloration, electrical failure through carbon chains, arcing, contact point failure, and varnish deposits.

Repairing the damage from smoke contamination is a job for a professional. Fans can eliminate smoke. Protective covers can be arranged. The entire unit might need to be dismantled so that it can be hand-washed with suitable solvents. In any case, the system should not be turned on until a competent restorer has checked it and approved it for use.

Contamination

Contamination includes water and smoke as well as other types of material. The major concerns are dust and dirt, but oil, oil vapor, and other airborne fumes or contaminants can damage a computer.

In any loss by contamination, the machine should *not* be turned on. Attempts to do so to test its operation can be very costly. The best solution is to have the unit opened by a competent restoration service person and checked for foreign matter. If a contaminant is gaseous, the clean-up routine suggested for smoke should be followed. If the material is solid or fluid, the suggested recovery from water loss should be followed.

Head Crash

Often called the "read/write head," the head is a combination of a magnetic head suspended above a revolving disk. The disk revolves at 700 rpm, and the magnetic head repositions itself inward and outward above the disk in swift movements, selecting a magnetic track on the disk. In general terms, this arrangement can be compared to a record turntable. However, in a computer, the magnetic head never actually touches the spinning disk. They are adjusted to operate about three microns apart. A speck of dust could measure eight to ten microns. If a small particle of dust or grit enters this chamber, it could lodge between the revolving disk and the head. The results can be disastrous because the dust can scrape the disk, destroying the magnetic intelligence recorded on it.

Occasionally, the head (magnetic) units move out of alignment. If they strike the rotating disk, they could destroy it. Thus, a head crash alone does not automatically signify a contamination. These read/write heads are in a sealed unit in the computer. To reach the read/write heads; a contaminant must not only get into the computer, but must also penetrate this sealed chamber. A variety of causes can result in a **head crash**, and contamination is only a remote cause in most cases. More evidence than a head crash is necessary to identify contamination as the cause of loss.

Repair bills for "head crash" losses are often paid with little inquiry as to the cause. A deeper inquiry could reveal that the unit failed because of an internal defect or misalignment, either of which is generally excluded from coverage.

Impact or Crushing

Although computers are generally sturdy machines, if a cabinet is struck and bent by a lift truck or other heavy equipment, wires could be pinched, or connections could be stressed or broken.

Special preparations, as outlined by the manufacturer, should be done before a computer is shipped. Damage to a computer or one of its components can occur during shipping. Most freight carriers recognize the units as "special handling" cargo. Even so, units get dropped, overturned, rained on, and otherwise abused along the way. Most physical damage from impact or crushing occurs while the units are in transit.

Voltage Variation

Voltage is the "pressure" exerted by electricity. If the voltage along a wire is doubled, twice as much electricity will flow through the wire. However, wire has a limit as to how much current it can safely carry. When the voltage increases and causes the current to surpass the wire's capacity, the wire heats up and melts—just like a fuse. Upon melting, the wire cannot carry current. Whatever appliance was receiving current at the output end of the wire would be deprived of power, and the system would be disabled.

This condition occurs when lightning strikes a power line and momentarily increases the voltage on that line. That increased pressure could travel down the line to a computer. The voltage at the wall plug could increase momentarily from 115 volts to 170 volts or to 500 volts, which is one type of line surge. Tiny wires in the computer, sometimes smaller than a human hair, would become overstressed and melt. The computer would become disabled.

Determining the cause of a power surge is often difficult. Circumstances must be investigated since several factors other than lightning can cause power surges. Bad switching practices at a power station might cause a momentary voltage jump. The sudden unloading of a power system, as when a pole is hit by a car, might cause a momentary increase of voltage. A near miss by lightning could also induce voltage increases in a power source.

Many computers are fitted with voltage regulators to smooth out line surge. They should also have special grounding to intercept any lightning surges that come in on the power line. If a computer is fitted with these attachments, machine failure caused by lightning is unlikely. In looking at the circumstances surrounding a computer loss allegedly caused by lightning, the adjuster should examine the local weather records for the time when the computer failed. Many power companies keep detailed records of their line voltages and lightning strikes to their lines, which are often available to an adjuster.

Magnetic Field Intrusion

Computer data are recorded in magnetic spots on a disk or tape that has an iron oxide face. These disks and tapes could be erased by simply passing them through a magnetic field that would rearrange the electrons in a uniform direction. In so doing, the intelligence encoded on the disk would be lost. The same effect would be produced by bringing a magnetic field near a computer. The magnetic field would also rearrange the electrons in the computer—on disks or on tape—and the intelligence stored in the computer would be lost.

Certain welding equipment generates a magnetic field. Induction heating coils operate through use of magnetic fields, as do some other systems. Anything with an electromagnet has a magnetic field. Office workers often have magnets or magnetized objects on their desks. These objects can destroy computer disks. If the computer and its media are not shielded from magnetic fields, the data and programs on the disks could be accidentally erased.

Movement of recorded data through a magnetic field and vice versa can be equally damaging. Whenever data are missing or scrambled, the adjuster must consider the possibility that data were exposed to a magnetic field of enough strength to wipe it clean.

Coverage

Generalizing about computer coverages is difficult. This section presents some of the most important features of such coverage.

Loss Exposures

An insured computer owner could suffer various kinds of loss, including the following:

- Physical loss to equipment or media
- Costs to replace data or programs
- Extra expense to continue computer operations
- Loss of business income

In working with any computer loss, an adjuster must be aware that these systems can be expensive and very complicated and also that they might be the nerve center for many other operations of the business. As a result, continuous disablement can have far-reaching effects.

The BPP

This standard commercial property policy provides valuable coverage for computer losses, but with significant limitations. Coverage for business personal property extends to "equipment" and "all other personal property owned by you and used in your business." Nothing in this language would exclude computer equipment and media. In addition, the BPP provides a $1,000 coverage extension for the cost to research, restore, and replace valuable records, including those on electronic media. The BPP does not cover certain types of property, including "accounts, bills,. . .evidences of debt. . .," and other specifically described property that other policies cover. The exclusion of the last type of property is significant because computer equipment can be covered specially under inland marine forms.

The BPP contains exclusions for power failure and for "artificially generated electric current, including electric arcing, that disturbs electrical devices, appliances or wires," as well as for mechanical breakdown and changes in temperature or humidity. In addition, the enumerated covered causes of loss in the basic and broad forms might not adequately address the exposures related to computer equipment.

Inland Marine Policies

Computer policies are a recognized part of the inland marine market. They are a nonfiled line of business, which means that policy forms can be adapted with much greater flexibility than under the traditional commercial property lines of coverage. Indeed, inland marine forms covering computer exposures are so varied that they cannot be discussed in great detail. Generally, inland marine policies are "all-risks" and can be flexible enough to cover the exposure to maintenance and repair problems. An adjuster who finds an inland marine policy applicable to a loss must review the coverage very carefully, especially in regard to settlement options. Following are key issues to consider with nonstandard computer coverages:

- Standard homeowner policies can have dollar limitations or can exclude personal property used at any time for business purposes. Most personal computers are periodically used for business purposes. Inland marine coverage of personal computers could eliminate this problem.

- The primary reason to get computer coverage in the inland marine market is for broadened perils, particularly causes of loss that are typically excluded, such as electrical surges, mechanical breakdown, and changes in temperature or humidity. Nevertheless, some nonstandard computer policies might contain the same exclusions. An adjuster handling a computer loss must carefully read all coverages, exclusions, and definitions.

- Common exclusions in specialized computer coverages are for programming error or processing error. These are essentially "operator error" exclusions.

- **Computer viruses** are programs that disrupt or destroy existing programs and data. They are normally covered by any policy that covers programs and data, but they might not be covered if an employee intentionally introduced them. Dishonest acts of employees are excluded from all policies, except those designed specifically for that purpose.

- Equipment can be valued on a **modified**, or **upgraded**, **replacement cost basis**. The reality of the computer market is that a piece of equipment bought only a few years ago might be obsolete. Any replacement machine would likely include features and capabilities that the old machine did not possess. Most standard insurance policies would not pay for such upgrades, but many nonstandard policies would.

- Data and programs are usually valued at the cost to replace or reconstruct. Alternatively, they can be valued on a stated value basis. Some policies provide that irreplaceable data are covered only for the value of the blank media on which they were stored.

- Certain underwriting criteria can be written into the policy as conditions, the effect of which is that the policyholder must continue to live up to such criteria or the coverage will be void. These criteria might include requirements that a mainframe be housed in a separate, secure room with its own air conditioning and fire suppression systems or that data be systematically backed up and stored off site.

- Some nonstandard policies have coverage for extra expense and loss of business income built in. Some have only extra expense coverage.

- Some nonstandard policies include additional coverage for the cost of recharging a discharged halon or carbon dioxide system.

Other Insurance

Other coverage for computer losses is common. An agent can cover the computer system as a separate entity in addition to the coverage that exists on the BPP form. Inland marine contracts can also be in force. Coverage can be in effect through a finance company or bank. As with many commercial losses, boiler and machinery coverage might apply. This might contribute to the payment for the loss, or in some cases it might be the primary coverage. Adjusters should conduct a reasonable exploration to find additional coverage when adjusting a loss.

Computer Loss Adjusting

Losses to computer equipment, media, and data present the adjuster with unique loss mitigation and settlement challenges and opportunities. This section presents several of these challenges and opportunities.

Initial Assessment and Response

The adjuster's first obligation at the site of a computer loss is to be sure that the entire system is shut down and that it stays shut down until a full analysis of the loss is made and a qualified repair person is on site to monitor and initiate any restart. The adjuster must talk to whoever was present when the incident occurred to identify the specific cause of this loss. Examining the equipment and the loss site often reveals evidence that identifies the reason for failure. Adjusters are not expected to analyze the internal failures of the system, but should take charge, advise the insured of its duty to protect the machine against further damage, and help the insured obtain the services of a competent repair technician.

Detailed Identification of Equipment

Another initial duty of an adjuster is to identify the damaged machine or system. A form similar to the one shown in Exhibit 13-2 should be used for that purpose. The information on this form can enable the adjuster to talk by phone to an expert who would be involved in repairing the machine or system or in deciding how to proceed.

Backup of Data

In most well-run computer operations, the data in the system are copied at specific intervals. The copy is stored as a backup in anticipation of a malfunction or damage to the computer system. An adjuster should ask the insured whether such a procedure is used, at what intervals the data are copied, and how the backup is preserved. Is it retained on site? Is it sent to a secure off-site storage and, if so, where? How often?

The retrieval of stored data usually depends on the ability to use another similar machine. This can occur only if the insured's read/write head unit has been properly adjusted. As noted earlier in this chapter, if the head is maladjusted, it might work perfectly when it rereads its own output, but no other

Exhibit 13-2
Adjusters' Field Identification for Computers
(For Completion During *First* Inspection of Loss)

Insured:_____

Date of Loss:_____

Equipment—purchased new _____ or used _____ Date _____

Purchased from whom? _____

Maker: _____

Model: _____

Serial #: _____

Size of hard disk _____ of soft disks _____

Number of hard disks _____ of soft disks _____

Monitor-detail _____

Printer(s) _____ Type: _____ Model: _____

Operating system: _____

Modem: yes _____ no _____ Type _____

Internal added cards: 1. _____

                               2. _____

                               3. _____

Microprocessor—speed: _____

Number of users on system: _____

Describe software: _____

Describe what software did: _____

_____

_____

Was equipment energized at time of loss? yes _____ no _____

Signed _____

Inspection date _____

computer could read that same tape or disk. When the insured's read/write head has been damaged, the output tape is useless because no other unit can retrieve the data.

Some technical processes can circumvent this problem. Tapes and disks that are faulty in their creation can occasionally be deciphered by use of special techniques in computer labs. The adjuster should be aware that experts can help to recover data.

After a loss, contaminated tapes or disks should not be run until a trained technician has cleaned them. Failure to do so might result in damage to the read/write heads.

Settlement Options

An important factor in computer settlements is obsolescence, which results from the speed with which computer technology evolves. As a new model reaches the market, the related older models sharply lose value even if they are unsold. When these units become technically obsolete, they lose their salability. With small units, such as personal computers, new but obsolete models go on sale, and the inventory is quickly absorbed at reduced prices. However, larger obsolete components might languish in warehouses for months or years waiting to be sold. This inventory can be the adjuster's salvation. Finding and obtaining just the right replacement unit to fit into an existing system take patience but can result in dramatic savings.

Computers often contain a set or group of related items. Even a personal computer is usually made up of three or more components, each of which can be replaced as a unit. Replacing a single element without replacing an entire system might be possible and economical.

During repair evaluation, the adjuster often discovers that repairs, though possible, might take several weeks because of a delay in obtaining parts. At this point, the insured and the adjuster must decide how to proceed. The options are as follows:

1. Wait for the repairs to be complete
2. Purchase a new unit
3. Purchase a used unit
4. Rent a temporary unit

The analysis of how to make this decision is beyond the scope of this text. However, if the insured has business interruption coverage, the insurer providing such coverage would play a major role in the physical damage settlement. As explained in Chapter 11, extra expense coverage pays for increased costs to repair underlying physical damage to the extent that such payments reduce the business interruption loss. The adjuster must agree with the insured on a course that will best serve all concerned.

Insureds often lease computer equipment. An adjuster who identifies equipment as leased must review the written lease. Usually, the lessee is required to insure the equipment; however, this is not always the case. Sometimes a lease expires upon destruction of the equipment. In any case, the lessor is usually not named on a lessee's policy, so an adjuster can make settlement directly with the lessee.

Computer Consultants

Computer consultants have access to two types of printed lists of available replacement units: one for new, never used units, and one for units that are rebuilt and warranted to be good as new. Obtaining a replacement unit can save other components of the overall system. This option might solve the problem of an insured who sees the need for an entirely new system.

The key to successful replacement is to have the help of a good consultant. The cost for a consultant is probably not warranted on a small personal computer loss, but even in such a case, many consultants are willing to discuss the matter by phone. They hope that providing help on small matters will encourage others to hire them on a fee basis for large matters.

These consultants have at their disposal several references on the value of used units and components. This valuation is not an exact science, and market conditions must be considered. Valuation is probably best determined by someone who is familiar with the industry, changes that are occurring, the history of any problems, the number of sales made, and the current quantity of unsold merchandise.

Most experienced adjusters can determine the value of a personal computer with an original cost under $3,000. Enough of a market exists in most communities to create a mutually acceptable value. By contrast, valuation of a $200,000 mainframe requires research on a national scale. No one locality will have a sufficiently large market to guide the adjuster. Using a paid consultant is advisable in such a case.

Service Contract

Service contracts protect owners of many computers. Through those contracts, service agencies maintain and repair the units during the life of the agreements. These agreements are generally void in the event of certain casualty losses to the unit. Thus, loss to a computer by fire would likely void the service contract protection.

A computer with a service contract is more valuable than one without a contract. When computer coverage extends to "direct physical loss," a voided service contract as described above is probably not covered. Although the loss of the contract is real, it is not a "physical" loss. When the computer coverage extends to "direct loss" (whether physical or not), the loss of a service contract might be covered and might require settlement by the adjuster. The purchase of new equipment with a new service contract is probably an unnecessary expense.

After repairs, the service contract provider might be unwilling to reactivate the contract in anticipation that some fault or defective repair might still emerge. However, in these situations, the adjuster could obtain contracts from service agencies at prices anticipating further problems, including the need for frequent computer service. After six months or one year, if the computer has proven sound and has not developed a history of excessive service needs, the original provider might reinstate the original service contract.

Contamination Claims

In the late nineteenth and early twentieth centuries, the environment became polluted by discharge in areas where large concentrations of people worked and lived. Both industrial and private waste was dumped in streams. Polluters gave little thought to other people downstream and gave no thought to the effect of the pollution on the ocean. These discharges were considered small, easily diluted, and of no long-range importance.

Today, the magnitude of contamination and the toxicity of materials are thousands of times more severe than in earlier times. Huge spills of contaminants into important waterways have been extensively publicized, thus raising public awareness of the environment. Other types of contamination are more subtle, and, to some extent, more insidious, such as the consequences of asbestos fiber exposure to a worker or to the population in general. Asbestos was recognized as a potential health problem by asbestos manufacturers as early as the 1930s, but it continued to be mined, refined, handled, and installed, and the excess was discarded into open areas. Asbestos contamination is now a national problem.

Radiation is another type of environmental contamination. Vast improvements have been made in the detection of radiation, but with these has come the realization that radiation occurring in nature is much more of a threat than ever before understood. Without detection devices, the radon gas epidemic would never have been known.

Another general source of contamination arises from the use, transportation, storage, or disposal of chemicals, many of which are extremely toxic. Chemicals in transit are especially vulnerable to accidents. They are usually transported over water or land in barges, boats, ships, trains, or trucks. Even chemicals in storage represent a contamination threat. Some are explosive or combustible. Many produce gases, creating pressure within containment vessels, which then have the propensity to explode. The container might leak or be damaged, allowing the chemicals to seep under ground, spread across the surface, or evaporate into the air. Each of these conditions creates a different set of problems for control, dissipation, and cleanup.

This section presents a brief introduction of the law concerning pollution/contamination cleanup because it might affect first-party insurance and a brief explanation of the coverage difficulties in this area. This is a rapidly evolving area of the law and of insurance coverage. Furthermore, the courts will probably play a major role in interpreting both the law and insurance policies.

Legal Aspects of Contamination

Both state and federal law affects legal rights and duties concerning contamination. This section presents the most important of these laws, the federal Superfund law.

Superfund

The Comprehensive Environmental Response, Compensation, and Liability Act (CERCLA), popularly known as the **Superfund** law, was enacted in 1980. It was not the first major federal environmental law, but it has had the greatest effect on first-party insurance claims. Under this law, the Environmental Protection Agency (EPA) is required to discover and clean up dangerous waste sites. The EPA must consider whether a site has shown evidence of release of a hazardous substance or whether such a release appears imminent. The EPA is required to create a list of hazardous waste sites that need attention in order of priority. It is authorized to order **potentially responsible parties (PRPs)** to eliminate the contaminants and to clean up the sites. If these parties fail in this effort, the EPA is authorized to take remedial measures to protect public health and welfare and to pay for these efforts out of Superfund.

The EPA may impose liability for cleanup costs retroactively against those who deposited hazardous waste before the statute became law on December 11, 1980. Because of the magnitude of the cleanup problem, both in cost and technical skill, there has been and will continue to be great emphasis on the recovery of costs from responsible parties, as well as encouragement of private cleanup efforts.

The EPA can seek recovery of its costs from the following "potentially responsible parties":

1. The current property owner

2. The owner of the facility/property when the hazardous waste was deposited

3. Any person who contracted or arranged for disposal of the hazardous waste

4. Any person who accepted the hazardous waste for transportation or disposal

Past owners are liable only if hazardous waste was disposed of on the property during their ownership. Current owners are liable for all existing contamination as soon as they take title to the land. The statute does not require that the "potentially responsible party" be negligent in disposing of its waste. The courts have deemed this to be an absolute liability standard.

Only a few defenses can be effective against the absolute liability standard. An act of war or Acts of God are valid defenses if appropriate. Likewise, the act or omission by an unrelated third party could serve as a defense, provided the defendant could not foresee the negligence of that third party. In addition, the parties can have no contractual relationship, not even by deed. Although the statutory defenses to liability are limited, the best defense might be the EPA's problems of proof. The EPA's inability to prove a defendant's status as a "potentially responsible party" can limit or eliminate CERCLA liability.

The 1986 amendments to the Superfund law created an **innocent landowner** defense, which applies to an owner who purchased a contaminated site without knowledge of the problem and after an appropriate investigation into its prior use. Ignorance of the problem is not the same as innocence. Investigation into prior use must be made.

Insurance Implications of Superfund

The most significant aspect of the Superfund law from the perspective of first-party insurance is that it makes the owner responsible for his or her own property. Since the owner's property is alleged to be damaged or defective from contamination, many owners have sought recovery from their first-party insurance.

Landowners have submitted many claims against third-party coverage as well. Indeed, most of the insurance litigation arising out of environmental claims concerns third-party coverage. This text discusses the problems of environmental claims under first-party coverages only.

Possible Coverage for Pollution/Contamination

Claims for pollution/contamination might be covered, depending on the circumstances of the loss and the wording of the applicable policy. The most important basis for coverage has been "all-risks" policies and the debris removal coverage.

"All-Risks" Coverage

These policies cover "risks of direct physical loss" to covered property, unless excluded. Pollution or contamination usually involves loss that is "direct" and "physical." The only remaining issues are whether the loss is to covered property and whether pollution/contamination or its cause is excluded. The most significant type of property *not* covered in a pollution claim is land itself. Exclusions for pollution/contamination are also common, as discussed in the section on the BPP that follows.

Debris Removal

Insureds have sought coverage for pollution cleanup under their debris removal coverage by asserting that the polluting material itself was debris once it had contaminated the insured property or that the contaminated property constituted debris. The merit of this argument depends on the wording of the applicable debris removal clause. The ISO forms have been modified to prevent coverage for pollution cleanup under the debris removal clause.

Exclusions and Limitations for Contamination/Pollution

Since 1987, ISO policies have been drafted to exclude loss by contamination unless that event is preceded by a covered loss. That is, pollution/contamination is now covered only as a consequence of a prior covered loss, and then only within narrow limits of coverage. Some losses (to land, for instance) are absolutely excluded. The ISO policies exclude pollution unless it is caused by a peril specifically named in the coverage. Additionally, an annual aggregate limit has been imposed. Contamination of soil or water is specifically excluded from the debris removal coverage.

Property Not Covered—BPP

Coverage under the BPP is limited to "direct physical loss to covered property." Following are some types of property not covered:

  f. The cost of excavations, grading, backfilling or filling

  h. Land (including land on which the property is located), water, growing crops or lawns

m. Underground pipes, flues or drains

Debris Removal

The additional coverage for debris removal includes the following:

a. Debris Removal

(1) We will pay your expense to remove debris of Covered Property caused by or resulting from a Covered Cause of Loss that occurs during the policy period. . .

(2) The most we will pay under this Additional Coverage is 25% of:

(a) The amount we pay for the direct physical loss of or damage to Covered Property; plus

(b) The deductible in this policy applicable to that loss or damage

But this limitation does not apply to any additional debris removal limit provided in the Limits of Insurance section.

(3) This Additional Coverage does not apply to costs to:

(a) Extract "pollutants" from land or water; or

(b) Remove, restore or replace polluted land or water.

Coverage extends to removal of debris of *covered property* caused by a *covered cause of loss*. Any debris that does not satisfy both of these conditions is not included under this additional coverage. Furthermore, the coverage is restricted to 25 percent of the direct covered loss. Debris removal is an "additional coverage." It is not intended to replace other coverages or to become a "coverage" in its own right. It is contingent on the occurrence of a covered loss and is limited by the size of the covered loss. Because of this provision, the possibility of a $100 oil spill with a $10,000 cleanup cost is avoided.

If the insured has suffered a loss that in combination with debris removal exceeds the policy limit, or if the debris removal cost exceeds 25 percent of the covered loss, an additional $5,000 is provided for this "additional coverage."

Pollutant Cleanup

The policy specifically states that it will *not* respond to pollution claims under the Debris Removal Additional Coverages section. Instead, another type of additional coverage is specifically designed for pollution cleanup:

d. Pollutant Clean Up and Removal

We will pay your expense to extract "pollutants" from land or water at the described premises if the discharge, dispersal, seepage, migration, release, or escape of the "pollutants" is caused by or results from a Covered Cause of Loss that occurs during the policy period. . . ..

Here, the policy affirms its intent to pay for pollution that is a consequence of a covered loss that occurs during the policy period. An annual aggregate limit of $10,000 is included.

Exclusions From the "All-Risks" Causes of Loss Form

The causes of loss—special form, because of its "all-risks" format, has a long list of excluded risks, including the following:

> Discharge dispersal of "pollutants" unless the discharge, dispersal, seepage, migration, release, or escape is itself caused by any of the "specified causes of loss." But if loss or damage by the "specified causes of loss" results, we will pay for the resulting damage caused by the "specified cause of loss."

The term "specified causes of loss" means fire; lightning; explosion; windstorm or hail; smoke; aircraft or vehicles; riot or civil commotion; vandalism; leakage from fire extinguishing equipment; sinkhole collapse; volcanic action; falling objects; weight of snow, ice, or sleet; and water damage. Water damage means accidental discharge or leakage of water or steam as the direct result of the breaking or cracking of any part of a system or appliance containing water or steam.

Summary

The insurance industry treats the four types of losses discussed in this chapter differently. Both crime and boiler and machinery losses are major exposures that the industry has addressed with specialized, standardized policies. Electronic data processing losses are a major exposure that the industry is trying to address. Standardized coverage forms have not yet evolved. Losses from pollution/contamination are an exposure the industry has tried to avoid except when incidental to a covered loss.

In crime insurance, adjusters must be keenly aware of how carefully tailored the coverage might be in a specific case and must carefully investigate the claim to determine whether the circumstances of a loss match the coverage.

Boiler and machinery coverage fills a gap left by ordinary commercial property policies. An adjuster must understand how these coverages fit together and must be fully aware of the meaning of "accident" to an "object" in a boiler and machinery policy.

Although standard policies provide substantial coverage for EDP losses, special EDP policies are becoming more common. EDP losses present the adjuster with important loss mitigation and settlement opportunities.

Pollution and contamination claims can present difficult coverage issues. The insurance industry has tried to avoid coverage for most such losses. Whether it can continue to do so depends on the specific policy language applicable and on the attitudes of the courts.

Bibliography

"The Arson Epidemic." *Insurance Backgrounder*. Public Relations Department of State Farm Insurance Companies, 1994.

Blank, Douglas D. "Investigating and Preventing Insurance Fraud." *For the Defense*, November 1994, pp. 11-12.

1995 Property/Casualty Insurance Facts. New York, NY: Insurance Information Institute, 1995.

"State Beat." *Claims*, September 1994, p. 17.

Thorness, Bill. "The New SIU Team." *Claims*, September 1994, p. 58.

Index

A

Access time, 12
Accident, 260
Accommodation coverage, 243
Accounting, basic, for organizations, 166
   retail method of, 138
Actual cash value (ACV), 19, 137
Actual loss, 181
Additional, optional, and extended
   coverages under the BIC, 191
Additional coverages, limits of insurance
   apply to, 194
Additional items and unit cost, 12
Additional living expense, 202
Additional living expense losses, 205
Adjusting considerations, 214
Adjusting requirements, NFIP, 226
Adjustment, loss, 158, 238
   preparation of file for, 158
Adjustment of bailment losses, 217
Adjustment difficulties with book inven-
   tory, 145
Adjustment process: Step I—conduct the
   initial survey, 3
Adjustment process: Step II—prepare
   diagrams and sketches, 3
Adjustment process: Step III—scope the
   damage, 3
Adjustment process: Step IV—consider
   coverage, 4
Adjustment process: Step V—document
   with photographs, 4
Adjustment procedures, 225

Advantages of computer estimating, 21
Adverse selection, 219
Agreed value, business income, 202
Agreement, condominium association,
   231
Air conditioning, 125
Air conditioning system, central, 125
All-encompassing concept, 232
"All-risks" causes of loss form, exclusions
   from, 278
"All-risks" coverage, 276
"All-risks" or specialized coverage, 210
Allowances, trade discounts and, 136
Alterations and new buildings, 192
Alternative repairs, 18
Aluminum siding, 65
Amount of loss, 254
Application of estimating methods, 10
Application of overhead and profit, 8
Appraisal, 218
Area, calculating, 60, 65
   roof, 71
   surface, 23
   total, 74
Arithmetic for estimating, 23
Armored cable, 128
Articles, scheduled, 243
Asphalt, 68
Asphalt composition shingles, 70
Assets, 167
Association, condominium, 228
Authorities, civil, 204
Authority, civil, 192
Authorization, NFIP, 225

Average-quality cabinets, 110
Awning windows, 105

B

Backup of data, 269
Bailee, 215
    bailment for the benefit of, 215
Bailee and bailor, bailment for the mutual
        benefit of, 215
Bailee coverages, 215
Bailee liability policy, 216
Bailee losses, 215
Bailee's customers policy, 216
Bailment, 215
    commercial, 215
Bailment for the benefit for the bailee,
        215
Bailment for the benefit of the bailor, 215
Bailment losses, adjustment of, 217
Bailment for the mutual benefit of the
        bailee and bailor, 215
Bailment situations, liability in, 215
Bailor, 215
    bailment for the benefit of, 215
Bailor coverages, 216
Balance sheet, 140, 166
    effects of property losses on, 172
Balloon construction, 82, 84
Barewalls concept, 231
Base cabinets, 108
Base moldings, 113
Baseboards, 113
Basic accounting for organizations, 166
Beams, 85
BIC (Business Income Coverage form),
        165
    additional, optional, and extended
        coverages under, 191
Bill of lading, 214
Blackboard, 90
Blanket coverage, 250
Block or parquet flooring, 102
Board, ridge, 93

Board feet, 26
Board feet formula, 28
Board foot calculations, 97
Board foot formula, 99
Boards, corner, 115
Boiler and machinery business interrup-
        tion, 261
Boiler and machinery coverage, 255, 258
    need for, 256
    small business, 261
Boiler and machinery exposures, 257
Boiler and machinery market, 257
Book inventory, adjustment difficulties
        with, 145
Book value, determining, 140
Book value method, summary of, 143
Books and records, 139
BOP (businessowners policies), 134
Bottom line, 171
Box cornice, 115
BPP, 134, 244, 267
    limitations under, 256
Branch circuits, 127
Brand and labels clause, 162
Break point, 162
Bridging, 85
Builders' risk coverage, 234
Builders' risk exposures, 235
Builders' risk losses, 234
Builders' risk policies, types of, 235
Building loss, scope of, 1
Building losses, negotiating, 15
Built-up roofing, 71
Built-up roofs, 69
Bundles, 68
Burden, employer's, 7
Burglary, 241, 251
Business income, 178
    extended, 193
    loss of, 183
Business income agreed value, 202
Business Income Coverage form (BIC),
        165
Business interruption, boiler and machin-
        ery, 261

Business interruption losses, 166
Businessowners policies (BOP), 134
    limits under, 202
BX cable, 128
Bylaws, 231

C

Cabinet quality, identifying, 109
Cabinets, average-quality, 110
    base, 108
    economy-quality, 109
    kitchen, 108
        estimating, 112
    premium-quality, 110
    types of, 108
    utility, 108
    wall, 108
Cable, armored, 128
    BX, 128
    nonmetallic sheathed, 128
Calculating area, 60, 65
Calculating number of pieces in a section,
    99
Calculating square footage, 40
Calculations, board foot, 97
    extra expense and coinsurance, 201
    gable and hip area, 73
Cap, drip, 115
Carpentry, finish, 101
    frame, 81
    damageability and repair of, 95
        elements of, 82
    rough, 81
Carriers, 212
Casement windows, 104
Cash, 172
Casings, 106, 114
Causes of depreciation, 137
Causes of loss, 262
    covered, 180
Ceiling joists, 92
Ceiling moldings, 113
Ceilings, 56

water stains on, 34
Central air conditioning system, 125
Chair rails, 113
Changing values, handling, 237
Charges, freight, 136
Checking reported values, 153
Choice of estimating methods, 12
Circuits, branch, 127
Civil authorities, 204
Civil authority, 192
Claims, contamination, 273
Class (of a building), 20
Clause, brand and labels, 162
    full reporting, 152
Cleanup, pollution, 277
Closed cornice, 115
Code requirements, 18
Coinsurance, 195
    optional coverages instead of, 201
Commercial bailment, 215
Commercial property, 235
Commercial unit owners, 233
Common elements, 228
Comprehensive Environmental Response,
        Compensation, and Liability Act
        (CERCLA), 274
Computer consultants, 272
Computer estimating, advantages of, 21
Computer estimating systems, 20
Computer loss adjusting, 269
Computer losses, 261
Computer viruses, 268
Concept, all-encompassing, 232
    barewalls, 231
Conditions, 260
Condominium, 228
Condominium association, 228
    declarations of, 231
Condominium association agreement, 231
Condominium association coverage form,
    232
Condominium losses, 228
Conduit, 127
    rigid, 128
    thin-wall, 128

Considerations, adjusting, 214
Consignee, 212
Construction, balloon, 82, 84
    frame, estimating, 97
    platform, 82, 83
    western, 82
    wood sill, 85
Consultants, computer, 272
Contamination, 264
    legal aspects of, 274
Contamination/pollution, exclusions and
        limitations for, 276
Contamination claims, 273
Contract, service, 272
Contractor's equipment, 218
Contractor's equipment losses, 218
Contracts, salvage, 148
Contracts and documents, need to
        consult, 212
Contrast to finished estimate, 2
Contribution to surplus, 171
Cooling, and heating, systems, 120
Corner boards, 115
Cornice, 115
    box, 115
    closed, 115
    open, 115
Cost, replacement, 136
    total, 58, 61, 68
    unit, 12, 62, 68, 78
Cost data, 22
Cost of goods formula, 142
Cost of goods sold, 142, 169, 171, 175
    determining, 142
Cost-to-sales ratio, 143
Costs, "soft," 236
    handling, 137
Counter tops, 112
Coverage, 54, 134, 218, 266
    accommodation, 243
    "all-risks," 276
    "all-risks" or specialized, 210
    blanket, 250
    boiler and machinery, 255, 258
        need for, 256
    small business, 261
    builders' risk, 234
    NFIP, 220
    removal, 220
    scheduled, 250
    termination of, 238
Coverage aspects of estimating, 18
Coverage extension, 194
Coverage form, condominium association,
        232
    unit owner's, 233
Coverage Form A—employee dishonesty,
        249
Coverage Form C—theft, disappearance,
        and destruction coverage, 250
Coverage Form E—premises burglary, 251
Coverage Form H—premises theft and
        outside robbery, 251
Coverage forms, 232, 235
Coverage Forms D and Q—robbery and
        safe burglary, 251
Coverage questions, 35
Coverages, 178, 202
    additional, limits of insurance apply to,
        194
    bailee, 215
    bailor, 216
    crime, 242
Covered causes of loss, 180
Coverings, flocked, 54
Crash, head, 264
Crime coverages, 242
Crime general provisions form, 248
Crime losses, 241
    investigation of, 252
Crushing, impact or, 265
Cutting and fitting waste, 5

D

Damage, degree of, 2
    smoke, 35
    water, to drywall, 35
    wind versus water, 226

Damage to and repair of drywall and plaster, 59
Damage to and repair of roofing, 69
Damage to exterior paint, 50
Damageability and repair of frame carpentry, 95
Damageability and repair of wood fences, 101
Data, 262
  backup of, 269
  cost, 22
Debris removal, 14, 276, 277
Decimal equivalents, 23
Declarations of the condominium association, 231
Declarations page, 258
Deed, master, 231
Defense, 260
Degree of damage, 2
Delays caused by strikers, 191
Demolition, 14
Denials and rejections, 226
Depreciation, 226
  causes of, 137
Destruction of records, 145
Detailed identification of equipment, 269
Determination of values for last reported date, 153
Determining the actual cash value of a repair estimate, 19
Determining book value, 140
Determining cost of goods sold, 142
Determining loss of business income and extra expense, 182
Determining the method of repair, 34
Determining the period of restoration, 187
Determining settlement for loss of use, 204
Differences, price, resolving, 17
Differences in conditions (DIC) insurance, 238
Differences in scope, resolving, 16
Dimensions, nominal versus actual, 27
Direct costs, miscellaneous, 9

Discussions with the insured, 160
Door stop, 106
Door trim, 113
Doors, 106
Double-hung windows, 104
Double roll, standard, 54
Drain/waste/vent systems, 119
Drip cap, 115
Drywall, 58
  estimating, 60
  installation of, 60
  water damage to, 35
Drywall and plaster, damage to and repair of, 59
Due diligence requirement, 187
Dwelling form (DF), 220

E

Economy-quality cabinets, 109
Effect of a loss on expenses, 174
Effect of a loss on net income, 176
Effect of a loss on revenue, 174
Effects of a loss, 172
Effects of property losses on the balance sheet, 172
Effects of property losses on the income statement, 174
Electric heating, 121
Electrical metallic tubing (EMT), 128
Electrical service, entrance of, 127
Electrical systems, 126
Elements, common, 228
Elements of frame carpentry, 82
Elements of a proper scope, 2
Employee involvement, 254
Employer's burden, 7
Entrance of electrical service, 127
Environmental Protection Agency (EPA), 274
Equipment, contractor's, 218
  detailed identification of, 269
  tools and, 8
Equity, owners', 167

Equivalents, decimal, 23
Essential coverage provision, 258
Estimate, final, 11
   pricing, 5
   total, 77, 99
   trade, 22
Estimates, painting, factors in, 36
   roofing, 71
Estimating, arithmetic for, 23
   computer, advantages of, 21
   coverage aspects of, 18
   exterior paint, factors in, 51
   other considerations in, 13
Estimating drywall, 60
Estimating frame construction, 97
Estimating interior trim, 114
Estimating kitchen cabinets, 112
Estimating methods, 10, 39
   application of, 10
   choice of, 12
Estimating procedures, 9
Estimating references, 31
Estimating siding, 65
Estimating systems, computer, 20
Estimating the value at risk, 20
Estimating wallpaper, 55
Estimating windows, 106
Estimating wood flooring, 102
Event, verification of, 252
Excess of revenue over expenses, 171
Exclusions, 221, 239
Exclusions from the "all-risks" causes of
   loss form, 278
Exclusions and limitations for contamina-
   tion/pollution, 276
Exercise and nonwaiver of rights, 160
Expense, additional living, 202
Expenses, 168, 169
   effect of a loss on, 174
   extra, 179
   incurred, 206
   necessary, 205
   revenue over, excess of, 171
Exposure, 63
Exposures, boiler and machinery, 257

builders' risk, 235
   loss, 266
Extended business income, 193
Extension, coverage, 194
Exterior paint, damage to, 50
Exterior paint estimating, factors in, 51
Exterior siding, 62
Exterior wood trim, 115
Extra expense and coinsurance calcula-
   tions, 201
Extra expense loss, 183
Extra expenses, 179

F

Fabric-backed foil, 54
Factor, waste, 5
Factors affecting the costs of wallpaper
   losses, 53
Factors in exterior paint estimating, 51
Factors in painting estimates, 36
Fair rental value, 207
Federal Emergency Management Agency
   (FEMA), 220
Federal Insurance Administration (FIA),
   220
Fees, salvage, 150
Feet, board, 26
   square, 24
Felt, 76
Felt paper, 68
Fences, wood, 100
FICO (Flood Insurance Claims Office),
   226
Field notes, 1
Final estimate, 11
Financial records, types of, 140
Financial statement, 140
Finish carpentry, 101
Finish flooring, 101
Finish plumbing, 118
Finish wood floors, 101
Finished estimate, contrast to, 2
Finished goods, 133
Finished stock, 181

Fire and heat, 36
Fixtures, plumbing, 120
Flashing, 69
Flocked coverings, 54
Flood (defined), 220
Flood Insurance Claims Office (FICO),
    226
Floor framing, 85
Floor joists, 85
Flooring, block or parquet, 102
    finish, 101
    plank, 102
    strip, 102
    types of, 102
    wood, estimating, 102
Floors, finish wood, 101
Foil, fabric-backed, 54
Form, crime general provisions, 248
    dwelling, 220
    general property, 220
    reporting, 151
Forms, coverage, 232, 235
    manuscript, 236
Formula, board feet, 28
    board foot, 99
    cost of goods, 142
Frame carpentry, 81
    damageability and repair of, 95
    elements of, 82
Frame construction, estimating, 97
Framing, floor, 85
    wall, 90
    window and door, 90
Fraud, indicators of, 253
Freight, 136
Freight charges, 136
Full dimension lumber, 27
Full reporting clause, 152
Full values, reporting, 152
Furnace puff-back, 126

G

Gable, 73
Gable and hip area calculations, 73

General property form (GPF), 220
Girders, 85
Goods, 133
    finished, 133
    hard, 134
    soft, 134
Goods in process, 133
Goods sold, cost of, 142, 169, 171, 175
Gross area method, 40
Gross area method—Step 1: calculate the
    surface area, 41
Gross area method—Step 2: deduct open-
    ings of 100 square feet or more, 41
Gross area method—Step 3: estimate the
    materials, 41
Gross area method—Step 4: estimate the
    labor, 42
Gross area method—Step 5: total the
    estimate, 42
Gross margin, 169
Gross profit, 169
Gypsum board, 58

H

Handling changing values, 237
Handling costs, 137
Hard goods, 134
Hardware, 262
Head crash, 264
Header joist, 85
Headers, window and door, 90
Heat, 263
    fire and, 36
Heat pump, 125
Heaters, space, 126
Heating, electric, 121
    warm-air, 121
Heating and cooling systems, 120
    miscellaneous, 125
Heating systems, solar, 125
    steam and hot-water, 121
Hinges, 106
Hip, 73

Hip rafters, 93
Homeowners loss of use, 202
Hopper, 105
Hot-water, and steam, heating systems, 121
How to Estimate Building Losses and Construction Cost, 5, 7

I

Identifying cabinet quality, 109
Impact or crushing, 265
Improvements, real estate and, 172
Income, 172
    business, 178
    net, 171, 172
Income statement, 140, 167, 168
    effects of property losses on, 174
Increases only, 205
Incurred expenses, 206
Indemnity, maximum period of, 201
    monthly period of, 201
Indicators of fraud, 253
Initial assessment and response, 269
Initial survey, 3
Inland marine insurance, 210
Inland marine losses, 209
Inland marine market, 210
Inland marine policies, 236, 267
Innocent landowner, 275
Inspection of roofs, 70
Installation of drywall, 60
Insurable interest, 135
Insurance, differences in conditions (DIC), 238
    inland marine, 210
    motor truck cargo, 214
    other, 268
    specific, 153
    transit, 214
Insurance claim receivable, 169
Insurance implications of Superfund, 275
Insurance for loss of business income and extra expense, 176
Insured, discussions with, 160

Insured value of merchandise, 134
Insured's liability to salvor, 150
Insured's statement, 253
Interest, insurable, 135
Interior trim, 104, 113
    estimating, 114
Intrusion, magnetic head, 266
Inventories, perpetual, 146
Inventory, 172
Investigation of crime losses, 252
Involvement, employee, 254
ISO Crime Program, 245

J

Jack rafters, 93
Jalousie windows, 105
Jambs, 106
Joist, header, 85
Joists, 85
    ceiling, 92
    floor, 85

K

Key, 60
King-post truss, 93
Kitchen cabinets, 108
    estimating, 112

L

Labor, 6, 11, 38, 52, 55, 57, 61, 67, 71, 76, 99
    quantity of, 6
Labor and materials method, 10
Lading, bill of, 214
Landowner, innocent, 275
Large losses, 15
Layaways, 139
Legal aspects of contamination, 274
Length, rafter, 26, 74
Liabilities, 167
Liability in bailment situations, 215

Liability policy, bailee, 216
Limitation—electronic media and data, 190
Limitations under the BPP, 256
Limits under businessowners policies, 202
Limits of insurance apply to additional coverages, 194
Lines, personal, 243
Living, normal standard of, 206
Living expense, additional, 202
Locksets, 106
Loss, 171
   actual, 181
   amount of, 254
   causes of, 262
   effect of, on expenses, 174
      on net income, 176
      on revenue, 174
   effects of, 172
   extra expense, 183
   responsibility for, 213
Loss adjusting, computer, 269
Loss adjustment, 158, 238
Loss of business income, 183
Loss of business income and extra expense, determining, 182
   insurance for, 176
Loss exposures, 266
Loss of use, determining settlement for, 204
   homeowners, 202
Losses, additional living expense, 205
   bailee, 215
   bailment, adjustment of, 217
   builders' risk, 234
   business interruption, 166
   computer, 261
   condominium, 228
   contractor's equipment, 218
   crime, 241
      investigation of, 252
   inland marine, 209
   large, 15
   property, effects of, on the balance sheet, 172
      on the income statement, 174
   small, 15, 163
   time element, 165
   transportation, 212
      parties in, 212
Losses under the National Flood Insurance Program, 219
Lumber, full dimension, 27
   true dimension, 27

M

Magnetic field intrusion, 266
Manuscript forms, 236
Margin, gross, 169
Mark-up, 170
Markdowns, 138
Market, boiler and machinery, 257
   inland marine, 210
Market value, 137
Master deed, 231
Material, 51, 75
Material prices, 6
Materials, 5, 10, 54, 61, 66
   quality of, 2
   sheet, 63
   siding, 63
Maximum period of indemnity, 201
The Means Repair and Remodeling Estimator, 7
Measurement, multiple system of, 43
Measurements, raw counts of, 2
Mechanical systems, 116
Media, 262
"Meeting of the minds" requirement, 182
Merchandise, 133
   insured value of, 134
   out-of-sight, 140
Meter socket, 127
Method, gross area, 40
   labor and materials, 10
   net area, 42, 55
   time and materials, 10
   unit cost, 10, 12, 47, 58
Method of repair, determining, 34

Methods, estimating, 10, 39
Milling waste, 6
Miscellaneous direct costs, 9
Miscellaneous heating and cooling systems, 125
Modified (upgraded) replacement cost basis, 268
Moldings, base, 113
   ceiling, 113
   picture, 113
Monthly period of indemnity, 201
Motor truck cargo insurance, 214
Multiple parties, 211
Multiple system of measurement, 43
Mutual advantage of percentage damage settlements, 161

N

Nails, 76
Nation-Wide Marine Definition, 210
National Construction Estimator, 7
National Flood Act of 1968, 219
National Flood Insurance Program (NFIP), 219
   losses under, 219
Nature of the unit owner's interest, 231
Necessary expenses, 205
Necessary suspension of operations, 180
Need for boiler and machinery coverage, 256
Need to consult contracts and documents, 212
Negotiating building losses, 16
Negotiation, 162
Net area method, 42, 55
Net area method—Step 1: calculate the surface area, 43
Net area method—Step 2: calculate the openings, 43
Net area method—Step 3: estimate the materials, 46
Net area method—Step 4: estimate the labor, 47

Net area method—Step 5: total the estimate, 47
Net income, 171, 172
   effect of a loss on, 176
Net worth, 167
New buildings, alterations and, 192
NFIP (National Flood Insurance Program), 219
NFIP adjusting requirements, 226
NFIP authorization, 225
NFIP coverage, 220
Nominal size, 6
Nominal versus actual dimensions, 27
Nonmetallic sheathed cable, 128
Normal standard of living, 206

O

Object, 258
Occupancy (of a building), 20
One square, 68
Open cornice, 115
Operation of reporting forms, 152
Operations, 179
   necessary suspension of, 180
Optional coverage—extended period of indemnity, 194
Optional coverages instead of coinsurance, 201
Options, settlement, 271
Other considerations in estimating, 13
Other insurance, 268
Out-of-sight merchandise, 140
Overhead, 8
Overhead and profit, 226
   application of, 8
Owners' equity, 167

P

Paint, 37
   exterior, damage to, 50
Painting, 33
   preparation before, 36

Painting estimates, factors in, 36
Panel, service, 127
Paper, 55
    felt, 68
Parallelogram, 24
Parquet, or block, flooring, 102
Parties, multiple, 211
Parties in transportation losses, 212
Paste, 56
Percentage damage settlements, 161
    mutual advantage of, 161
    use of salvors in, 162
Period of indemnity, maximum, 201
    monthly, 201
Period of restoration, 187
    determining, 187
Perpetual inventories, 146
Personal lines, 243
Picture moldings, 113
Pitch, 73
Plank flooring, 102
Plaster board, 58
Plates, sill, 85
    sole, 83, 90
    top, 84, 90
Platform construction, 82, 83
Plumbing, 117
    finish, 118
    rough, 118
Plumbing fixtures, 120
Point, break, 162
Policies, builders' risk, types of, 235
    inland marine, 236, 267
    reporting form, 151
Policy, bailee liability, 216
    bailees customers, 216
Policy inception, values projected from, 196
Policy release, 218
Policy requirement, 195
Pollution cleanup, 277
Possible coverage for pollution/contami-
    nation, 276
Posts, 85
Potentially responsible parties (PRPs),
    274

Preliminary survey, 159
Premises, residence, 203
Premium-quality cabinets, 110
Preparation, 51, 53
Preparation before painting, 36
Preparation of file for adjustment, 158
Price, selling, 139
Price differences, resolving, 17
Prices, material, 6
Pricing an estimate, 5
Primers, 38
Procedures, adjustment, 225
    estimating, 9
Proceeds, salvage, 150
Profit, 8, 171, 172
    gross, 169
    overhead and, 226
        application of, 8
Profit and loss statement, 140
Program, Write Your Own (WYO), 220
Programs, 262
Proofs of loss, 226
Property, commercial, 235
    recovery of, 255
Property covered, 236
Property covered—dwelling form, 221
Property covered—general property form,
    222
Property held for rental, 203
Property losses, effects of, on the balance
    sheet, 172
        on the income statement, 174
Property not covered, 224
Property not covered—BPP, 276
Provision, essential coverage, 258
    waiver of rights of recovery, 233
Puff-back, furnace, 126
Pump, heat, 125

Q

Quality (of a building), 20
Quality of the materials, 2

Quantity of labor, 6
Questions, coverage, 35

R

Rafter, valley, 93
Rafter-cord, 93
Rafter length, 26, 74
Rafters, hip, 93
    jack, 93
Rails, chair, 113
Ratio, cost-to-sales, 143
Raw counts of measurements, 2
Raw materials, 133
Real estate and improvements, 172
"Reasonableness" standard, 188
Records, books and, 139
    destruction of, 145
    financial, types of, 140
Recovery of property, 255
Rectangle, 24
References, estimating, 31
Rejections, denials and, 226
Release, policy, 218
Removal, debris, 14, 276, 277
Removal coverage, 220
Rental, property held for, 203
Rental value, fair, 207
Repair, determining the method of, 34
Repair estimate, determining the actual
    cash value of, 19
Repair and Remodeling Quarterly, 19
Repair or replace, time needed, 188
Repairs, alternative, 18
    spot, 70
Replacement cost, 136
Replacement cost basis, modified (up-
    graded), 268
Reported values, checking, 153
Reporting form, 151
Reporting form policies, 151
Reporting forms, operation of, 152
Reporting full values, 152
Reports, 228

timeliness of, 153
Requirement, due diligence, 187
    "meeting of the minds," 182
    policy, 195
Requirements, code, 18
Residence premises, 203
Residential unit owners, 234
Resolving differences in scope, 16
Resolving price differences, 17
Response, initial assessment of, 269
Responsibility for loss, 213
Restoration, determining the period of,
    187
    period of, 187
Retail method of accounting, 138
Revenue, 168
    effect of a loss on, 174
Revenue over expenses, excess of, 171
Ridge board, 93
Rights of recovery provision, waiver of,
    233
Rigid conduit, 128
Rise, 73
Robbery, 241, 251
Role of salvor in settlement, 147
Roof area, 71
Roof sheathing, 93
Roof surface, tar and gravel, 69
Roofing, 68
    built-up, 71
    damage to and repair of, 69
Roofing estimates, 71
Roofs, built-up, 69
    inspection of, 70
Rough carpentry, 81
Rough plumbing, 118

S

Sale before settlement, 150
Sale of salvage, 147
Salvage, 146
Salvage contracts, 148
Salvage fees, 150

Salvage proceeds, 150
Salvor, insured's liability to, 150
   role of, in settlement, 147
Salvors, 146
   services of, 146
   use of, in percentage damage settlements, 162
Sash, 104
Scabbing, 96
Scheduled articles, 243
Scheduled coverage, 250
Scissors truss, 93
Scope, 1
   differences in, resolving, 16
   proper, elements of, 2
   suggested sequence for, 2
Scope of a building loss, 1
Scope and estimating process, 1
Selection, adverse, 219
Selling price, 139
Service contract, 272
Service panel, 127
Services of salvors, 146
Settlement, role of salvor in, 147
   sale before, 150
Settlement for loss of use, determining, 204
Settlement options, 271
Settlements, percentage damage, 161
Sheathing, 68
   roof, 93
   wall, 90
Sheet, balance, 140, 166
Sheet materials, 63
Sheetrock, 58
Shellac, 50
Shingles, 76
   asphalt composition, 70
   wood, 63
Shipper, 212
"Shortest time" standard, 204
Shrinkage, 145
Siding, aluminum, 65
   estimating, 65

exterior, 62
vinyl, 65
wood, 63
Siding materials, 63
Sill plates, 85
Sistering, 96
Size, nominal, 6
Sizing, 53
Slate, 69
Sliding windows, 104
Small business boiler and machinery coverage, 261
Small losses, 15, 163
Smoke, 263
Smoke damage, 35
Socket, meter, 127
"Soft" costs, 236
Soft goods, 134
Solar heating systems, 125
Sole plates, 83, 90
Soot, 35
Space heaters, 126
Specific insurance, 153
Specifications, 1
Splicing, 96
Spot repairs, 70
Square, 24
Square feet, 24
Square feet versus square yards, 24
Square footage, calculating, 40
Stain, 50
Stains, on ceilings, 34
   water, 34
Standard, "reasonableness," 188
   "shortest time," 204
Standard double roll, 54
Standard of living, normal, 206
Statement, financial, 140
   income, 140, 167, 168
   insured's, 253
   profit and loss, 140
Stationary windows, 105
Steam and hot-water heating systems, 121
Stock, 133

finished, 181
Stop, door, 106
Strikers, delays caused by, 191
Stringer joist, 85
Strip flooring, 102
Studs, 84, 90
Subflooring, 85, 90
Subrogation, 228, 237
Suggested sequence for a scope, 2
Superfund, 274
    insurance implications of, 275
Supply, water, 118
Surface, 51
Surface area, 23
Surface features, 53
Surfaces, types of, 37
Surplus, contribution to, 171
Survey, 1
    initial, 3
    preliminary, 159
Suspension of operations, necessary, 180
Sweating, 119
System, central air conditioning, 125
    drain/waste/vent, 119
    electrical, 126
    heating and cooling, 120
    mechanical, 116
    miscellaneous heating and cooling, 125
    solar heating, 125

T

Table, water, 115
Take-off, 1
Tar and gravel roof surface, 69
Tear-out, 14
Termination of coverage, 238
Theft, 241, 251
Thin-wall conduit, 128
Tiles, 69
Time, access, 12
Time element losses, 165
Time and materials method, 10
Time needed to repair or replace, 188

Time in which repairs should be complete, 189
Timeliness of reports, 153
Tools and equipment, 8
Top plates, 84, 90
Total area, 74
Total cost, 58, 61, 68
Total estimate, 77, 99
Trade discounts and allowances, 136
Trade estimate, 22
Training, 21
Transit insurance, 214
Transportation losses, 212
    parties in, 212
Trapezoid, 24
Triangle, 24
Trim, door, 113
    exterior wood, 115
    interior, 104, 113
        estimating, 114
    window, 113
True dimension lumber, 27
Truss, king-post, 93
    scissors, 93
    W-type, 93
Trusses, 93
Types of builders' risk policies, 235
Types of cabinets, 108
Types of financial records, 140
Types of flooring, 102
Types and methods of wiring, 128
Types of surfaces, 37
Types of windows, 104

U

Unit, 10
Unit cost, 12, 62, 68, 78
    additional items and, 12
Unit cost method, 10, 12, 47, 58
Unit owner's coverage form, 233
Unit owner's interest, nature of, 231
Unit owners, commercial, 233
    residential, 234

Universal pricing code (UPC), 139
Use of salvors in percentage damage
    settlements, 162
Utility cabinets, 108

V

Valley rafter, 93
Valleys, 93
Valuation, 136
Value, fair rental, 207
    market, 137
Value of merchandise, insured, 134
Value at risk, estimating, 20
Values, determination of, for last reported
    date, 153
Values against which compliance is
    measured, 196
Values projected from policy inception,
    196
Variation, voltage, 265
Varnish, 49
Verification of the event, 252
Vinyl, 54
Vinyl siding, 65
Viruses, computer, 268
Voltage variation, 265

W

W-type truss, 93
Waiver of rights of recovery provision,
    233
*Walker's Building Estimators Reference
    Book*, 5, 7
Wall board, 58
Wall cabinets, 108
Wall framing, 90
Wall sheathing, 90
Wallpaper, estimating, 55

Wallpaper losses, factors affecting the
    costs of, 53
Wallpapering, 52
Warm-air heating, 121
Waste, 5, 55, 65
    cutting and fitting, 5
    milling, 6
Waste factor, 5
Water damage to drywall, 35
Water/humidity, 263
Water stains, 34
Water stains on ceilings, 34
Water supply, 118
Water table, 115
Western construction, 82
What happens to an organization after a
    loss?, 166
Wind versus water damage, 226
Window and door framing, 90
Window and door headers, 90
Window trim, 113
Windows, 104
    awning, 105
    casement, 104
    double-hung, 104
    estimating, 106
    jalousie, 105
    sliding, 104
    stationary, 105
    types of, 104
Wiring, types and methods of, 128
Wood fences, 100
    damageability and repair of, 101
Wood flooring, estimating, 102
Wood floors, finish, 101
Wood shingles, 63
Wood siding, 63
Wood sill construction, 85
Wood trim, exterior, 115
Worth, net, 167
Write Your Own (WYO) program, 220